CLASSIC
COLORADO
HIKES

LAKES, LOOPS, AND
HIGH-RIDGE TRAVERSES

For Alex & Irina —

Anything is possible,

enjoy the

journey!

Snowmass Lake, Elk Range.

COLORADO
MOUNTAIN CLUB
GUIDEBOOK

CLASSIC COLORADO HIKES

LAKES, LOOPS, AND HIGH-RIDGE TRAVERSES

JON KEDROWSKI

The Colorado Mountain Club Press
Golden, Colorado

Classic Colorado Hikes: Lakes, Loops, and High-Ridge Traverses
© 2022 Jon Kedrowski

Published by:
The Colorado Mountain Club Press
710 10th Street, Suite 200, Golden, CO 80401
303-996-2743 | cmcpress@cmc.org | cmc.org

Founded in 1912, The Colorado Mountain Club is the largest outdoor recreation, education, and conservation organization in the Rocky Mountains. Look for our books at your local bookstore or outdoor retailer or online at cmc.org

Corrections: We greatly appreciate when readers alert us to errors or outdated information by emailing cmcpress@cmc.org.

Jon Kedrowski: author and photographer, except where noted
John Fielder photographs copyright John Fielder, 2022. Visit johnfielder.com to see 1,000 Colorado images.
Takeshi Takahashi: composition
Sarah Gorecki: publisher

Front cover photo: Blue Lakes Basin and Mount Sneffels as seen from near the summit of Dallas Peak.
Back cover photo: Reflection in South Crestone Lake.

Distributed to the book trade by:
Mountaineers Books
1001 SW Klickitat Way, Suite 201, Seattle, WA 98134
800-553-4453 | mountaineersbooks.org

We gratefully acknowledge the financial support of the people of Colorado through the Scientific and Cultural Facilities District of greater metropolitan Denver for our publishing activities.

TOPOGRAPHIC MAPS created with CalTopo software.

Printed in the United States of America

22 23 24 / 10 9 8 7 6 5 4 3 2 1

ISBN 978-1-937052-75-1
Ebook ISBN 978-1-937052-83-6

CONTENTS

▬▬ CHAPTER 1: FRONT RANGE NORTH
(RMNP AND INDIAN PEAKS WILDERNESS)

▇▇ CHAPTER 2: FRONT RANGE SOUTH (I-70 CORRIDOR)

▇▇ CHAPTER 3: TENMILE/MOSQUITO RANGE

▇▇ CHAPTER 4: GORE RANGE/VAIL VALLEY

CHAPTER 5: STEAMBOAT AREA/ PARK RANGE/RAHWAH/FLAT TOPS

CHAPTER 6: SAWATCH RANGE

CHAPTER 7: ELK RANGE

CHAPTER 8: SANGRE DE CRISTO RANGE

Lake Isabelle, Indian Peaks Wilderness.

FOREWORD

BOOM! Another lightning strike hit close by, and my 7-year-old brother, Joe, cried as we huddled for warmth under our old army ponchos in an intense afternoon thunderstorm. After multiple attempts, I was finally able to get an old fuel pellet to light, and we both put our hands over its meager heat to try to thaw out our numb, frozen hands.

I suppose most would argue we were too young at the time to be out there by ourselves. I was only 15, and my stepdad had left us to climb the fourteeners Windom, Sunlight, and Eolus in the remote Weminuche Wilderness of southern Colorado. We were hiding out in a small alcove near the summit of Sunlight Peak, and I was regretting my decision to lead us through the snowfields.

Earlier that day, we woke up and climbed Windom Peak, then traversed over to Sunlight. It was early in the climbing season, and we found it easy to stick to the snowfields. However, this resulted in hours of getting soaked by the snow, and by the time the clouds rolled in, we were already freezing.

Joe was still cold when the intensity of the storm let up, but we continued with our descent. After navigating treacherous terrain in the rain, we made it down to Twin Lakes. These two beautiful lakes are well-known in the Chicago Basin area and sit near 12,500 feet. For whatever reason, I put my hand in the water. It seemed crazy considering half of the lake was covered in snow and ice, but to my surprise, the freezing lake water felt warm. We were excited at the opportunity to thaw our frozen fingers and toes, so we sat, with our hands and feet submerged in the water, feeling immediate relief from the cold.

Unbeknownst to me, this was an experience that impacted the direction of my life and shaped who I would become. My passion for seeking adventure in Colorado's mountains, specifically the fourteeners, only grew from there.

No matter where my life takes me or what path I choose, I always find myself drawn back into our mountains. Is it the experience of solitude in the remote parts of Colorado or piecing together a challenging linkup combined with the thrill of traversing spectacular ridges to get from peak to peak? Is it the great workouts the crowded mountains of the Front Range have to offer or simply the breathtaking views of turquoise-colored lakes where the tranquil scene quiets the stress of life?

Jon Kedrowski (right) with Andrew Hamilton and Andrea Sansone on Mount Adams in the Sangre de Cristo Range.

For whatever reason, the mountains are part of a place where I find my thrill and purpose for existence.

In recent years, as some of the more well-known peaks and hikes in Colorado have become crowded, I have found myself searching for new, unique ways to connect multiple peaks together on routes rarely seen by human eyes. Taking the "road less traveled" or leading yourself off the beaten path opens the door to infinite opportunities of adventure and discovery. Lakes you never knew existed, views you'll never forget, and experiences of a lifetime are waiting for you, for us all.

You don't have to travel to the far reaches of the earth to discover these amazing climbs and solitude. You can stay right here in Colorado for a lifetime of exploring the peaks, like I have. And you can use Jon's extensive knowledge and experience from his years of climbing in the backcountry and skiing Colorado's peaks, along with the wealth of knowledge and places in this guidebook to help you find some of those hidden adventures. All the best on your journeys!

—*Andrew Hamilton, October 2021*

Fastest Known Times (FKTs)

♦ Climbed all 58 Colorado fourteeners in 9 days 21 hours 51 minutes (2015) ♦ First and only person to climb each of the 58 Colorado fourteeners in one single calendar winter season (Dec. 21, 2017 to March 16, 2018) ♦ Climbed Colorado's Centennials (103 highest peaks) in 22 days 16 hours and 54 minutes (2021)

OVERVIEW MAP NORTH

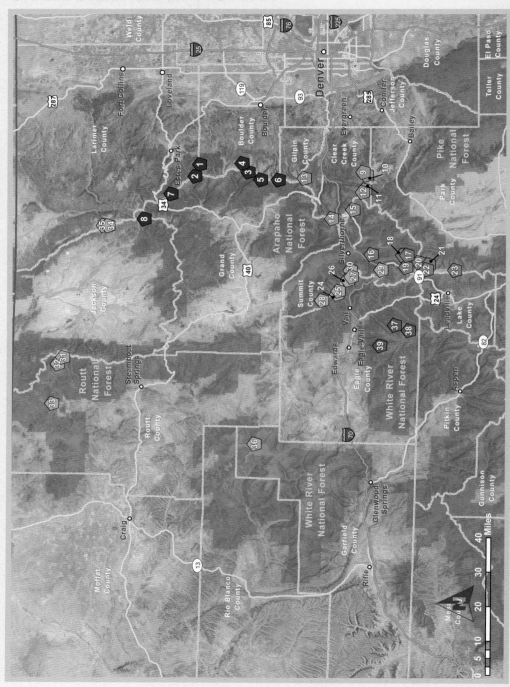

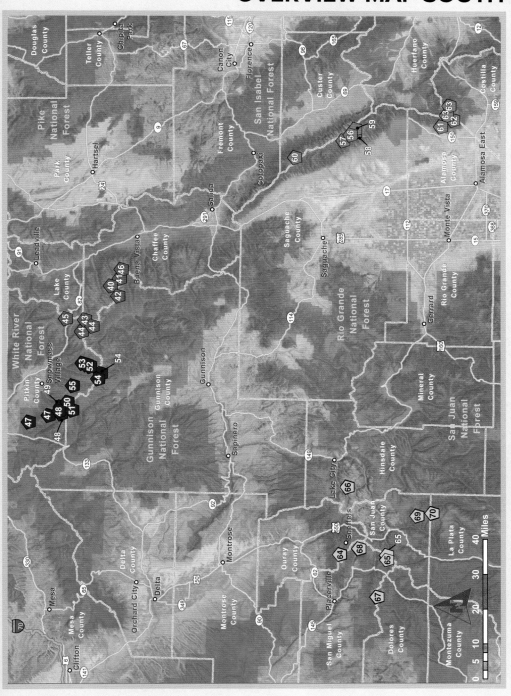

Climbing near the summit of Capitol with Pierre Lakes far below.

INTRODUCTION

Hiking and climbing in Colorado certainly aren't new. In some circles, if you aren't out there every weekend heading to the most beautiful place you can find in the wilderness, snapping a photo for social media (or better yet, just for you), and showing off how amazing your latest find is, you aren't cool. Spending time in the wilderness, whether it includes taking the dog, bringing the family along, or even taking a cool dip in a mountain lake, is surely becoming one of Colorado's favorite pastimes. Don't forget to pack the tasty snacks and the beer! Some people are obsessed; they need fresh air and their favorite view. Some have also created checklists that go far beyond the reaches of the fourteener denizen peakbagger; they have to now climb every ridgeline on their favorite thirteeners and twelvers. There truly are no limits when it comes to exploring the beautiful lakes, loops, and high-ridge traverses in the highest places in our state.

This book is for everyone who desires the Colorado hiking and climbing wilderness experience. I have outlined and selected some of my favorite backcountry lakes, but I've added a whole lot more. Have you ever sat down for a break at a high-mountain lake and wondered: *Can that peak be climbed?* Or, *I wonder if it's possible to traverse that ridge?* For every lake, there is a loop, and for every loop, I suggest a high-ridge traverse. And in the "Dr. Jon's Extra Credit" sections, I suggest even more options for creating your own adventures. Tap into your desire to be an explorer, take your map, and use your imagination. Enjoy making your own adventures throughout our great state of Colorado! I look forward to seeing you out on the ridgeline and on the summit!

—*Jon Kedrowski, May 2022*

HOW TO USE THIS GUIDE

Nearly every entry in this guidebook highlights a lake or several lakes that are destinations along the trail or route described. Beyond the lake, most entries include the difficulty rating and options for further exploration. Some hikes are loop hikes, meaning you can hike to a lake or series of lakes and return to the trailhead by taking a loop. Then, "The Loop and High-Ridge Traverse" and "High-Ridge Traverse" sections highlight an extra route, such a climbing route to a peak or a peak-to-peak high-ridge traverse. Some high-ridge traverses are out-and-back routes, and in most other cases, the route will be an actual loop, so please read the descriptions and study the provided maps (and your own maps) carefully.

In the sections of this book that discuss the lakes, the loops, and the high-ridge traverses as well as in "Dr. Jon's Extra Credit" sections, the routes are described using the climbing classifications explained in the next section.

CLIMBING CLASSIFICATIONS

When a climbing route is described in this guide, the following descriptions are used:

Steepness Ratings

Easy:	0–30 degrees
Moderate:	30–45 degrees
Steep:	45–60 degrees
Very Steep:	60–80 degrees
Vertical:	80–90 degrees

Rock Ratings

The climbing difficulty of the routes listed in this guide is classified under the Yosemite Decimal System (YDS).

Class 1: Trail hiking or any hiking across open country that is no more difficult than walking on a maintained trail. The parking lot at the trailhead is easy Class 1, groomed ski trails are midrange Class 1, and some of the big step-ups on rocks, such as those near the top of the Barr Trail of Pikes Peak, are difficult Class 1.

Class 2: Steep trail, climbers'-trail, or off-trail hiking. Class 2 usually involves bushwhacking or hiking on a talus or loose rock slope. You are not yet using handholds for upward movement. Occasionally, a Class 2+ rating is used for a pseudo-scrambling route where you will use your hands but do not need to

A never-ending ridgeline in the Elk Range.

search hard for handholds. Most people are able to downclimb Class 2+ terrain facing out and without the use of hands while using superb balance and careful stepping.

Class 3: The easiest climbing (not hiking) category. People usually call this "scrambling." You are beginning to look for and use handholds for upward movement. Basic climbing techniques are used, which are noticeably beyond the level of any walking movements. Although you must use handholds, you don't have to look hard to find them. Occasionally putting your hand down for balance while crossing a talus slope does not qualify as Class 3; this is still Class 2. About half of Class 3 climbers feel the need to face in toward the rock while downclimbing Class 3.

Class 4: This level of climbing is within the realm of "technical climbing." You are not just using handholds; you have to search for, select, and test them. You are beginning to use muscle groups not involved with hiking, those of the upper body and abdominals in particular. Movement at Class 4 is more focused, thoughtful, and slower. Many people prefer to rappel down a serious Class 4 pitch that is exposed rather than downclimb it. Many Class 3 routes in California would be rated Class 4 in Colorado.

Class 5: Technical climbing and nothing less. You are now using a variety of climbing techniques, not just cling holds. Movements may involve stemming with your legs, cross-pressure with your arms, pressing down on handholds as you pass them, edging on small holds, smearing, chimneying, jamming, and using heel hooks. Any lack of flexibility will be noticeable and can hinder movement, and Class 5 movement totally occupies the mind of the individual. Most people choose to rappel down Class 5 pitches.

Class 5 Climbing Described within the YDS

Class	Description
5.0–5.7	Easy for experienced climbers; where most climbers begin. Two or three great handholds or footholds are present for upward movement using the four extremities.
5.8–5.9	Where most weekend climbers become comfortable; employs the specific skills of rock climbing, such as jamming, liebacks, and mantles. One or two good handholds or footholds are present for upward movement using the four extremities.
5.10	A dedicated weekend climber may attain this level; strong fingers and great footwork are necessary. There is only one good handhold or foothold per four extremities for upward movement.
5.11–5.15	The realm of true experts; demands much training and natural ability, and often, repeated working of a route using very few handholds of solid grip. Many times there are zero handholds per four extremities.

THE BASICS: TIPS FOR THE TRAIL

Do you want to hike or backpack in Colorado's backcountry and safely enjoy your adventure?

Entire books of hundreds of pages have been written on how to hike, gear to consider when hiking, and backcountry travel, so I've merely provided a few tips to consider, and the rest of how you go about being safe and smart while enjoying your adventures is up to you.

Here's what I've learned after many years of hiking, camping, exploring, and backcountry ski mountaineering:

The most important variable to consider is the weather. Before packing a single bag, be sure you understand the weather forecasts inside and out. Equally as important is educating yourself on mountain meteorology as well as avalanche safety (for snowy winter and spring climbs). Being able to diagnose the weather you see unfolding in the field as well as the type of snow conditions (even in summer) can save your life. This kind of wisdom will help you decide whether to attack the summit or turn around and go home. Consult local weather experts for information, take a college class on weather climate and outdoor education, or attend personalized mountain meteorology workshops (such as outdoor "how-to" seminars at your local gear shops). Don't forget those valuable avalanche safety courses as well.

Brainard Lake.

Know the mountain geography, specifically the route topography. Research the peak and know the escape routes in case bad weather rolls in. Knowing the route will also give you a good estimate of how long it will take you to reach the summit and how you can descend. Keep in mind the weight of your pack and that you'll only be as fast as the slowest group member. Understanding topography can also help you select the route safest from rockfall and avalanches. Terrain selection is often the most critical factor in managing risk in the mountains.

Increase your fitness and acclimatization ahead of time. Efficiency is a key piece of the puzzle, and if you're in great shape, you can move faster and feel better. Sleep in a high-mountain town or backcountry hut first, and then increase the elevation gradually to backcountry experiences on twelvers or thirteeners to further acclimatize. As you climb bigger objectives, you'll want to have the stamina, speed, and fitness to escape almost any situation that comes up. This guidebook progresses in the same way. Each entry allows you to first hike to a lake for a shorter goal and then build up to more difficult challenges, such as peak ascents and high-ridge traverses. Your endurance will improve as you begin to tackle larger objectives and even multiday objectives.

Lighten your load. The more weight you carry, the slower you will move. Heavy weight also increases fatigue. Here are my three components to traveling lighter and more efficiently:

- **Bare essentials:** I am a bare minimalist during most of my travels, but it's up to you to experiment to see what you can survive without. My bare essentials are my whippet/ice ax, ultralight down hoody jacket, waterproof jacket and pants (which also act as wind breakers), water reservoir/water bottle, headlamp, energy bars, hat, gloves, cameras, sunscreen, sunglasses, toilet paper, lighter, ultraviolet water purifier, and prepacked pizza (among other snacks and food for the backcountry). If you are headed for a hut trip or winter camping, you'll need to add a –15- to 15-degree ultralight down sleeping bag (depending on how cold you get), a sleeping pad, an ultralight one- to three-person tent, and maybe an additional ultralight bivy sack.

- **Stoves:** Don't forget your stove either, as it might come in handy to melt snow for water or boil up your favorite dehydrated meals! On multiday peaks or hut trips, a stove is sometimes needed, and if I do carry one, it's a very small and light MSR PocketRocket.

- **Avalanche gear:** In avalanche terrain, a beacon, probe, and shovel are essential, and an inflatable avalanche bag is nice, but remember that they won't prevent you from being caught in an avalanche; they will only help you be located by others if you are caught in a slide. A beacon will also facilitate your own rescue, or help you to find others, should you be caught in an avalanche. Make sure your probe extends enough (15 feet or more), otherwise it will be useless if your companions are buried!

Know your limits. You'll want to climb smaller peaks in this guide in traditional alpine style (with fast and light day gear only) before attempting overnight camping as well. If camping, even in the summer, isn't quite your thing, hut trips in Colorado are becoming very popular and are available near some of the entries in this book through the 10th Mountain Division Hut Association (huts.org) and other hut options (see the appendix).

Before you leave on any trip, browse websites for avalanche information (spring and winter), and in summer, you can often Google your objective to see recent trip reports. Start easy and build from there. After guiding numerous groups up fourteeners, volcanoes, and other peaks throughout the world, including everywhere in Colorado and across the Himalayas, I've found that wilderness trips are often one of the most difficult things hikers, skiers, and boarders have ever done. Being educated and having a good level of fitness can give you the edge you need to enjoy your trips rather than suffer, so do your homework before launching.

Select your team carefully and conserve your energy in the backcountry. Traveling in small groups of fewer than five people is usually the safest practice in the mountains. Too many people tend to slow things down, and if you are climbing a relatively narrow objective or small mountain face, managing slough, rockfall, or other hazards with more than five people can be a chore. I prefer a party of two to four for maximum enjoyment, unless the hazards are minimal. But I also have a few

Wildflowers galore in Ice Lakes Basin.

rules for groups when it comes to setting skin tracks, breaking trail in snow, or navigating tough terrain and helping to conserve energy on big objectives:

- Have the youngest and strongest members break trail or set the skin track, but don't be afraid to rotate through to keep everyone fresh to reach your summits in a timely, efficient manner.
- Always stop to rest with the group and evaluate terrain in safe zones that are out of the way of rockfall and avalanche paths. In addition, stopping every hour to take a heavy pack off, eat a snack, review the route and direction with the group, and just enjoy being there are good practices to get into. When it comes to taking breaks, stopping in a safe area but also an area that is sunny and in a windbreak on a cold day is a good idea. And on very warm days, seek a shady area.

Practice Leave no Trace (LNT). Take only pictures and leave only footprints. Pick up all of your trash and basically leave the wild places you find wild and pristine for future generations. To review the seven principles of Leave No Trace visit lnt.org. We are fortunate to still have this land to explore, and before that the Native Americans, primarily the Ute tribes, roamed and protected these places. We should continue their legacy to protect and preserve these mountains for all who come after us.

GEAR AND EQUIPMENT

Although I mention the basic and standard equipment I tend to use, my best advice for you is go to a local rental shop and demo some gear. A thirty-liter backpack is a great size for most single-day outings and is large enough to hold the "ten essentials" described in the next section. I work with clients on a regular basis to dial in their gear for any mountain anywhere in the world, so for more on gear advice and training for mountain objectives visit jonkedrowski.com and drjonsadventures.com, and shoot me an email!

The Ten Essentials Systems

Rather than refer to specific products, I categorize essential backcountry equipment according to its purpose. Increase your survival chances in extreme environments by always having all ten systems in your pack.

1. Navigation
2. Sun protection
3. Insulation
4. Illumination
5. First-aid supplies
6. Fire
7. Repair kit and tools
8. Nutrition
9. Hydration
10. Emergency shelter

Dream Lake, Rocky Mountain National Park.

Nutrition and Hydration

As I mentioned earlier, it's important to take breaks, but you should also experiment to find out which foods help you feel strong out on the trail. I always say that my favorite thing about doing big adventures in the mountains is the food. There are so many bars and gels out on the market these days. Supplement those with real foods that are high in energy. I love making avocado and peanut butter and jelly sandwiches. But also taking tasty trail mixes and real fruit is a good way to enjoy the journey! I often carry peaches, bananas, apples, and lots of dried fruit too. When it comes to dehydrated food on multiday trips, many of the brands these days have tons of sodium. Shop carefully to choose products with less salt, fewer preservatives, and more natural ingredients. Don't forget the chocolate, too, and drink and carry plenty of water—up to four liters per day is best. I will simply carry a Steripen and one Nalgene bottle to purify water right out of the lakes and streams.

Footwear

Probably the most important component of your backcountry adventures is your footwear. Find a pair of shoes or boots that is warm enough, breathable enough, and correct for the season you are in (snow, mud, rain). While high-top boots give plenty of protection for spring or fall and into winter, once the days get long and the trails are snow-free, I prefer trail runners. Waterproof is usually a good thing too. But you also have to have a pair that you can do hundreds of miles in, that don't give you blisters, and that you can hike, climb, scramble, and do anything in.

Ice Ax, Crampons, and Trekking Poles

While this book is intended to be used primarily in the summer for hiking, we can't ignore the fact that most peaks in Colorado hold snow well into June and July, and sometimes snow lingers into August. Carrying an ice ax and crampons is also a personal decision based on terrain selection and the difficulty of your climbing objective combined with seasonal snow conditions. For example, you might not need crampons even if the couloir you are climbing is 40 degrees—maybe the snow is punchy or powdery, allowing for good steps. If the snow is icier (likely in June or July), your ice ax might come in handy. However, if the slope is moderately steep but powdery, a tool called a whippet could be a better choice. A whippet is an adjustable ski pole with an ice ax on the end. It can also double as a walking stick or trekking pole. I prefer whippets for moderate couloirs where you need to stand taller, but also where I might like to have the security of an ax for traversing or climbing relatively steep terrain or tricky sections. Trekking poles for long days on the trail can really come in handy for taking the pressure off your knees. This is especially true if you are

Always expect the best when exploring Colorado's high ridgelines!

descending with a heavy pack. It's important to be prepared for various terrain in Colorado, especially if you decide to venture past the lakes described in this book.

METEOROLOGY: REGIONAL WEATHER AND CLIMATE

Despite this being a summer hiking guidebook, it is important to understand and consider how the previous winter weather and snowfall will impact your summer hiking season and conditions. During an average year, the Colorado mountains receive anywhere from 250 to 750 inches of snow. Most of the snow falls between November and May in the higher elevations and areas near timberline (12,000 feet). Generally, in May, the change of seasons produces high pressure that combines with warm and long days that will settle the snowpack and make it ideal for skiing and backcountry travel, eventually melting out for hikers and peakbaggers. In spring, the high pressure can settle in for days, providing warm, stable weather, which becomes prolonged by summer's arrival in late June. If you decide to try to hike in June in Colorado above 10,000 feet, remember that you might have to deal with remaining snowpack. Because the seasons are changing, bad weather days can also occur. It could be raining in the valleys below 9,000 feet but snowing at higher elevations for days at a time. For example, in 2015 and 2021, Colorado's high country above 10,000 feet saw upwards of 48 inches of snow during May. The highest peaks, especially at and above timberline, benefited from the snow, while mountain towns in the valleys only saw rain. Big upslope snowstorms commonly hit the Front Range during May, providing the sticky snow coverage (along with lack of wind) needed for skiing many peaks that can only be navigated for a month or two each year. We also all remember the winter of 2018–2019 when 9 to 12 feet of snow fell on most of Colorado's great ranges from March 1 to March 15. Big winter snows can determine how much snow lingers far into the summer and may impact your summer objectives, so be aware of that.

At lower elevations, the distinct continental dry climate lends itself to evergreen, conifer, and aspen forests. It's a good rule of thumb to remember that the higher elevations (with tundra vegetation above the timberline) not only receive the lion's share of the seasonal snowfall, as well as summer rains, but can also experience intense blizzards and strong winds at any time of year, even in August!

The orographic (rain shadow) effect also plays a significant role in weather and highland climate in the Colorado mountains. There is generally less snowfall and overall precipitation east of the Continental Divide, and the eastern aspects of the Front Range generally receive less precipitation than the windward and wetter sides of the Divide (with the exception of upslope springtime snow events on the Front Range peaks). For the same reason, there is typically more snowfall (and summer monsoonal rainfall) in the southern mountains like the San Juans and the central Elk Range, versus the Sangre de Cristos. Even the Sawatch Range can be hit with a bit more snow and rain in the summer than the Tenmile/Mosquito Range because it is located farther to the south and west and catches the prevailing fronts coming from the western United States, either from the California coast or the Pacific Northwest. In summer, the monsoon comes from the south predominately, so ranges in southern Colorado often get more rain activity than the northern Colorado ranges. The eastern side of the Sawatch Range is very dry, also due to the orographic effect.

The routes in this guidebook are generally best during June through October. By June, a very dry period of pre-monsoonal weather takes place in Colorado. The days are long, and usual afternoon thunderstorm activity is absent for the most part. In typical years, at the beginning of June, the frontal precipitation that takes place moves into the state from the northwest or the west. Thunderstorms can happen with this frontal precipitation, so it's always imperative that you start your adventure early in the day and get below tree line before noon. This will become even more important by the end of June and into July and August, as the summer monsoon fully kicks in by that time.

During this time, most weather fronts come in from the southwest by way of prevailing winds traveling from the southwest and south. Warmer monsoonal moisture travels into Colorado, combining with warm sunshine, and it's pretty common to have thunderstorms every afternoon, sometimes starting as early as 11:00 a.m. It is never fun to get nearly struck by lightning while coming down a peak too late or while sitting at a mountain lake in the afternoon.

Always start early to lower your chances of getting caught in a thunderstorm. Personally, my favorite time to hike and go for these very long high-ridge traverses on the peaks is in the post-monsoon season of September and October before the winter snow begins. Bluebird days in Colorado are a special treat: you can still start early for the sunrise, but you don't have to rush. The air is cooler and crisper, the sunshine is warm, and there won't be any storms to ruin your day.

Furthermore, "Wild Ice" on Colorado's lakes is a very short season to take advantage of, primarily in late October through December, depending on elevation and location. The ice above 10,000 feet will freeze with overnight temps in the teens or lower, but without snowfall, you can hike to the lakes on 40- to 50-degree days with a lower sun angle and enjoy an incredible mountain lake experience on skates. (More on wild ice on high mountain lakes later in this guide.)

BEING SAFE IN COLORADO'S MOUNTAINS

There are many steps an educated and experienced backcountry explorer, hiker, and alpinist can take to decrease the chances of being caught in a life-threatening situation in the wilderness of Colorado's mountains. In this section, we will explore strategies to keep you and your hiking companions safe in the mountains on all of your trips. It only takes a little thoughtful planning and decision-making to make every adventure you go for safe and enjoyable.

Four Human Factors for Backcountry Safety

1. **Become experienced and educated.** Take wilderness first-aid, leave-no-trace, and even rock-climbing courses, and if you have never been out hiking in the backcountry before, go with someone who knows what they are doing. You can always learn something from others. Get out and explore as often as possible. You can learn a great deal from just being out on the peaks all the time.

2. **Practice good terrain-selection and routefinding habits.** Carrying the proper equipment is important, but if you steer clear of extremely steep slopes, avoid overhanging cornices (even if they linger into the summer on ridges), and stay away from glaciers that are heavily crevassed (this applies mainly to other parts of the world), you can minimize your risk. Proper backcountry travel is a skill that is learned over many years. Always consider what is above you when climbing, think often about your escape route, and never linger in an area that might be prone to snow slides or rockfall.

3. **Never go out alone.** I approach this one with discretion—many of my adventures are done solo, as I enjoy solitude. Going solo is a matter of preference and can be very rewarding for the experienced alpinist. The rewards can also be great if you have an equal partner because you can learn a great deal from one another in the mountains. If you do plan to go out alone, consider

bringing one of the many GPS trackers available these days. It will give your family your location just in case.

4. **Start early.** Many mistakes in the backcountry are created and compounded from other mistakes. The root of the problem is often not starting early enough and running out of time, which makes us rush and make rash decisions, leading to mistakes and accidents. For example, in April, May, and June, the Colorado snowpack is generally more predictable and stable compared to winter months. Snow heats up and softens in the afternoons from warmer temperatures and direct sunlight. The snowpack settles, freezes, and stabilizes overnight when it gets cold. It is generally a good rule to begin an ascent in safe, frozen, and stable snow well before dawn and to be on the summit at sunrise or at least before 9:00 a.m. on a very warm day. Starting early is also a good rule so you are down and out of harm's way before noon. Especially for the summer months, START EARLY. From the end of June to early September, afternoon thunderstorms are always a concern and will likely happen nearly every day in the mountains of Colorado. If your objective is high, is challenging, and makes for a long day, a predawn start is mandatory. Be aware of monsoon surges that could linger overnight and make entire days total washouts. If that's the case, choose a better weather day in addition to starting early or just postpone your day completely.

A Note for Out-of-State Visitors

Conditions in Colorado can vary greatly from those in other parts of the country and differ within separate parts of the state. For example, conditions in the Wasatch Mountains of Utah are very different from those in Colorado's Rocky Mountains. And snow conditions as well as summer monsoon surge timings on a daily basis in the San Juan Mountains can vary from those in the Elk Range and the Front Range. Learn about the snowpack melt-out for June and July and forecast trends for afternoon thunderstorms of the specific location of your outing to help you determine how safe conditions might be.

Before heading out into Colorado's backcountry, study the general conditions reports and forecasts from NOAA.gov. Don't be afraid to Google and consult local resources, such as trip reports from others and local weather apps to gather more forecast information. ALWAYS START EARLY in consideration of afternoon thunderstorms. Ask close friends or people you know about what has been happening in the same season. They may be able to refer you to people or agencies that have local information.

TYPICAL SEASONAL CONDITIONS

The following conditions are typically encountered when exploring in Colorado's backcountry:

June–July: Wildflowers and green meadows explode with color, and trails dry out significantly for the peak of the summer hiking season. Keep an eye out for afternoon thunderstorms with the arrival of the summer monsoon season in July. Summer snow conditions arrive, which are optimal conditions for this guidebook. Snow has settled, but may be sloppy, wet, and slippery by 8:00 a.m. Climbing, hiking, and skiing early can be good but sticky. Watch for unpleasant sun-cupped snowfields on some aspects.

August–October: Lack of snow coverage usually means that everything in the mountains becomes accessible. Not only can you climb peaks and visit lakes, but you can swim in them too! You can also go for a run, mountain bike, or rock climb!

November–December: This is the tail end of the hiking season as backcountry ski season begins in Colorado, but the lack of snow can lead to exposed terrain hazards (rocks, bushes, tree stumps) and bare areas on peaks. Most lakes freeze over for the winter during this period. Use caution, but it may even be possible to ice skate on some of them!

January–March: Snow is accumulating, and snowpack is growing, but with large storms that dump a lot of snow and the lack of warmth and low sun angles, snow layers may not bond until well into March.

April–May: Spring ski season arrives with longer days, excellent snow coverage, warmer temperatures, and stable snowpack. (See Dr. Jon's backcountry ski guidebook, *Classic Colorado Ski Descents.*) With midday to afternoon warming, predawn starts for big objectives should be routine. Steeper lines must be climbed and skied before 9:00 or 10:00 a.m. depending on slope aspect, solar heating, and overall snow coverage. Lower elevation trails begin to become snow-free but will be wet and muddy for hiking.

COLORADO'S "WILD ICE" —BEST ICE-SKATING LAKES

Weather and Conditions for Good Ice

Bluebird days in Colorado in the fall slowly transition into winter. Late fall days deliver sunshine that feels warm, and there won't be any storms to ruin your day. Consistently bitter cold nights ranging from 25°F all the way down to 0°F begin to freeze the surface of many lakes above 10,000 feet. Ice-skating adventures on Colorado's lakes have a very short season to take advantage of, primarily in late October through December, depending on elevation and location. This is called "Wild Ice." The high-altitude lakes, especially above tree line, will freeze with overnight temps combined with long dry spells and no snowfall. Because snowpack hasn't been created yet, you can hike to the lakes on 35- to 50-degree days on snow-free trails with a lower sun angle and enjoy an incredible mountain lake experience on skates.

The best places for Wild Ice are north-facing cirques that are tucked into glacial basins. These lakes are more shadowed and stay colder all day long as the sun angle gets lower. The lakes might still get some sun, but they tend to stay cold into the later fall, which helps create good, smooth ice coverage. Ice will freeze solid and become very smooth in places that are high and dry. A second great location for ice-skating lakes is on eastern slopes. These places will get nice sunshine on a crisp fall morning, which can help you warm up once the sun hits you. But even with the sun still setting later in the day, the ice won't be getting direct sunlight, thus keeping it from melting or becoming sunbaked. When you are watching weather forecasts and temperatures, look for a period of one to two weeks of completely dry weather with no snowfall. Conversely, west-facing lakes might get some afternoon melt and refreeze easily too, but be skatable only in the early mornings. In October

Smooth ice skating on Chihuahua Lake on a crisp fall morning. *Photo by Connor Drumm*

Skating Maroon Lake in early November. *Photo by Naomi Jane Atherton*

or November and into early December if temperatures in a mountain town like Vail, Aspen, Breckenridge, or Telluride have been showing highs in the 40s to 50s and lows in the 20s at 8,000 feet, it's a good bet that a dry spell would create perfect ice on your favorite mountain lake at 11,000 feet or higher.

When it comes to safety, you can never be too careful. Ice thickness of 4 inches or more is the safest, but bear in mind that ice doesn't form on a lake uniformly. When inspecting a lake for ice-skating possibility, look for complete coverage and no openings in the entire lake. Avoid inlets and outlets from creeks and streams. These tend to bring in warmer moving water and let water flow out, often impacting the thickness of the ice and making it more dangerous.

Considerations for Gear

Ice skates, of course! You'll need to strap your skates on your backpack. Skate guards are a must. So are gloves, and kneepads or elbow pads if you are worried about taking a tumble. If you are worried about breaking through while skating, you can carry a life preserver just in case. A towel can be nice to wipe off your blades and also have something to sit on and set your feet on while changing footwear when you get off the lake. Toe warmers and hand warmers can help for those really chilly mornings. Bring a few of your friends and play a little, but be safe out there.

Suggested Lakes—My Top Ten

Here are my top ten lakes to skate on, with their entry numbers in this book. Be sure to check with local land managers regarding seasonal closures or other restrictions and minimize your impact in these alpine and wilderness areas.

1. Maroon Lake and Willow Lake—#55
2. Chihuahua Lake—#15
3. Missouri Lakes and Fancy Lake—#38
4. Capitol Lake—#48
5. Vestal Lake—#69
6. Cathedral Lake—#52
7. Thomas Lakes—#47
8. Dream Lake and Sky Pond—#2
9. Deluge Lake—#26
10. South Crestone Lake—#57
    Extra Credits: Lake Ann—#42 and Bear Lake—#46

Enjoy the journey and please have safe adventures! —Dr. Jon

CHAPTER 1

FRONT RANGE NORTH
(RMNP AND INDIAN PEAKS WILDERNESS)

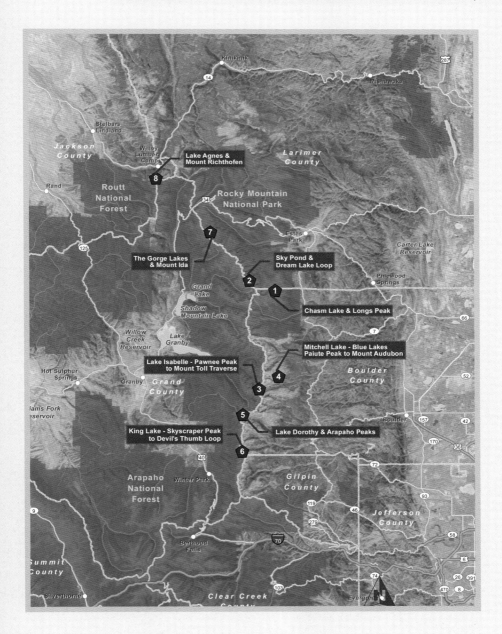

- Lake Agnes & Mount Richthofen — 8
- The Gorge Lakes & Mount Ida — 7
- Sky Pond & Dream Lake Loop — 2
- Chasm Lake & Longs Peak — 1
- Mitchell Lake - Blue Lakes Paiute Peak to Mount Audubon — 4
- Lake Isabelle - Pawnee Peak to Mount Toll Traverse — 3
- King Lake - Skyscraper Peak to Devil's Thumb Loop — 6
- Lake Dorothy & Arapaho Peaks — 5

CHASM LAKE AND LONGS PEAK

1

Elevation Gain	2,600 feet for Chasm Lake; 4,856 feet for the summit of Longs Peak
Round-Trip Distance	9.5 miles to Chasm Lake; 15 miles for ascent of Loft to Longs and descent of the Keyhole route
Trailheads	Longs Peak (9,400 feet); Copeland Lake/Sandbeach Lake/Wild Basin (8,320 feet)
Difficulty Ratings	Class 1 hike to the lake on trail; Class 3 hike/climb for Longs Peak Loop
Optimal Season	June through October
Maps	Trails Illustrated #200 and #301; Roosevelt National Forest

COMMENT: Longs Peak is the icon of Rocky Mountain National Park (RMNP). Its lofty and prominent summit is seen in the northwest skyline from the Denver metropolitan area on a clear day. While visiting Chasm Lake is a relatively easy adventure, be ready for windy conditions and plan on a full-day outing and predawn start to attempt Longs Peak.

Chasm Lake illuminated by the Diamond on Longs just after sunrise.

Left: The Homestretch ascending to the flat summit of Longs. **Right:** Descending the north-face Cables route with two rappel pitches; note Chasm Lake to the right.

GETTING THERE

Longs Peak Trailhead (9,400 feet). This trailhead is located at the Longs Peak Ranger Station just off Colorado Highway 7. If approaching from the north from Estes Park, travel 9 miles from the US Highway 36/Colorado Highway 7 junction in Estes Park. Turn right on the paved road marked for Longs Peak Trailhead and follow the road 1 mile to the parking area and ranger station. From the south, travel 10.5 miles north from the junction of Colorado Highway 7 and the Peak to Peak Highway (Colorado Highway 72). Turn left on the paved road marked for Longs Peak Trailhead and follow the road 1 mile to the parking area and ranger station.

Copeland Lake (Sandbeach Lake/Wild Basin) Trailhead (8,320 feet). Copeland Lake Trailhead is also called the Sandbeach Lake Trailhead and is located at the entrance to Wild Basin just off Colorado Highway 7. If approaching from the north from Estes Park, travel 13 miles from the US Highway 36/Colorado Highway 7 junction in Estes Park. Turn right on the paved road marked for Wild Basin and follow the road 0.4 mile to the parking area just north of the Wild Basin park entrance. From the south, travel 6.5 miles north from the junction of Colorado Highway 7 and the Peak to Peak Highway (Colorado Highway 72). Turn left on the paved road marked for Wild Basin and follow the road for 0.4 mile to the parking area just north of the Wild Basin park entrance. For more information on timed entry permits and trailhead status in RMNP visit nps.gov/romo and recreation.gov.

THE LAKE

1. Chasm Lake (11,780 feet) (Class 1–2). Start from the Longs Peak Trailhead and follow the East Longs Peak Trail for 4.5 miles to Chasm Meadows below Chasm Lake. On the way, you will cross a stream near timberline at 2 miles. Turn left at Jims

Grove junction at 2.5 miles and reach Chasm junction (11,540 feet) at 3.5 miles, where you will continue to the left toward Chasm Meadows. Once in the meadows and you are traveling to Chasm Lake, head toward the east face of Longs by hiking and ascending some solid granite steps for about 150 vertical feet before dropping into a deep glacial cirque that holds the magnificent Chasm Lake. From here, you will be staring directly at Longs Peak's impressive Diamond face. Enjoy where you are and don't be surprised to hear an echo from other people in the area in this unique amphitheater, although it's not always easy to match the sound of others with where they are actually located.

THE LOOP/HIGH-RIDGE TRAVERSE

2. Longs Peak Summit (14,256 feet) via Loft ascent and Keyhole descent (Class 3). From Chasm Meadows, instead of traveling to Chasm Lake and toward the east face of Longs (or after you have visited Chasm Lake), climb to the southwest toward a moderate face that rises to a saddle between Mount Meeker and Longs Peak. The key to reaching the flat saddle, known as the Loft, is to take a left (south) and traverse a narrow but obvious ledge that heads south then southwest up Class 3 slopes to reach the flat saddle. From the Loft, continue west for 0.25 mile, descending around the mountain for 150 feet. Then climb up and around into Keplinger's couloir. Just before starting to gain elevation below the rock formations known as the Palisades (beautiful west-facing rock slabs), you will pass an arrow painted on the rocks known as Clark's Arrow.

From Clark's Arrow, scramble north and descend slightly; then ascend a broken set of ledges up a couloir to 13,600 feet. From here, the top of the couloir can be reached at a feature called the Notch, but before you get to the Notch, traverse left (northwest) on a snow-covered ledge and ramps for 200 yards to join the Homestretch at 13,900 feet. Follow the relatively easy slope of rocky slabs to the summit of Longs.

Once you are ready to descend, take care to leave the broad summit of Longs by heading back down the Homestretch. In the summer, you can easily spot the bull's-eyes painted on the rock to keep you on your route. At 13,900 feet, the Homestretch slabs give way to some rocky and narrow ledges and eventually head west then northwest around the mountain. The "Narrows" can be a bad place to be late in the day, and you also want to be aware of other people on this pure granite slab traverse. It crosses a sheer vertical granite face on a narrow ledge. Upon your arrival at the top of the Trough on the southwest corner of the ridgeline of Longs at 13,750 feet, you will be peering down a glacial trough gully and must downclimb the steep initial 50 feet of Class 3 granite to get into the Trough itself. Once in the Trough, you

Top: Longs Peak is very scenic, seen here from the junction to Chasm Lake. *Photo by Chris Tomer* **Right:** Torrey Udall climbing a fun section of Kiener's, an exciting route that peers down the Diamond.

will descend about 600 feet of loose rock in a Class 2+ gully. Near 13,150 feet, look north (right) and locate the exit and the ascending traverse to the start of the Ledges. Ascend for a hundred yards or so on the Ledges, then descend for 300 yards more to the obvious exit to the west aspect of Longs Peak where you will pass through the Keyhole and head east at 13,200 feet. There is a historic stone shelter on the east aspect of the Keyhole. From here, you'll drop several hundred feet onto the boulder field and make your way back to the trailhead in 6 miles by way of the Longs Peak Trail. The trail wraps around Mount Lady Washington in a clockwise circle, northeast, then east, then southeast, and at 2.5 miles, you will reach Chasm Lake junction. From here, it's 3.5 miles back to the Longs Peak Trailhead where you started. You can always do this route in reverse too: climb the Keyhole and descend the Loft.

DR. JON'S EXTRA CREDIT
A. Longs backpacking options. After obtaining the necessary permits from the National Park Service, choose to camp one night at either Chasm Lake or in the boulder field near the Keyhole and do the Longs Peak Loop in either direction following the route descriptions above. Additional route options to the top of Longs include the Keyhole, the North Face Cables, and Kiener's. A classic route is Kiener's via Lambslide and Broadway with a descent of the north face.
B. Sandbeach Lake. From the Copeland Lake/Wild Basin Trailhead, get an early start and hike to Sandbeach Lake, and from there, it is possible to climb Longs Peak via Keplinger's couloir. If you really want a challenge, add Mount Meeker, one of Colorado's one hundred highest peaks at 13,911 feet.

CHASM LAKE AND LONGS PEAK

SKY POND—LOCH VALE —LAKE OF GLASS —DREAM LAKE LOOP

2

Elevation Gain	2,200 feet for Sky Pond and return via Dream Lake Loop
Round-Trip Distance	9.5 miles; up to 13 miles if you visit many of the side lakes and extra credit locations
Trailheads	Glacier Gorge (9,240 feet); Bear Lake (9,475 feet)
Difficulty Ratings	Class 1–2 hike on trail; Class 3 hike/climb for 150 feet for scrambling above Timberline Falls; easy hiking on the national park's constructed trails overall
Optimal Season	June through November; December and January can be common for winter snowshoeing with trails scoured by wind
Map	Trails Illustrated #200

COMMENT: Sky Pond is one of the major highlights of a beautiful network of glacially carved valleys and nearly a dozen lakes that create the identity of Rocky Mountain National Park. While this lake and loop route are very stunning, providing an abundance of lakes, they also can be very crowded for that same reason. Consider doing these hiking options during the week or in the shoulder season of fall or later in the year when the snow begins and the summer crowds are gone. You can do the loop in either direction too; starting at Dream Lake for sunrise can be quite rewarding. Winter is possible too; just be ready for the wind if you go.

Dream Lake during a late summer snowstorm.

GETTING THERE

Glacier Gorge Trailhead (9,240 feet). Glacier Gorge Trailhead is located on Bear Lake Road, 8 miles from US Highway 36 inside Rocky Mountain National Park. Because this trailhead is inside the national park, consider using the free park shuttle to access the trailhead during the busy summer months, especially weekends.

Bear Lake Trailhead (9,475 feet). Bear Lake Trailhead is another mile up the road and can also be used to start or finish this loop. For more information on timed entry permits and trailhead status in RMNP visit nps.gov/romo/planyourvisit/index.htm and recreation.gov.

THE LAKE

1. Sky Pond (10,900 feet) (Class 2–3). Start from the Glacier Gorge Trailhead or Bear Lake Trailhead and follow a series of signs and trails for 4.5 miles to the spectacular cirque basin that holds Sky Pond. In a quick 0.25 mile from the parking area, just after crossing Chaos Creek, the trail briefly converges with the Glacier Creek Trail. After a brief distance (less than a tenth of a mile) the Glacier Creek Trail heads to the right toward Bear Lake. Travel toward Sky Pond by turning left at this junction in the direction of Alberta Falls. If coming from Bear Lake Trailhead, leave the parking lot over a large bridge, and after 100 yards, head left and down the hill toward Alberta Falls.

At just over 0.8 mile, you will reach Alberta Falls, one of the more popular hiking destinations in Rocky Mountain National Park. This scenic 35-foot waterfall thunders down a small gorge on Glacier Creek, named after Alberta Sprague, the wife of Abner Sprague, one of the original settlers in the Estes Park area.

Left: Emerald Lake. **Right:** Lake Haiyaha among the boulders.

Loch Vale on the way to Lake of Glass and Sky Pond.

At 1.6 miles, after travelling through some pine forest, you will arrive at the North Longs Peak Trail junction. To continue on toward Sky Pond, turn right (southwest) here. About a half mile farther up the trail, you'll reach Mills Lake junction. The trail to the left (south) leads to Mills Lake and Black Lake up Glacier Gorge, while the side trail to the right leads north to Lake Haiyaha. (You'll take this trail later to complete the loop portion of this route.) To continue on toward Sky Pond, proceed straight ahead onto the Loch Vale Trail. Note that some trails in this area were heavily reconstructed through a 2012 project but are still in excellent condition.

Above the junction, the route becomes quite steep as it climbs over a pair of short switchbacks through an impressive gorge, while Icy Brook cascades down the valley on your left. On the third switchback, you'll reach a vantage point that offers a nice view of a waterfall tumbling down the gorge.

At roughly 2.8 miles from the trailhead, you will reach Loch Vale, known as "The Loch." The word "loch" is the Scottish Gaelic and Irish term for a lake or a sea inlet. This stunning subalpine lake, at 10,190 feet, is located within one of the most studied watersheds in the world. For more than thirty years, scientists have monitored chemical inputs to the watershed and performed climate change research here.

Views across from the lake include 13,153-foot Taylor Peak and Taylor Glacier (to the southwest). Framing the spectacular gorge on either side is 12,668-foot Thatchtop Mountain (south) and 12,829-foot "Sharkstooth" toward the southwest. As you hike around the north shore of the lake, 13,208-foot Powell Peak will begin to reveal itself to the south.

Beyond The Loch, the trail begins to climb again, and at just over 3.6 miles, you'll come to the Sky Pond/Andrews Glacier split. The trail to the right leads to Andrews Glacier and the Andrews Creek Backcountry Campsites, the only campsites in this area. Continue on toward Sky Pond by staying to the left at this junction.

At 0.33 mile above the junction, you'll have your first good view of Timberline Falls, high above the trail. At 4.1 miles from the trailhead and 0.5 mile above the trail junction, you will reach the base of Timberline Falls. From this vantage point, the trail begins to climb a series of rock steps. This next section of trail is steep and climbs nearly 200 feet in just under 0.25 mile.

The main portion of the waterfall drops roughly 100 feet and continues cascading down the valley below you. Look out across the valley to the northeast for a bird's-eye view of The Loch in the far-off distance.

When facing the falls, you will need to climb/scramble up 100 feet or so of Class 3 rock. The first 30 feet are the most challenging, and then the route eases up after that. Be cautious if there is water on the route, and then above the falls, enjoy the view and continue on to the Lake of Glass a mere football-field length beyond. Travel along the Lake of Glass on a rocky and rugged trail on the west side of the lake, and then continue up toward a prominent moraine in the middle of the valley farther south and westerly to ascend another 0.4 mile to Sky Pond. This lake is amazing with sheer cliff walls on three sides, including views of the Sharkstooth spires, Taylor Peak, and Powell Peak, all over 12,000 feet.

THE LOOP

2. Lake Haiyaha to Dream Lake (Class 1). After enjoying the vistas from Sky Pond, return to Mills Lake junction by hiking for 2.5 miles back down the way you came up. Pass Lake of Glass, carefully downclimb to the base of Timberline Falls, proceed through the Andrews Glacier junction, then hike past the Loch, and arrive at the Mills Lake junction. Turn left (north) and hike 0.75 mile to Lake Haiyaha. "Haiyaha" is a Native American word meaning lake of many big rocks. There will be a small spur trail leading to the left toward the lake at roughly 0.6 mile from the Mills Lake junction. At this point, you can enjoy some of the oldest pine trees in Rocky Mountain National Park and take in the magnificent view of Chaos Canyon.

Left: Signs clearly mark the way in RMNP, so it is easy stay on track. **Right:** Alberta Falls in early fall.

From Lake Haiyaha, it's nearly 2 miles back to the Glacier Gorge Trailhead, and the hike is stellar. Follow the spur trail back to the main trail and stay left at the trail junction that you had originally come from when you came over from Mills Lake junction. In less than 0.5 mile, as you head north along a flat zone, you will come to an opening with excellent panoramas of Bear Lake and Nymph Lake to the north and Longs Peak to the south.

In about a mile from Lake Haiyaha, there will be a trail junction where another short spur trail to the left takes you, in about 100 yards, to visit Dream Lake, and the trail to the right heads east to Nymph Lake and then back to either trailhead. Enjoy this gorgeous set of lakes and remember to go early in the morning to avoid the crowds and to be able to take reflection photos. Consider the loop in reverse order as well because Dream Lake at sunrise is stunning!

DR. JON'S EXTRA CREDIT
A. Andrews Creek campsites for backpacking (Class 2). After obtaining the necessary permits from the National Park Service, choose to camp one or two nights at the Andrews Creek campsites, which are not very far from the Andrews Glacier. From here, it's possible to launch other ambitious adventures of your own, including any number of peak climbs or high-ridge traverses in the alpine. Technical rock climbing can be found in abundance on many of the jagged peaks mentioned in these descriptions.

B. Emerald Lake (Class 1). From the Dream Lake junction, travel west for 0.5 mile to Emerald Lake. This lake is worth the side trip and can be an excellent place to have lunch depending on how early you start your day on the loop.

SKY POND—LOCH VALE
—LAKE OF GLASS—DREAM LAKE LOOP

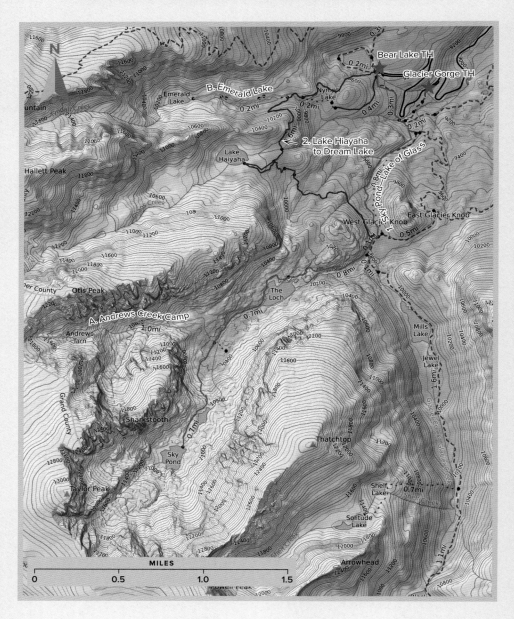

LAKE ISABELLE —PAWNEE PEAK TO MOUNT TOLL TRAVERSE

3

Elevation Gain	400 feet for Lake Isabelle; 2,500 feet for Pawnee Peak; 2,950 feet for Mount Toll Traverse
Round-Trip Distance	4.5 miles for Lake Isabelle; 10.5 miles for Pawnee Peak; 11.5 miles to Mount Toll for the traverse
Trailhead	Long Lake (10,505 feet) at Brainard Lake Recreation Area
Difficulty Ratings	Class 1 hike on trail to lake; Class 2–3 hike/climb for Pawnee Peak (12,943 feet) to Mount Toll (12,979 feet) Traverse
Optimal Season	June through October; Brainard Lake Recreation area is accessed by the Gateway Trailhead along the access road from October 15 to Memorial Day generally. This will add 5 miles each way to your destination.
Maps	Trails Illustrated #102 and #1304

COMMENT: Lake Isabelle is one of the most scenic glacial trough lakes and basins in the entire state of Colorado. Moose can be abundant here and so will the wildflowers in July and August. The Indian Peaks Wilderness encompasses 76,000 acres of wilderness in Colorado, with many of the peaks named in honor of Native American

Lake Isabelle, Shoshoni Peak, and the Isabelle Glacier in the distance.

Lake Isabelle reflection.

tribes. This adventure to Pawnee Pass and Pawnee Peak is a great way to honor their namesake. Arrive early to ensure you get a parking spot as this popular destination does fill up quickly, especially on weekends. In 2021, Brainard Lake Recreation Area began using a reservation system. Get your reservation online in advance at recreation.gov. Your national parks pass or other federal lands passes are valid at Brainard Lake Recreation Area. Without a pass, the daily fee is $12.

GETTING THERE

Long Lake Trailhead (10,500 feet). Travel Colorado Highway 72 to the town of Ward. Ward is 13 miles north from Nederland coming from Boulder via Colorado Highway 119 or by traveling Colorado Highway 7 from the north from Lyons or Estes Park. From the north side of Ward on Colorado Highway 72, turn west on Brainard Lake Road (County Road 102). Travel 2.5 miles to the Brainard Gateway Trailhead and then travel another 2 miles to Brainard Lake. Continue past the lake for 0.5 mile and take a left at a split in the road in a pine forest. After another 0.5 mile, the road dead-ends in a parking lot with a public toilet, which is at the trailhead.

THE LAKE

1. Lake Isabelle (10,868 feet). Start from the Long Lake Trailhead and enter the Indian Peaks Wilderness almost immediately upon leaving the parking lot to the southwest. In 0.25 mile, you will arrive at the east Jean Lunning Trail junction. This trail loops around the south side of Long Lake and will reunite with the trail you are on (Pawnee Pass Trail) about a mile farther up the trail. Continue southwest on the Pawnee Pass Trail by staying right and traveling along the north and west sides of the lake in some pine forest with several openings to the lake on your left.

After 1 mile, continue into the forest and stay right at the reemergence of the Jean Lunning Trail. The trail will continue westward, and you will be treated to some spectacular mountain scenery with jagged peaks in the distance as the trees give way to meadows of flowers. Ascend some rocky meadows and arrive at the junction of a trail at mile 2.1. The Pawnee Pass Trail heads to the right, and the Isabelle Glacier Trail heads to the left. Take a left and proceed to the banks of the lake in less than 150 yards. The lake will appear right in front of you. The basin behind the lake offers views of Niwot Ridge to your left, 13,409-foot Navajo Peak, Navajo Glacier, 13,441-foot Apache Peak, and 12,967-foot Shoshone Peak to the right. The banks of the lake are an excellent place for a picnic or a relaxing summer nap.

THE HIGH-RIDGE TRAVERSE

2. Pawnee Peak (12,943 feet) and Mount Toll (12,979 feet) via Pawnee Pass, south slopes/south ridge (Class 2–3). Start at the Long Lake Trailhead. From the trailhead gate, hike up the Pawnee Pass Trail to the southwest toward Lake Isabelle. At 2.1 miles, you will reach the junction of the Isabelle Glacier Trail and the Pawnee Pass Trail. Instead of heading to the lake, travel to your right and head north on the Pawnee Pass Trail as it switches back up some steeper terrain to the north and then veers off to the northwest, arriving at Pawnee Pass after 2.5 miles. From the pass, you can see Pawnee Peak to the north. Hike along a social trail and rocky ridge to reach the flat summit of Pawnee Peak. The views from here

Leaving the Long Lake Trailhead toward Isabelle Lake.

Passing a creek in the basin, Shoshoni Peak above.

are spectacular. You can look directly to the north and see Mount Toll roughly a half mile away. Descend the ridge for a short distance to a flat saddle between the two peaks and climb the southwest ridge of Mount Toll for 0.25 mile from the 12,540-foot connecting saddle between the two peaks. Follow the ridge north and ascend 400 feet by staying on the southwest aspect of the ridgeline. A couple of Class 2–3 moves are required on the ridge, but they are enjoyable, and the small summit of Mount Toll appears abruptly. On your return, in favorable weather, you can also take advantage of visiting Shoshoni Peak (12,967 feet), which is a mere 0.9 mile south of Pawnee Pass on an easy ridgeline.

DR. JON'S EXTRA CREDIT

A. Isabelle Glacier (Class 2). Continue along the north and west shores of Lake Isabelle up the Isabelle Glacier Trail for 1.7 miles to the base of the Isabelle Glacier below the stunning faces of Navajo and Apache Peaks. This is one of Indian Peaks Wilderness's signature natural amphitheaters.

B. Pawnee Pass to Pawnee Peak, Mount Toll, Paiute Peak, and Mount Audubon Traverse Loop (Class 3–4). Start early from the Long Lake Trailhead and travel the 5.75 miles to Mount Toll as described in the previous section. From Mount Toll, carefully navigate the southwest ridge and then travel along the connecting ridge (on the west side as you head north) between Mount Toll and Paiute Peak (13,088 feet). From Paiute Peak, descend east for several hundred feet to the connecting saddle on boulders before finding a climbers' trail and traveling east for 0.9 mile from Paiute Peak's summit to the top of Mount Audubon (13,223 feet). This is the high point of the loop. From here, descend the Mount Audubon Trail for 3.7 miles to the Mitchell Lake Trailhead, which is less than 0.5 mile from the Long Lake Trailhead. This very scenic and challenging loop offers a full day of 11.5 miles and 10,500 feet of total elevation gain. (See Mitchell Lake—Blue Lakes—Pauite Peak to Mount Audubon, entry #4, for the trailhead directions for Mitchell Lake.)

LAKE ISABELLE—PAWNEE PEAK TO MOUNT TOLL TRAVERSE

MITCHELL LAKE —BLUE LAKES—PAIUTE PEAK TO MOUNT AUDUBON

4

Elevation Gain	200 feet for Mitchell Lake; 850 feet for Blue Lake; 1,350 feet for Upper Blue Lake; 2,564 feet for Paiute Peak; 3,150 feet for Paiute Peak to Audubon Loop Traverse from Upper Blue Lake starting from trailhead
Round-Trip Distance	2.0 miles for Mitchell Lake; 5.5 miles for Blue Lake; 7.0 miles for Upper Blue Lake; 9.0 miles for loop of Blue Lakes to Paiute Peak and Mount Audubon
Trailhead	Mitchell Lake (10,524 feet) at Brainard Lake Recreation Area
Difficulty Ratings	Class 1 hike on trail to lakes; Class 2–3 hike/climb for Paiute Peak and Mount Audubon Traverse/Loop
Optimal Season	June through October; Brainard Lake Recreation area is accessed by the Gateway Trailhead along the access road from October 15 to Memorial Day generally. This will add 5 miles each way to your destination.
Maps	Trails Illustrated #102 and #1304

COMMENT: Mitchell Lake Basin and the Blue Lakes are some of the hidden gems of the Indian Peaks Wilderness. The Indian Peaks Wilderness encompasses 76,000 acres of wilderness in Colorado, with many of the peaks named in honor of Native American tribes. Mount Audubon is a very popular thirteener with a steady trail, but an early start can give you plenty of solitude. Arrive early to ensure you get a parking spot as this popular destination fills up quickly, especially on weekends. In 2021, Brainard Lake Recreation Area began using a reservation system. Get your reservation online in advance at recreation.gov. Your national parks pass or other federal lands passes are valid at Brainard Lake Recreation Area. Without a pass, the daily fee is $12.

GETTING THERE
Mitchell Lake Trailhead (10,524 feet). Travel Colorado Highway 72 to the town of Ward. Ward is 13 miles north from Nederland coming from Boulder via Colorado Highway 119 or by traveling Colorado Highway 7 from the north from Lyons or Estes Park. From the north side of Ward on Colorado Highway 72, turn west on Brainard Lake Road (County Road 102). Travel 2.5 miles to the Brainard Gateway

Pawnee · Toll · Paiute · Audubon · Notabon

A look at the peaks described here, left to right: Toll, Paiute, Audubon, Notabon.

Trailhead, and then travel another 2 miles to Brainard Lake. Continue past the lake for 0.5 mile, follow the signs, and take a right at a split in the road in a pine forest. After another 0.5 mile, the road dead-ends in a parking lot with a public toilet, which is at the trailhead.

THE LAKES

1. Mitchell Lake (10,720 feet) and Blue Lake (11,310 feet). Start from the Mitchell Lake Trailhead and enter the Indian Peaks Wilderness right after crossing Mitchell Creek on a footbridge toward the northwest. You will travel through a forest and cross another footbridge at the base of the lake close to the end of the first mile. You will see Mitchell Lake in some pine forest with several openings to the lake on your right.

After 1 mile, leave the lake and the dark forest behind as you climb into the basin heading west. Travel for 1.5 miles more along the creek to reach Blue Lake at 11,350 feet. You will see the pyramid of Mount Toll to your west, and this lake is stunning. Proceed for another 0.75 mile as the basin becomes very rocky before a social trail climbs up into a steeper portion of the basin. Follow it into a cirque and up on some flat rocky benches, and you'll arrive at Upper Blue Lake at 11,840 feet. The views of both Mount Toll and Paiute Peak's eastern aspects are imposing, but it's clear to see why these lakes were named.

Left: Mount Toll (right) from Blue Lake with Pawnee Peak and Little Pawnee Peak to the left.
Right: Mitchell Lake on a windy day with Audubon towering above.

THE LOOP AND HIGH-RIDGE TRAVERSE

2. Paiute Peak (13,088 feet) and Mount Audubon (13,223 feet) via Upper Blue Lake (Class 2–3 for the southeast face to west ridge). Start at the Mitchell Lake Trailhead. From the west side of Upper Blue Lake, travel west and ascend the steep slope of rock and rock slabs to reach a prominent rib or bump on the southeast face of Paiute Peak. At 12,300 feet, follow this Class 2+ rib directly north for nearly 400 feet to reach the south ridge crest of Paiute at 12,700 feet. Finish the climb by carefully ascending some Class 3 sections to the summit for almost another 400 feet of rock. This route is super fun, and the view of the basin and lakes below gets more and more dramatic as you get higher. From Paiute Peak, descend east for several hundred feet to the connecting saddle at 12,640 feet on boulders before finding a climbers' trail and traveling east for 0.9 mile from Paiute Peak's summit to the top of Mount Audubon (13,223 feet). This is the high point of the loop. From here, descend the Mount Audubon Trail for 3.7 miles to the Mitchell Lake Trailhead.

DR. JON'S EXTRA CREDIT

A. Mount Audubon Trail (13,223 feet) and Mount Notabon (12,620 feet). Instead of taking the challenging loop of Audubon with Paiute Peak and Blue Lakes as described in the previous section, consider a fun and easy alternative. Follow the Mount Audubon Trail to the north from the Mitchell Lake Trailhead. This popular 3.7-mile trail rises and reaches the east ridge of Mount Audubon and provides a gorgeous day on a Colorado thirteener that is the sixth-highest peak in the Indian Peaks Wilderness. You can even tag 12,260-foot Mount Notabon on the way.

MITCHELL LAKE—BLUE LAKES —PAIUTE PEAK TO MOUNT AUDUBON

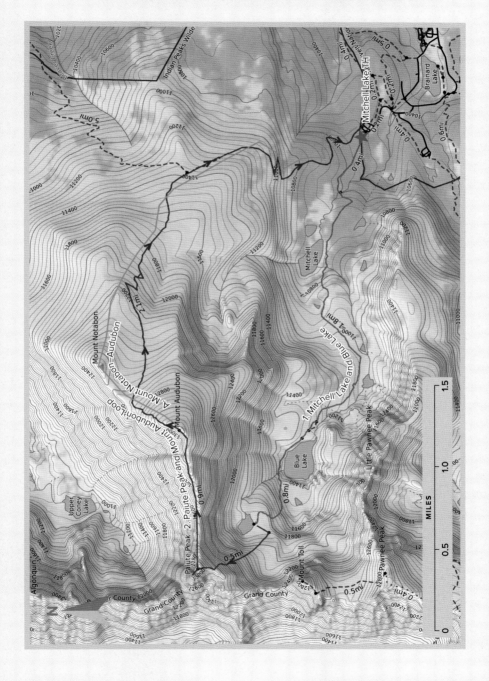

LAKE DOROTHY —ARAPAHO PASS —ARAPAHO PEAKS TRAVERSE

5

Elevation Gain	1,950 feet for Lake Dorothy; 3,400 feet for North Arapaho Peak from South Arapaho Peak
Round-Trip Distance	7 miles for Lake Dorothy, 8 miles for South Arapaho Peak, and 9 miles for the South to North Arapaho Peaks traverse out-and-back
Trailhead	Fourth of July (10,100 feet)
Difficulty Ratings	Class 1 hike on trail (Lake Dorothy); Class 2 hike for South Arapaho Peak; Class 3–4 hike/climb for 80 to 100 feet for scrambling the high ridgeline between South and North Arapaho Peaks
Optimal Season	June through October
Maps	Trails Illustrated #102; Arapaho National Forest

COMMENT: You can be to the trailhead in less than ninety minutes from most Front Range locations, making Arapaho Peaks and Lake Dorothy excellent options. These peaks are the sentinels of the Indian Peaks Wilderness, offering stunning views or a nice trail to a scenic lake if you prefer to stay in the basin instead.

Arapaho Reservoir, and what is left of Arapaho Glacier in the eastern cirque of the peaks, serve as Boulder County's water supply.

GETTING THERE

Fourth of July Trailhead (10,100 feet).
Follow Colorado Highway 119 south from Boulder to the small town of Nederland. From Nederland, head south on Colorado Highway 119 for 0.6 mile. Turn west (right) onto County Road 130, signed for Eldora. Follow the paved road through the town of Eldora, where the pavement ends. Continue on the road for 1.5 miles. Turn right at the signed junction and continue 4.5 miles to the trailhead, which is near the Buckingham and Fourth of July Campgrounds. Typically, the road at the end of the pavement gets plowed toward the trailhead by mid-April. By early May, it is possible to drive all the way to the trailhead, and four-wheel-drive is not mandatory.

THE LAKE

1. Lake Dorothy (12,050 feet). Follow the Arapaho Pass Trail for 1.6 miles as it climbs steadily to the west. To your south, you will see Diamond Lake and Falls in the basin across the valley as you emerge to near tree line. At 11,250 feet, the Fourth of July Mine ruins will be to your left, and you will pass the Arapaho Pass Trail junction but continue straight as you gradually climb out of the basin, get above the timber, and see the flat expanse of Arapaho Pass ahead of you to the west. The steady-grade trail is an old wagon road to Caribou Pass. After 1.1 miles from the Fourth of July Mine ruins and 2.7 total miles, you will reach Arapaho Pass. Stay along the ridgeline and travel west for

Top: The author ascending a Class 5 wall variation en route to North Arapaho's summit. Lake Dorothy is visible upper right in the distance. *Photo by Torrey Udall* **Bottom:** There's one Class 4–5 crack move on the ridge that is a fun downclimb when returning from North Arapaho. *Photo by Torrey Udall*

Lake Dorothy—Arapaho Pass—Arapaho Peaks Traverse

about 0.4 mile. Look into a cirque basin between the ridgeline you are on and Mount Neva to the southwest. Leave the trail, and you will arrive at Lake Dorothy in another 0.3 mile.

THE HIGH-RIDGE TRAVERSE

2. South and North Arapaho Peaks (13,502 feet) (Class 2 for the south slopes/southeast ridge). Start at the Fourth of July Trailhead. From the trailhead gate, hike up the Arapaho Pass Trail to the west. At 1.6 miles, you will get close to tree line. At the Fourth of July Mine ruins (11,250 feet), double back to the northeast on the Arapaho Glacier Trail, which is signed and well beaten. Travel northeast up relatively gentle slopes for 0.75 mile to reach the southeast ridge at 13,000 feet, where you will be able to see the Arapaho Glacier to the north in the basin. Continue 0.3 mile to the summit of South Arapaho Peak. From the basin at 11,500 feet, below South Arapaho's south face, it is possible to snow climb the steep Skywalker couloir, which heads directly north toward the summit. From the summit of South Arapaho Peak, traverse 0.7 mile to North Arapaho Peak via the Class 3–4 ridgeline. Generally, the safest way to traverse the ridge is to stay on the crest but avoid the east (right) side drop-offs. After some initial knife-edge sections, a short slab and chimney crack with access to the crest of the ridge will make you commit to the crux of the route, but after that, the difficulty eases as you ascend to the summit on some easy Class 2 and 3 ledges. Avoid the summit pyramid's steep cliffs by traversing left (west) near the summit and scramble/hike your way to the top. The route is heavily cairned these days, but always be aware of cairns that are false and misleading.

DR. JON'S EXTRA CREDIT

A. Diamond Lake or Lake Dorothy for backpacking. Travel into this area and camp one or two nights at either Diamond Lake or Lake Dorothy. You can travel over Arapaho Pass to the north of Lake Dorothy for a scenic excursion to Caribou Lake for a fun adventure.

B. Mount Neva to Mount Jasper Traverse Loop. Start early from the Fourth of July Trailhead. Travel the 2.7 miles to Arapaho Pass. From the pass, follow the ridgeline to the west and then head south on the north ridge of Mount Neva (Class 3 and 4) to reach the summit of Mount Neva (12,814 feet). From Mount Neva, traverse for 1.2 miles to the summit of Mount Jasper (12,923 feet). From the top of Mount Jasper, head east along a ridgeline, descend to Upper Diamond Lake, Lower Diamond Lake, and eventually the trailhead. (This loop is 4,000 feet of elevation gain in more than 11 miles.) This is a very scenic tour and best in late September on a bluebird day to enjoy the fall colors.

LAKE DOROTHY—ARAPAHO PASS —ARAPAHO PEAKS TRAVERSE

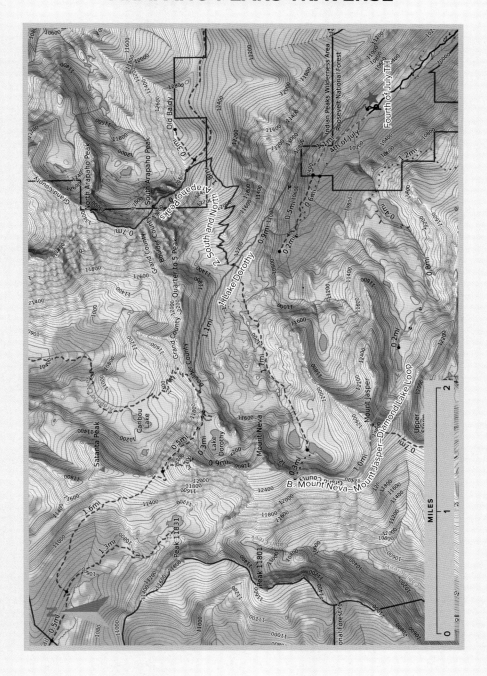

KING LAKE —BOB AND BETTY LAKES —SKYSCRAPER PEAK TO DEVILS THUMB LOOP

6

Elevation Gain	3,100 feet for King Lake; 2,800 for Bob and Betty Lakes
Round-Trip Distance	11 to 12 miles for either King Lake or Betty and Bob Lakes; 15 miles for King Lake to Devils Thumb Loop
Trailhead	Hessie (8,975 feet)
Difficulty Ratings	Class 1 hike on trail (King Lake); Class 2 hike for Loop to Devils Thumb Lake
Optimal Season	June through October
Maps	Trails Illustrated #102; Arapaho National Forest

COMMENT: This is a stunning setting in the Indian Peaks Wilderness to escape the crowds that flock to fourteeners in the summer. Consider a backpacking adventure to visit up to six lakes in the process. The Hessie Trailhead can be a bit tricky due to the nature of creek crossings and multiple trails in the area, but if you know how to read your map and understand landmarks and directions, you should be good to go!

A gorgeous day above King Lake, Indian Peaks Wilderness. *Photo by John Fielder*

GETTING THERE

Hessie Trailhead (8,975 feet). Follow Colorado Highway 119 south from Boulder to the small town of Nederland. From Nederland, head south on Colorado Highway 119 for 0.6 mile. Turn west (right) onto County Road 130 (Eldora Avenue), signed for Eldora. Follow the paved road through the town of Eldora, where the pavement ends. Continue on the road for 0.75 mile and park right on the road. The actual Hessie Trailhead is an additional 0.5 mile away and inaccessible by car. Walk to the trailhead by crossing the creek and staying on the dirt road to the left (west).

THE LAKES

1.   King Lake (11,400 feet) or Bob and Betty Lakes. Follow the Devils Thumb Trail as it climbs steeply for 0.5 mile on the old four-wheel-drive road. Once leaving the road, continue for another 0.8 mile in the pine forest, then cross a bridge (left), and stay on the main Devils Thumb Trail. Refrain from taking the bypass trail or any side trails and continue to the Lost Lake Trail turnoff after 1.6 total miles. Continue west on the gradual King Lake Trail for 4 miles as it steadily climbs into the basin. If you look closely, you will see remnants of the Old Moffat Road on the hillside. The final mile to King Lake is steeper with several switchbacks. At 11,120 feet and 0.5 mile below King Lake, you will pass the trail junction with the Bob and Betty Lakes Trail #810. Before or after visiting King Lake, follow Trail #810 north for 250 feet and 0.4 mile to the southern end of Betty Lake and for another 0.4 mile and 150 feet to reach Bob Lake at just under 11,600 feet.

THE LOOP AND HIGH-RIDGE TRAVERSE

2.   Devils Thumb Lake Loop and Jasper Lake (Class 2). Start at the Hessie Trailhead. This can be done as a fun full-day hike or an overnight backpacking trip by staying at either King Lake or Bob Lake. From the trailhead, hike up the King Lake Trail to the west. At almost 6 miles, you will arrive at King Lake. From King Lake at 11,400 feet, travel southwest above the lake for 0.2 mile, gaining a couple hundred feet of elevation to a very flat saddle on the Continental Divide. When you reach the top, you will intersect with the High Lonesome Trail. Rollins Pass is to the southeast, but instead, travel northwest along the ridgeline on a gradual uphill for the first 0.75 mile. Next, turn due north for an additional 1.25 miles. Skyscraper Peak will be visible to your east as you travel along the ridge. You are traveling essentially along the Continental Divide at this point. Continue for 0.5 mile more to the north from a subtle trail junction between the main trail you are on and the Skyscraper Peak Trail. You will reach a vantage point and a trail junction where you can look down into a basin to the northeast and see the Devils Thumb Lake. This area is known as Devils

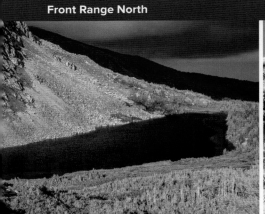

Left: Storm over Devils Thumb Lake, Indian Peaks Wilderness. *Photo by John Fielder*
Right: Exploring glacial tarns in the Indian Peaks Wilderness near Jasper Lake can be fun.

Thumb Pass. Follow this trail to the northeast from 11,800 feet down to the 11,150-foot Devils Thumb Lake for a mile to reach the lake in a gorgeous basin. From Devils Thumb Lake, travel 1 mile east to Jasper Lake. There are good campsites at both Jasper and Devils Thumb Lakes. The Devils Thumb Lake Trail will descend for 4 miles from Jasper Lake back to the Hessie Trailhead.

DR. JON'S EXTRA CREDIT

A. Skyscraper Peak (12,383 feet) (Class 2). You can climb the gentle ridgeline between Devils Thumb Pass and Skyscraper Peak for 0.75 mile to the east to reach the small summit of Devils Thumb Peak along the broad then narrowing ridgeline. This can be a side trip to the major loop as described previously, or you can travel from Hessie Trailhead by using the Devils Thumb Trail. This makes your day 13.5 miles and just shy of 3,500 feet of elevation gain.

B. Woodland Lake and Skyscraper Reservoir (Class 1). The basin below and to the south of Skyscraper Peak holds Skyscraper Reservoir and Woodland Lake and is accessed via the Woodland Lake Trail. With careful research, this area is worth exploring and makes for a shorter day.

C. Devils Thumb, Peak 12,640', Storm Lake Loop (Class 2+). From Devils Thumb Pass, travel the ridgeline north 1.8 miles to the summit of Peak 12,640'. As you ascend to this high point along the Continental Divide, you will get a nice view of the Devils Thumb to your east. From Peak 12,640', some research of the surrounding basin on your map to the north will allow you to descend into the drainage that feeds into Jasper Lake with a visit to Storm Lake on the way. This clockwise loop, starting from Devils Thumb Lake to Peak 12,640', then to Storm Lake and Jasper Lake, and back to Devils Thumb Lake, is 6.5 miles.

KING LAKE—BOB AND BETTY LAKES
—SKYSCRAPER PEAK TO DEVILS THUMB LOOP

THE GORGE LAKES AND MOUNT IDA

7

Elevation Gain	3,150 feet for Azure Lake; 2,475 feet for Mount Ida
Round-Trip Distance	10.8 miles for Azure Lake; 11.1 miles with Inkwell Lake Loop; 9.5 miles for Mount Ida
Trailhead	Poudre Lake/Milner Pass (10,760 feet)
Difficulty Rating	Class 1–2+ hike both on trails and across tundra with no trails
Optimal Season	July through October
Maps	Trails Illustrated #200 and #301; Roosevelt National Forest

COMMENT: This is the most scenic and beautiful hike in all of Rocky Mountain National Park. The views not only from the top of Mount Ida are some of the best in all of the American West, but those who choose to descend into "The Gorge" to visit Lake Azure and other lakes in the basin will be rewarded with the pristine beauty that is the signature of Colorado. In July and August, please start early, even predawn on this hike, because by noon on some days, the thunderstorms will be strong and most of this hike is above timberline with no safety from the dangers of lightning. Check the forecast carefully before starting and always know the prevailing wind direction so you can watch the weather to allow for good decision-making.

GETTING THERE

Poudre Lake Trailhead (8,975 feet). Drive Trail Ridge Road (US Highway 34) west from Estes Park. The trailhead is located at Milner Pass, which is 4.2 miles south of the Alpine Visitor Center and 15.7 miles north of the Grand Lake entrance of Rocky Mountain National Park.

THE LAKES LOOP

1. Azure to Inkwell Lakes Loop (11,940 feet) (Class 1–2). Follow the trail on the south side of Poudre Lake, where you'll find signs for Milner Pass and Mount Ida at the trailhead. The well-maintained trail gains elevation quickly through a subalpine forest for the first 0.6 mile using four switchbacks and a single log bridge to the well-signed Milner Pass/Mount Ida Trail junction at 11,075 feet. Turn right (south) on the Mount Ida Trail and ascend steadily to tree line for 0.6 mile to 11,400 feet.

There will be two more switchbacks, and after that, you will traverse some gladed trees and begin to get some great views. You will have traveled 1.2 miles so far. The broad open slopes of the ridgeline will be visible, and the trail will next head south-southeast just west of and below the Continental Divide. Follow this trail for another 1.6 miles to a cairn that is very prominent in some distinguishable quartzite rocks at mile 2.8 after ascending a steeper portion of the ridgeline (12,140 feet). At the fork, stay right. Next the trail descends across a saddle with stellar views to the north across wide-open alpine bowls slightly above 12,000 feet. At mile 3.5, the trail becomes rocky and almost fades away; continue on to the 4.25-mile mark and traverse left (directly east) to mile 4.5 where you will reach the rim of the gorge at 12,650 feet, and Azure and Inkwell Lakes will be easily seen below you. Azure Lake will be almost directly to your southeast from the rim at 12,600 feet.

In early summer, use caution here and watch for snow cornices left over from the winter. From the rim of the gorge, you should be able to locate a reasonable patch of grass heading southeast and down into the gorge toward the west end of Azure Lake. You can always walk farther east along the rim to find the best place to descend. Careful routefinding and sure feet will allow you to descend 550 feet and 0.3 mile to a flat sandy area and then farther down for less than a football-field length to the banks of Azure Lake (11,940 feet) at nearly 5.5 miles from the trailhead.

Hikers enjoy the view from Mount Ida with Azure and Inkwell Lakes below. Longs Peak and Chief Cheley Mountain are visible upper right.

Left: Once you reach timberline, it's 3 more miles to Mount Ida in the distance. **Right:** Looking back to timberline and back toward Trail Ridge Road.

From Azure Lake, descend north along the creek outlet on some rocky granite slopes to 11,500 feet to your north and then east for 0.25 mile to reach Inkwell Lake. From Inkwell, you can finish this small loop back to the gorge rim by finding a route back up grassy Class 2 slopes directly west from the creek inlet of Inkwell Lake to the gorge rim at 12,600 feet. Remember, most weather moves in from the west or southwest and even northwest in the summer months, so when you are down visiting the lakes, the gorge wall to the west won't allow you to see the weather that is moving in. Be cautious about this fact and visit these lakes in the morning to stay safe on the ridge when returning north to the Poudre Lake Trailhead on the Mount Ida Trail.

THE HIGH-RIDGE TRAVERSE
2. Mount Ida 12,889 feet (Class 1). Start at the Poudre Lake Trailhead and follow the previous description for 3.5 miles on the Mount Ida Trail south to the base of Mount Ida along the ridgeline at 12,000 feet. Here the trail becomes rocky and fades away. It is best to veer to the right (west) while ascending Mount Ida along the final 1.2 miles to the summit, as this will allow you to avoid the largest unpleasant boulders closer to the eastern edge of the ridgeline. There is a pretty good trail most of the way, and people have left cairns behind to mark trail segments at times. Once you are near the top, you will know it because you get 360-degree views in all directions and you will see the gorge lakes to your east in the basin below you. Other points of interest in the distance include the Mummy Range to the northeast, the Never Summer Mountains to the west, and Longs Peak to the southeast. Terrah Tomah Mountain, Mount Julian, and Cracktop Mountain are to the east, while the Kawuneeche Valley,

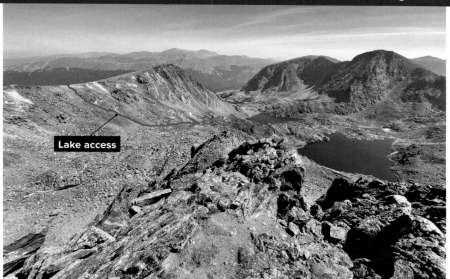

Looking north from the top of Ida, you can see the southeast-facing aspect of the gorge rim and where you should descend to the lakes from.

Julian Lake, Big Meadows, and Shadow Mountain Lake will be seen to the southwest. You are truly in the heart of the northern Colorado Rockies!

DR. JON'S EXTRA CREDIT

A. Chief Cheley Peak (12,829 feet) (Class 2). You can climb the relatively easy ridgeline between Mount Ida and Chief Cheley Peak for 0.5 mile to the southeast to reach the small summit, named for Frank Cheley, who founded a pre-Outward Bound–style summer camp in 1921 that is still running trips in the area today. Consider pushing farther west along the ridgeline from Chief Cheley Peak to the summits of Peak 12,800' and Cracktop (12,745 feet) if time and weather allow.

B. Gorge Lakes backpacking (Class 2–3). The basin below and to the east of Mount Ida not only hosts Azure and Inkwell Lakes, but many more lakes worth seeing. Consider camping in the basin near the lakes to be safe from afternoon thunderstorms. This will allow you plenty of time to visit some of the other lakes, such as Arrowhead, Doughnut, and Highest Lakes, and even do some fly-fishing in an idyllic setting. (Backcountry camping permits for Rocky Mountain National Park are $26 per party for May 1 through October 31; inquire at the Alpine Visitor Center.)

C. Milner Pass, Mount Ida, Timber Lake car-to-car (Class 2). You can leave a car at the Timber Lakes Trailhead off US 34/Trail Ridge Road in the far western portions of RMNP near Grand Lake and do a car-to-car traverse. It's all downhill through some stunning vistas from Mount Ida to Timber Lake.

The Gorge Lakes and Mount Ida

THE GORGE LAKES AND MOUNT IDA

LAKE AGNES AND MOUNT RICHTHOFEN

8

Elevation Gain	500 feet for Lake Agnes; 2,675 feet for Mount Richthofen
Round-Trip Distance	2.1 miles for loop around Lake Agnes; 4.1 miles for the Mount Richthofen loop
Trailhead	Lake Agnes (10,275 feet)
Difficulty Ratings	Easy Class 1 hike on trails around the lake; Class 2–3 across tundra/scattered alpine forest ecozone and rocky terrain with no trails for mountain climbing
Optimal Season	July through October
Maps	Trails Illustrated #200; Arapaho and Roosevelt National Forests

COMMENT: This tucked-away lake on the far northwestern edge of Rocky Mountain National Park located in State Forest State Park is an excellent option for a gorgeous hike in the middle of the summer. The fishing in Lake Agnes is excellent, and if you choose to climb to the top of Mount Richthofen, you'll be treated to some stellar mountain views.

Left: Lake Agnes with Mount Mahler behind. **Right:** Mount Richthofen's north ridge viewed from Static Peak.

GETTING THERE

Lake Agnes Trailhead (10,275 feet). Take US Highway 287 north from Fort Collins to Colorado Highway 14 (Poudre Canyon). Travel Colorado Highway 14 west for 52 miles over Cameron Pass. Continue to the west side of the pass and look for the well-signed Lake Agnes entrance to the State Forest State Park at mile 60 on Colorado Highway 14. Turn left (south), enter the guard shack for the State Forest State Park, pay $9 fee for your vehicle, and follow the signs on the dirt road to the Lake Agnes Trailhead.

THE LAKE LOOP

1. Lake Agnes (10,670 feet) (Class 1). This is an easy hike that is short and sweet. Head up to the lake on the relatively steep trail as it climbs quickly up many switchbacks for just under 1 mile to Lake Agnes. Spend some time in this place enjoying the stillness of the basin on a summer or fall morning. It's easy to circumnavigate the lake to see the reflections from all angles, and there is also a cool island out in the middle of the lake.

THE HIGH-RIDGE TRAVERSE

2. Mount Richthofen (12,951 feet) (Class 2–3 for the north slopes/west ridgeline). Start at Lake Agnes and follow a path around either side of the lake. Once on the south side, you can hike up some loose talus and scree while finding a climbers' trail and ascend for 1,300 feet to the 11,990-foot grassy saddle between Mount Richthofen (east) and Mahler (west). This flat saddle gives you a nice view back to Lake Agnes. Ascend the west ridge of Mount Richthofen for 1,000 feet to its summit. The crux of the route is a Class 3 gully just past some minor pinnacles along the ridgeline. The ridge is a bit airy but climbable on very solid rock.

DR. JON'S EXTRA CREDIT

A. Mount Mahler (12,495 feet) (Class 3–4). After descending back to the 11,990-foot connecting saddle between Richthofen and Mahler, ascend the Class 3–4 ridge to the summit of Mahler. Mahler is a step more challenging than Richthofen, but its east ridge will deliver. Enjoy problem-solving a small tower on the ridge (Class 4) to reach the top. It's possible to descend Mahler on its north side back to an unnamed lake near Lake Agnes to make a loop out of your adventure.

B. Snow Lake, Static Peak, Nohku Crags (Class 2, 3, 4). There are some other gorgeous destinations located nearby in State Forest State Park, so pack your bags and extend your weekend plans.

LAKE AGNES AND MOUNT RICHTHOFEN

CHAPTER 2

FRONT RANGE SOUTH
(I-70 CORRIDOR)

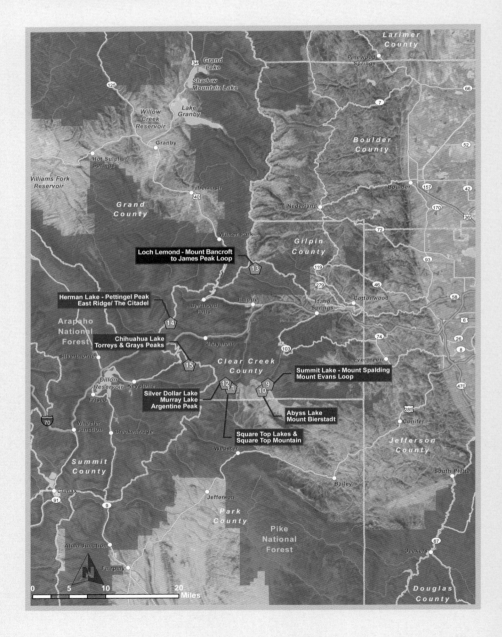

Loch Lemond - Mount Bancroft
to James Peak Loop

13

Herman Lake - Pettingel Peak
East Ridge/ The Citadel

14

Chihuahua Lake
Torreys & Grays Peaks

15

Summit Lake - Mount Spalding
Mount Evans Loop

9
10

Silver Dollar Lake
Murray Lake
Argentine Peak

12
11

Abyss Lake
Mount Bierstadt

Square Top Lakes &
Square Top Mountain

Larimer
County

Pinewood
Springs

Grand
Lake

Shadow
Mountain Lake

Lake
Granby

Willow
Creek
Reservoir

Granby

Hot Sulphur
Springs

Villiams Fork
Reservoir

Grand
County

Tabernash

Boulder
County

Boulder

Nederland

Winter Park

Gilpin
County

Empire

Arapaho
National
Forest

Silverthorne

Dillon
Reservoir

Keystone

Frisco

Wheeler
Junction

Breckenridge

70

Summit
County

Climax

91

Alma Junction

Fairplay

Cottonwood

Idaho
Springs

Clear Creek
County

Graymont

Evergreen

Conifer

Jefferson
County

South Platte

Webster

Bailey

Jefferson

Park
County

Pike
National
Forest

Deckers

Douglas
County

0   5   10   20
                    Miles

N

SUMMIT LAKE —MOUNT SPALDING —MOUNT EVANS LOOP

9

Elevation Gain	0 feet for Summit Lake; 992 feet for Mount Spalding; 2,050 feet for Mount Evans
Round-Trip Distance	1 mile for Mount Spalding; 5.5 miles for Mount Evans
Trailhead	Summit Lake (12,850 feet)
Difficulty Rating	Class 1–2 hike both on trails and across tundra/scattered alpine forest ecozone and boulders with no trails
Optimal Season	July through October
Maps	Trails Illustrated #104 and #1302; Pike and Arapaho National Forests

COMMENT: If you are looking for a beautiful high-mountain lake with an additional hike above timberline with spectacular views, make Summit Lake your destination. In midsummer, don't expect to have the lake all to yourself, but if you want an alpine Rocky Mountain–high experience with minimal effort, this little adventure is for you. Consider trying to visit this lake and hike to Mount Spalding at sunset, returning to Idaho Springs for dinner.

Mount Evans from Summit Lake near the trailhead.

Left: Follow the signs; the Mount Evans Trail will take you over Mount Spalding first. **Right:** Be prepared to greet the friendly goats on Mount Evans; they patrol the area!

GETTING THERE

Summit Lake (12,850 feet). Travel west from Denver on Interstate 70 for about 35 miles. Take Exit 240 at Idaho Springs and follow Colorado Highway 103 south for 13.5 miles to Echo Lake. Pay the entrance fee at the gate to the Mount Evans Highway (Colorado Highway 5) and travel 9 miles up the Mount Evans Highway to the Summit Lake parking area on the right.

THE LAKE

1. Summit Lake (12,800 feet) (Class 1). Start at the Summit Lake Trailhead and enjoy the trails right at the lake immediately from the parking lot.

THE LOOP AND HIGH-RIDGE TRAVERSE

2. Mount Spalding (13,842 feet) to Mount Evans (14,264 feet) (Class 2). Start at the Summit Lake Trailhead and walk north near an old rock building to follow the beginning of the trail that travels to the north end of the lake. Next locate a signed trail that travels to the west, climbing Mount Spalding's east ridge for 0.5 mile to the summit. Hike up through some rocks to reach the easier terrain on the ridge. At 13,250 feet, keep left below the ridge crest to get through some minor cliff bands. At 13,420 feet, emerge toward the ridge crest following broken trails and rocky slabs to the summit of Mount Spalding.

Scenic views along the ridgeline to Spalding with Chicago Lake behind.

From the summit of Mount Spalding, you get a nice view of the rest of the route to the summit of Mount Evans to your south. Follow a trail segment south and descend to the 13,600-foot connecting saddle along the ridge on your way to a flatter portion of the ridge. You will reach the west ridge of Mount Evans and be able to peer down south into Abyss Lake. At 13,800 feet, turn and continue southeast on the ridgeline to a hump at 13,900 feet. Follow a cairned trail that stays on the southern aspects of the ridgeline for 1 mile to the top of Mount Evans. Some of the trail will be rugged with lot of boulders to cross. Remember that it's important to stay along the western and southern aspects of the ridge and through many large granite slabs and boulders. You will more than likely be greeted by many people near the summit parking lot on Mount Evans. A quick way to complete this loop is to hike down to the summit parking lot 200 feet below you to the south, then turn north from the northern edge of the parking lot, and descend gentle grass and rocky slopes to the highway below in the direction of where you parked at Summit Lake.

DR. JON'S EXTRA CREDIT
A. Mount Evans express via the road. Feeling lazy and just want some spectacular views? Drop the kids off with Mom and have them hike to the summit; you can drive to the summit and meet them on top of Mount Evans!

SUMMIT LAKE—MOUNT SPALDING —MOUNT EVANS LOOP

ABYSS LAKE —MOUNT BIERSTADT —SAWTOOTH TO MOUNT EVANS TRAVERSE

10

Elevation Gain	3,330 feet for Abyss Lake; 4,440 feet for Mount Bierstadt; 5,500 feet for Mount Evans
Round-Trip Distance	18 miles for Abyss Lake; 22 miles for Bierstadt to Evans Traverse via Sawtooth
Trailhead	Abyss Lake (9,620 feet)
Difficulty Rating	Class 1–2 hike both on trails and across tundra/scattered alpine forest ecozone with no trails
Optimal Season	July through October
Maps	Trails Illustrated #104 and #1302; Pike and Arapaho National Forests

COMMENT: While Bierstadt and Evans are the easiest fourteeners to get to from Denver and the Interstate-70 corridor, consider this wild alternative for a backpacking adventure with a different approach to a beautiful lake. You can camp in several places en route to Abyss Lake or at the lake before launching an early-morning attempt on the classic Sawtooth ridge connecting both Evans and Bierstadt. The fall colors en route to the lake can be something special in mid-September. More than likely on this route to these fourteeners, you will only see people near the summit of each peak, while you'll have solitude everywhere else.

Looking west to Abyss Lake, Mount Bierstadt, and the Sawtooth.

A friendly goat near the top of Bierstadt and a lake deep in Abyss Basin below.

GETTING THERE

Abyss Lake Trailhead (9,620 feet). Travel west from Denver on I-70 for about 50 miles and take Exit 228 at Georgetown. Follow the signs into historical Georgetown. From downtown, continue following the signs out of town and head south above town on switchbacks on Guanella Pass Road. You will pass a power plant and a small lake in the deep valley on your left as you continue on a paved road for 10 miles from Georgetown to the top of Guanella Pass at 11,669 feet. Descend another 6.7 miles south from the top of Guanella Pass (the road will turn to dirt) to the trailhead at 9,620 feet, which is marked and on the east side of the road. If approaching from the south, follow the Guanella Pass Road (Park County Road 62) north for 5.5 miles from US Highway 285 near the town of Grant, which is 40 miles from Denver. The trailhead is just south of the Burning Bear Campground.

THE LAKE

1. Abyss Lake (12,650 feet) (Class 1). Start at the Abyss Trailhead and travel to the north then northeast on the Abyss Trail (#602). You will pass through a beautiful aspen forest as well as some lodgepole pines for the first mile. At 2.1 miles, the trail crosses over Scott Gomer Creek at 10,160 feet and then levels out through some dense aspen.

The trail crosses back over the creek at 3.2 miles and begins a steep climb on a rocky path arriving at a marshy meadow of willows at the 4-mile mark. You will arrive at the first of two Rosalie Trail junctions at 4.2 and the second one at 4.4 miles. Pass through this area and continue through a less dense forest with old signs of wildfire at mile 5 (11,275 feet). The meadows become more expansive with great campsites over the next half mile.

Left: Traversing the shoulder of Bierstadt. **Right:** Enjoying the summit view at 14,000 feet.

Continue on as the trail travels north then east around Helms Lake (11,750 feet). There is good camping here but keep an eye out for the trail as it can be hard to follow leaving the vicinity of the lake on the lake's east side. You'll continue to the northeast on the trail above the lake into open alpine meadows and wildflowers as the view will open up to both Bierstadt and Evans as well as Epaulet Mountain (13,523 feet). At mile 7.2, cross Lake Fork Creek and turn to the northwest, heading into rolling alpine tundra, eventually arriving at the south shore of Abyss Lake. Keep an eye out for mountain goats and bighorn sheep; this is their prime habitat.

THE LOOP AND HIGH-RIDGE TRAVERSE
2. Mount Bierstadt (14,060 feet) to Sawtooth to Mount Evans (14,264 feet) (Class 2–3). Start at the Abyss Trailhead and follow the Abyss Trail (#602) for 8.2 miles to Abyss Lake. You will either need to camp at Abyss Lake or start from the trailhead at 3:00 a.m. to safely do this loop and climb, especially in July and August. You can carefully travel around the lake's east side to get to the northern edge of the lake. From here, ascend 1,400 feet of grass and mainly large boulders to the west up the east-northeast face of Bierstadt for 0.75 mile to the summit (Class 2). From the top of Bierstadt, follow the northeast ridge of Bierstadt to a descending traverse to a notch of the 13,300-foot connecting saddle between Mount Bierstadt and the Sawtooth (13,768 feet). You can nearly stay on the crest of the ridge or slightly on the east side (right) of the ridgeline. After reaching the saddle, climb another 200 to 300 yards and ascend a shallow gully to a prominent notch on the ridge at the base of a gendarme of the ridgeline leading to the Sawtooth. This notch is the key to leaving the ridgeline and following ledges on the left side (west) of the ridge. Scramble up the ledges to an exit ledge from 13,300 to 13,600 feet. Once you come out to the

Quiet meadows below Mount Bierstadt at sunrise.

flat plateau (13,620 feet) north of the Sawtooth summit, you will see the flat summit of Sawtooth (13,786 feet) to your south. Hike to and stand on the Sawtooth if you wish—it's a stellar vantage point! From here, the final 1.3 miles of ridgeline to the summit of Mount Evans follows a climbers' trail along the western and southern aspects of the ridge and through many large granite slabs and boulders. You will more than likely be greeted by many people near the summit parking lot on Mount Evans. Your return to Abyss Lake can be done either by (1) following the Mount Evans Road south from the summit (0.5 mile) to a 13,300-foot switchback that overlooks the Abyss Lake basin to the southeast of Abyss Lake—from here, it's possible to drop in and contour a gully system to the southwest and west to drop back down to the Abyss Trail (#602) (see a topo map for this route) or (2) leave the Mount Evans Trail 0.75 mile west of the summit and descend steep boulders and rocks for 1,500 feet (0.7 mile) to the southwest to reach Abyss Lake from the westernmost 14,000-foot pinnacle along Mount Evans's west ridge.

DR. JON'S EXTRA CREDIT

A. Mount Spalding and Summit Lake (see entry #9). Feeling ambitious or have a completely clear day of nothing but blue skies in September or October? Consider taking a detour and traveling north 0.75 mile from the connecting ridge between Mount Evans and the Sawtooth to the 13,842-foot summit of Mount Spalding. You can also descend the east ridge of Spalding on a nice climbers' trail for 1 mile to the shore of Summit Lake. This entire high-altitude environment is very scenic with excellent views of the Front Range plains to the east (including the Denver metro area) as well as other peaks of the Front Range in all directions.

ABYSS LAKE—MOUNT BIERSTADT —SAWTOOTH TO MOUNT EVANS TRAVERSE

SQUARE TOP LAKES AND SQUARE TOP MOUNTAIN

11

Elevation Gain	490 feet for Lower Square Top Lake; 690 feet for Upper Square Top Lake; 3,656 feet for Square Top Mountain
Round-Trip Distance	4.2 miles for Upper Square Top Lake; 10 miles for Square Top Mountain; 11 miles for the Square Top Mountain to Silver Dollar Lake Loop
Trailhead	Guanella Pass (11,669 feet)
Difficulty Rating	Class 1–2 hike both on trails and across tundra with no trails
Optimal Season	June through November 1
Maps	Trails Illustrated #104; Argentine, Arapaho National Forest

COMMENT: Easily accessible from Denver and the Interstate-70 corridor, Square Top is one of Colorado's Bicentennial peaks, just shy of Centennial peak status. When the hordes of fourteener enthusiasts are bombarding Bierstadt to the southeast of Guanella Pass, choose this fresh alternative to the north for solitude and an enjoyable summer wildflower experience.

GETTING THERE

Guanella Pass (11,669 feet). Travel west from Denver on I-70 for about 50 miles and take Exit 228 at Georgetown. Follow the signs into historical Georgetown. From downtown, continue following the signs out of town and head south above town on

Upper Square Top Lake at sunset looking toward Mount Bierstadt.

Morning reflection in Lower Square Top Lake.

switchbacks on Guanella Pass Road. You will pass a power plant and small lake in the deep valley on your left as you continue on a paved road for 10 miles from George-town to the top of Guanella Pass at 11,669 feet. In winter, the road is generally plowed to the power plant, which is in the vicinity of the reservoir, and by May 1, the road is sometimes plowed and open to the pass (but this is not a CDOT priority). Note that a slog up the road in winter or early spring might add up to 4 miles one-way. In recent years, the road has been consistently open to Guanella Pass Campground and the Lower Silver Dollar Lake Trailhead, which is 1.7 miles from the top of the pass and has ample parking. If approaching from the south, follow the Guanella Pass Road north for 12.2 miles from US Highway 285 near the town of Grant.

THE LAKES

1.   Square Top Lakes (Class 2). Start at the top of Guanella Pass. At the south-west corner of the summit overlook parking lot, there is a detailed sign for the South Park Trail and Square Top Interpretive Trail. From the parking lot, you can also look to the west and see Square Top in the distance. Follow the Square Top Interpretive Trail through some rolling hills and willows for 1.6 miles to Lower Square Top Lake (12,050 feet). You will lose a little elevation (100 feet) initially upon leaving the park-ing lot. The trail to Upper Square Top Lake travels around the southern side of Lower Square Top Lake and climbs for 200 feet to the east and then north into the cirque below Square Top Mountain's east face, arriving at the stunning lake at 12,250 feet.

Left: Sign to Upper Square Top Lake marking the way. **Right:** Hiking up the southeast ridge.
Photo by Connor Drumm

THE LOOP

2. East slopes of Square Top Mountain (Class 2). From 12,250 feet at Square Top Lake, walk to the right (north) side of the lake. From here, you can climb directly up the steeper grassy slopes of the east bowl or trend right (ascending to your north and then northwest on some grassy benches) to the east ridge and eventually to the summit. Aim for a prominent flat spot at 12,750 feet on the east ridge of Square Top before the hiking on the ridge gets steeper and rockier. Hike the ridge for 0.5 mile to a flatter ridge crest at 13,400 feet where the broader southeast ridge meets the steeper east ridge. From here, follow the gentle ridge crest as it rolls and flattens for several football-field lengths (0.7 mile) to the 13,794-foot summit. On descent, return to the 13,400-foot ridge crest and look for climbers' trails down the southeast ridge, traveling along the east face cirques and back down to a trail that leads to lower Square Top Lake.

THE HIGH-RIDGE TRAVERSE

3. Murray Lake and Silver Dollar Lake. From the summit of Square Top, descend to the west and then the northwest ridge of the mountain on boulders and faint climbers' trails for 1 mile and 785 vertical feet to the 12,990-foot connecting saddle between Square Top and 13,743-foot Argentine Peak. Drop into the basin to the east (right) on relatively gradual grass and rock for 0.75 mile to Murray Lake. As you descend, you will also see Silver Dollar Lake 0.4 mile farther to the southwest. In the flat basin at 12,100 feet, you will meet the Silver Dollar Lake Trail. Travel left (north) to reach Murray Lake and right (southeast) for Silver Dollar Lake (11,950 feet). Proceed back east and down the Silver Dollar Lake Trail for 3 miles to the Lower Silver Dollar Lake Trailhead (10,850 feet). A vehicle shuttle for 1.7 miles to the top of Guanella Pass is required to get to your starting point.

DR. JON'S EXTRA CREDIT

A. Argentine Peak (13,743 feet) and Mount Edwards (13,856 feet). On a clear weather day, traverse from Square Top to Argentine to Mount Edwards and enjoy being up high on one of Colorado's longer and more desolate but gorgeous ridgelines. Just remember that it may be best to return and finish in the vicinity of Silver Dollar Lake or Murray Lake by returning over Argentine Peak. Better yet, perhaps you could attempt the Guanella Pass to Loveland Pass Traverse, described in the Torreys and Grays Peaks entry (#15). Nevertheless, start early and make it an excellent loop by hiking back to the east down to the Guanella Pass Road and campground and to the Lower Silver Dollar Lake Trailhead (Silver Dollar Road junction). It is about 3 miles from Murray Lake back to the Lower Silver Dollar Lake Trailhead (10,900 feet), and the Silver Dollar Road junction is only about a half mile south of the Guanella Pass Campground, but you might need a vehicle or shuttle of some sort to return to your starting point at Guanella Pass.

Square Top (13,795 feet) is dog-friendly and very uncrowded compared to its fourteener neighbors.

Square Top Lakes and Square Top Mountain

SQUARE TOP LAKES
AND SQUARE TOP MOUNTAIN

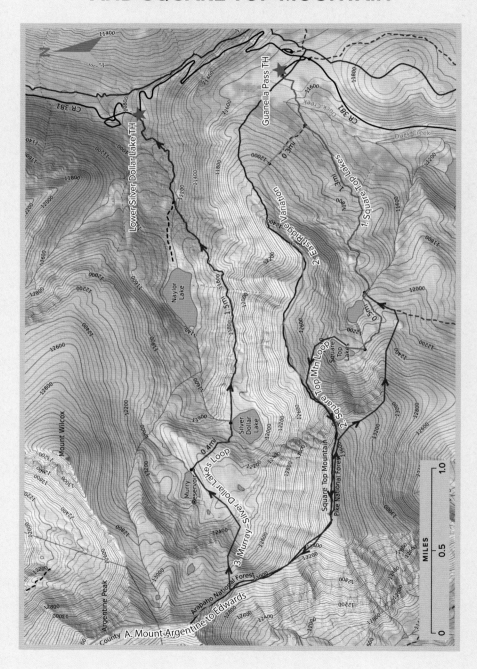

SILVER DOLLAR LAKE —MURRAY LAKE —ARGENTINE PEAK

12

Elevation Gain	1,050 feet for Silver Dollar Lake; 1,150 feet for Murray Lake; 2,833 feet for Argentine Peak
Round-Trip Distance	4.1 miles for Silver Dollar Lake; 4.7 miles for Murray Lake; 7.0 miles for Argentine Peak; 8.5 miles if you add Wilcox Peak
Trailhead	Lower Silver Dollar Lake (10,900 feet)
Difficulty Rating	Class 1–2 hike on four-wheel-drive road, trails, and tundra and rocks/scree off trails for high-ridge traverse only
Optimal Season	June through November, but July through September is ideal
Maps	Trails Illustrated #104; Arapaho National Forest

COMMENT: This is an easy day hike to some gorgeous lakes, so bring your friends and family out to these lakes to enjoy. Some will want to stay at the lakes, while others might choose to explore the vast basin above the lakes to get up on the Continental Divide to Argentine Peak, one of Colorado's Bicentennials, for an easy view that extends to the west to the Gore Range and toward Denver to the east. Start early to avoid the summer crowds but go beyond the lakes to find solitude.

From the top of Square Top, you get a great bird's-eye view of Silver Dollar and Murray Lakes.

GETTING THERE

Lower Silver Dollar Lake Trailhead (10,900 feet). Travel west from Denver on I-70 for about 50 miles and take Exit 228 at Georgetown. Follow the signs into historical Georgetown. From downtown, continue following the signs out of town and head south above town on switchbacks on Guanella Pass Road. You will pass a power plant and small lake in the deep valley on your left as you continue on a paved road for 10 miles from Georgetown to the top of Guanella Pass at 11,669 feet. In winter, the road is generally plowed to the power plant, which is in the vicinity of the reservoir, and by May 1, the road is sometimes plowed and open to the pass (but this is not a CDOT priority). Note that a slog up the road in winter or early spring might add up to 4 miles one-way. In recent years, the road has been consistently open to Guanella Pass Campground and the Lower Silver Dollar Lake Trailhead, which is 1.7 miles from the top of the pass and has ample parking.

THE LAKES

1.   Silver Dollar Lake (Class 1). Start from the Lower Silver Dollar Lake Trailhead and follow the four-wheel-drive road (FSR 79) to the west. You will ascend through

The greenish colors of Silver Dollar Lake look refreshing.

Murray Lake is tucked in not far up from Silver Dollar Lake.

pine forest for the first 0.75 mile. The route to this point is straightforward, following a four-wheel-drive road. The road takes a turn toward Naylor Lake on your right in the basin near buildings leading to a summer camp establishment. The actual trail to Silver Dollar Lake leaves the road and rises above the trees to the left (west). As you ascend the valley, Naylor Lake drops away from you to the right, and after 2 miles, you will arrive above timberline on a flat glacial basin with Silver Dollar Lake on your left. You can continue up the basin for another 100 feet and 0.5 mile to reach Murray Lake. The views to the east are stunning.

THE LOOP AND HIGH-RIDGE TRAVERSE

2. Mount Wilcox (13,175 feet) to Mount Argentine (13,733 feet) and back to Murray Lake (Class 2). After enjoying both Silver Dollar Lake and Murray Lake, head north through the grassy tundra and ascend easy slopes to the top of Mount Wilcox. Wilcox offers sweeping views of the basin. Next, continue west in the broad basin to the top of Mount Argentine along the Continental Divide. Grassy and rocky slopes mark the way, and it is possible to locate an old four-wheel-drive road that connects to Argentine Pass before following the ridgeline spine of the Continental Divide to the summit. Return to Murray Lake to locate the trail back to the trailhead. If Mount Wilcox isn't on your radar, simply travel directly through the tundra zone to reach Mount Argentine.

DR. JON'S EXTRA CREDIT

A. Traverse to Guanella Pass from Mount Argentine (Class 2). This little adventure requires a car shuttle or leaving a car at the top of Guanella pass before launching. Take a look at the high-ridge traverse for details of this traverse in the opposite direction in the Square Top Lakes and Square Top Mountain (#11) entry. Dr. Jon's extra credit in the same entry also offers some ideas for Mount Edwards north of Mount Argentine if you are really ambitious.

SILVER DOLLAR LAKE—MURRAY LAKE —ARGENTINE PEAK

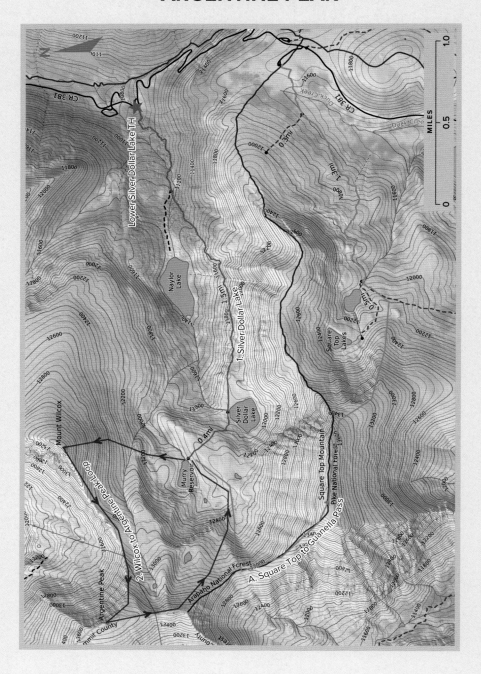

LOCH LEMOND —MOUNT BANCROFT TO JAMES PEAK LOOP

13

Elevation Gain	875 feet for Loch Lemond; 2,900 feet for Mount Bancroft; 3,615 feet for James Peak
Round-Trip Distance	4.6 miles for Loch Lemond; 9.2 miles for Mount Bancroft; 10 miles for James Peak Loop
Trailhead	Steuart Road (10,352 feet)
Difficulty Rating	Class 1–2+ hike both on four-wheel-drive road and trails and across tundra with no trails
Optimal Season	June through October
Maps	Trails Illustrated #103; Arapaho National Forest

COMMENT: The highest point in Gilpin County and the fifth-highest summit in the Indian Peaks, James Peak—along with Mount Bancroft—provides the perfect objective for a fun and scenic high-ridge adventure. There is also a great opportunity for a group outing on gentle ski terrain. A visit to Loch Lemond is part of the loop, but you can also up your game with visits to five additional lakes (Caroline, Reynolds, Ohman, Ice, and Steuart), which you will also get to see from above on this scenic circuit. You can get to the trailhead from Denver in less than an hour, making it easy to enjoy an outing close to home!

Bancroft's east ridge is a classic spicy ridge climb.

GETTING THERE

Steuart Road Trailhead (10,352 feet). This trailhead and access road is spelled "Steuart" and not "Stewart," named for one of the lakes in the upper basin. Traveling west from Denver on Interstate 70, take the Fall River Road Exit 238, 2 miles west of Idaho Springs. Travel 8 miles northwest on Fall River Road toward St. Mary's/ Alice. At Road 275 in Alice, turn left, and from here, you will go as straight as you can through Alice, a subdivision of houses and cabins. Alice was a mining town, renamed in 1868 when the Alice Mine was discovered. You will pass an old mine site that is in someone's yard, on your right after 0.75 mile, but keep going. Eventually you will come to a right turn into the woods that is marked but doesn't have any obvious houses along it. This is Steuart Road (but it's unlikely there is a sign), and this is the road to Loch Lemond. Turn right at Steuart Road, which turns into a four-wheel-drive road about a mile up from the right turn. If you are in a low-clearance vehicle, you will have to park once the road gets rougher, near a tailings pile at around 10,350 feet. A regular high-clearance vehicle can make it in the rest of the way, and drive until reaching the lake or until snow blocks the road. There are turnouts along the way where you can park one or two cars. Ideally, if you value your vehicle, park before the terrain gets too rough and hike up the valley.

Mount Bancroft to the west of Loch Lemond.

Left: A fun 120-foot rappel is necessary to descend Bancroft's east ridge (Class 5).
Right: Ascending easy slopes of Mount Bancroft with the traverse to James Peak visible along the ridgeline to the north.

THE LAKE

1. Loch Lemond (Class 1). Start from the Steuart Road Trailhead and follow the four-wheel-drive road (FSR 701.1) for 2.2 miles to the west, northwest, and the north to Loch Lemond at 11,200 feet. You will ascend through pine forest and into the high alpine of a scenic glacial trough and arrive at the southeast end of Loch Lemond. The route to this point is straightforward, following a four-wheel-drive road.

THE LOOP AND HIGH-RIDGE TRAVERSE

2. Mount Bancroft (13,250 feet) (Class 2) southeast ridge with traverse to James Peak (13,294 feet). After enjoying a break at Loch Lemond, from the south side of the lake, descend back down FSR 701.1 for less than a quarter mile to reach a junction with a closed FSR 701.2. Turn right (west) and follow FSR 701.2 for 0.75 mile as it travels southwest; first south, then west, and fully southwest to reach a small saddle near 11,933 feet on Bancroft's southeast ridge near timberline. From here, follow the relatively gentle and grassy southeast ridge of Bancroft first to the west and then to the northwest for 1.3 miles to the summit. Next, descend Bancroft's lofty northeast shoulder and traverse the connecting ridge between Bancroft and James Peak for 2.1 miles. The low point on the ridgeline is at 12,580 feet and directly to the west of Ice Lake in the beautiful cirque in the basin below you to the east. In this area, the rock along the traverse is solid but does not exceed Class 2+ with careful routefinding. The final slopes of James Peak's south ridge for 300 feet and 0.5 mile are enjoyable with many wildflowers in midsummer.

Ice Lake (frozen); looking east to Loch Lemond from the saddle to James Peak from Mount Bancroft.

To return to Loch Lemond and eventually the trailhead, follow a section of the Continental Divide Trail (CDT) for 2 miles south and southeast from the summit. Descend along the steep cliffs of the glacial cirque basin that holds the six lakes of interest for this tour. The views are stunning as you travel southeast between 12,600 and 12,000 feet. To the north of Loch Lemond at 12,000 feet, you will need to descend and stay right (southeast) following the trail for an additional 0.9 mile to the southeastern corner of Loch Lemond. From here, travel west across the southern end of the lake for 0.25 mile to meet FSR 701.1 and return to the trailhead from there.

DR. JON'S EXTRA CREDIT
A. Five-lake exploration (Class 2). Above Loch Lemond, you can take some time or even plan on camping in this spectacular cirque basin to discover the five additional lakes in this basin. Bring bug spray and your fishing rod for even more fun! For serious and skilled technical alpinists, a challenging mountaineering test-piece awaits to the north of Lake Caroline known as the Mount Bancroft East Ridge (Class 5+). Do your research and go for this challenge if you have the desire to enjoy an exciting high-alpine route.

LOCH LEMOND—MOUNT BANCROFT TO JAMES PEAK LOOP

HERMAN LAKE —PETTINGEL PEAK EAST RIDGE—THE CITADEL

14

Elevation Gain	Up to 3,200 feet for each peak
Round-Trip Distance	6.4 miles for Herman Lake; 9.5 miles for Pettingel East Ridge Loop; 10 miles for the Citadel
Trailhead	Herman Gulch (10,320 feet)
Difficulty Ratings	Class 1 and 2 for the trail to Herman Lake; Pettingel and Citadel routes require Class 3 and 4 scrambling
Optimal Season	June to October
Maps	Trails Illustrated #104; Arapaho National Forest

COMMENT: Easily accessible from Denver and the Interstate-70 corridor, Herman Lake is a fun and easy hike to bring the family or the dog. For loops and high-ridge traverses, Pettingel Peak and the Citadel are challenging scrambles where expertise and confidence without a rope are required. Pettingel Peak at 13,553 feet is the highest point in Grand County. The Citadel is sometimes called "Snoopy" because the double summits of the summit ridge resemble Snoopy sleeping on his doghouse. On a weekend day in July or August, don't expect to be the only party on these mountains as the routes on this peak are well-known. Nevertheless, you will still get much more solitude than on any of the fourteeners.

Jagged summit of Citadel; Pettingel's south ridgeline is visible upper right.

GETTING THERE

Herman Gulch (10,300 feet). Travel west from Denver on I-70. This trailhead is only a few miles east of the Eisenhower Tunnel. Use I-70 Exit 218 to access the trailhead on the north side of the interstate in a large parking lot with some outhouses.

THE LAKE

1. Herman Lake. Follow the well-worn trail through meadows for 3.2 miles to Herman Lake. It's best to avoid crowds by trekking to this lake in the early morning or on a weekday.

THE LOOP

2. Pettingel Peak (13,553 feet) (Class 3–4 for the east ridge to south slopes). Follow the Herman Lake Trail for 3 miles until you are nearly at the lake. From the lake, look east and then northeast to gain a steep southwest-facing ridge spine of talus and rock (Class 2+). Climb this spine following the path of least resistance for 1,000 feet to gain the east ridge of Pettingel. From here, you can see the aesthetic ridgeline and can hike and boulder hop for an additional 500 feet west to the summit. Next, drop southwest on more boulders and talus on the broad southwest shoulder of Pettingel. The ridge is easy at first, but the last 0.25 mile

Top: Herman Lake. *Photo by Chris Tomer*
Bottom: Thumbs-up from the author on a fun perch of the Citadel. *Photo by Mike Posner*

of traversing along to Citadel requires some scrambling and routefinding along some technical towers. You can bypass some of the steeper pinnacles on the right (west) as you ascend. Climb a nifty gully crack near the summit (Class 4) to reach the top of the higher west summit of the Citadel. Descend the southeast ridge route or ski either Snoopy's or Snoopy's back side couloir described next.

Left: Pettingel Peak's east ridge. *Photo by Chris Tomer* **Right:** Snoopy's back side couloir is a fun ski mountaineering route in May and a way to avoid loose rock.

THE HIGH-RIDGE TRAVERSE

3a. Citadel southeast ridge, south face/Snoopy's Collar (Class 3). Start at the Herman Gulch Trailhead. After about 2.5 miles, before the trail begins to steepen on its way up to Herman Lake, follow the line of the creek on a trail headed west through the valley, staying on the right side of the creek initially and then crossing over to the left side of the creek near tree line. Ascend southwest following the use trail as it climbs to a saddle at 12,500 feet to the east of the Citadel. This point is about 4 miles from the trailhead. Turn northwest from here and cross the high ridgeline to the south face of the eastern tower of the Citadel. Climb across the south face, below some cliffs, which leads to the couloir on the upper reaches of the face. Once reaching the top of the couloir, you can scramble left (west) on some rocks for 200 feet to reach the true summit.

3b. Snoopy's back side couloir (Class 3). A popular snow climb in May and June and ski mountaineering route. Ascend the basin to the southwest of Herman Lake into a deep cirque to the northeast of the Citadel. You can find a narrowing north-facing couloir to climb and connect to Snoopy's couloir at the tip and scramble up rocks to reach the true summit of Citadel.

DR. JON'S EXTRA CREDIT

A. Pettingel to Citadel Traverse Loop adding East Citadel. For seasoned mountaineers, climb Pettingel's east ridge to the summit and follow high ridges to the west and south, connecting the jagged ridge leading to the Citadel. Descend the southeast flank of the Citadel as described previously but before you head down, scramble from the connecting saddle between West Citadel and East Citadel and then back toward the basin of Herman Lake.

HERMAN LAKE—PETTINGEL PEAK EAST RIDGE—THE CITADEL

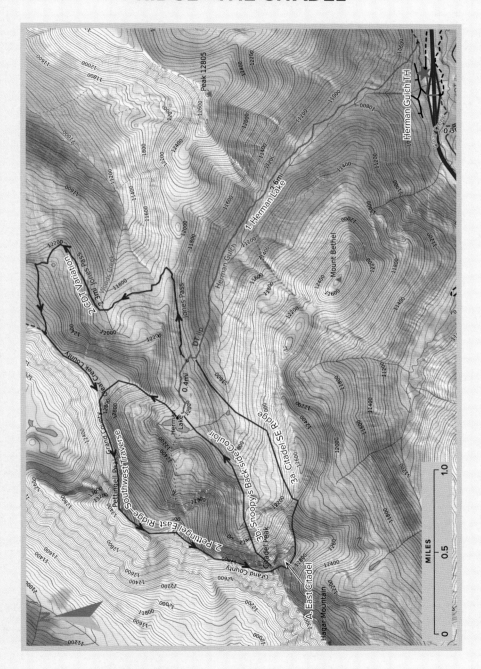

Herman Gulch TH

Peak 12805

Mount Bethel

1. Herman Lake 2.6 mi

Herman Gulch

2. CDT Variation

3.2 mi Jones Pass

Woods Creek

Jones Pass

DT Trip

0.4 mi

Citadel SE Ridge

3a. Citadel SE Ridge

3b. Snoopy's Back side Couloir

Citadel Peak

Bald Eagle Couloir

Herman Lake

Grand County/Clear Creek County

2. Pettingel East Ridge—Southwest Traverse

Pettingell Peak

Grand County/Clear Creek County

19. A. East Citadel

Hagar Mountain

MILES

0   0.5   1.0

CHIHUAHUA LAKE —TORREYS AND GRAYS PEAKS

15

Elevation Gain	1,900 feet for Chihuahua Lake; 4,667 feet for Torreys to Grays Loop
Round-Trip Distance	8.2 miles for Chihuahua Lake; 13.5 miles Torreys to Grays Loop
Trailhead	Peru Creek/Chihuahua Gulch (10,450 feet)
Difficulty Rating	Class 1–2 hike on four-wheel-drive road, trails, and tundra and rocks/scree off trails for high-ridge traverse only
Optimal Season	June through November, but July through September is ideal
Maps	Trails Illustrated #104; Arapaho National Forest

COMMENT: A very scenic and tucked-in glacial tarn, this approach to two of Colorado's tallest and most crowded fourteeners is very interesting when coming from the west. Not only can you avoid crowds, but a really fun visit to Chihuahua Lake might just prevent you from actually climbing any higher!

GETTING THERE

Chihuahua Gulch (10,450 feet). Travel west from Denver on I-70 to Exit 205 Silverthorne. This exit is west of the Eisenhower Tunnel. Follow US Highway 6 for sev-

Grays and Torreys Peaks at the head of the valley.

Left: Solid ice forms due to lack of afternoon sun by November, making Chihuahua Lake a great place to skate. **Right:** By November, the ice takes over on the lake.

eral miles east to the town of Keystone. Before Highway 6 leaves Keystone to climb up to Arapahoe Basin ski area and Loveland Pass, turn right on Montezuma Road. From the town of Keystone, travel east toward the settlement of Montezuma. Montezuma is the last exit off US Highway 6 when traveling toward Loveland Pass and the Arapahoe Basin ski area. From its start at US Highway 6 (Loveland Pass Road), drive on Montezuma Road (paved) for about 4.5 miles to the intersection with Peru Creek Road. Turn left on Peru Creek Road. The start of this dirt road has Forest Service signs and is well marked. Drive up Peru Creek Road for another 2.1 miles to the Chihuahua Gulch Trailhead. A four-wheel-drive road starts to the left (north) and gets very rough heading north into Chihuahua Gulch. There is ample parking at this junction on the south side of the road along some pine trees. Peru Creek Road isn't very rough, and there are several campsites along the trail.

THE LAKE

1. Chihuahua Lake (Class 1). Start from the Chihuahua Gulch Trailhead and follow the four-wheel-drive road (FR 78) for 2.2 miles to the northwest. You will ascend through pine forest and into high-alpine meadows of glacial moraine boulders and willows. Cross Chihuahua Creek twice on your way at 1.2 miles and 1.9 miles. The route to this point is straightforward, following a four-wheel-drive road. The road ends near some pine trees after a very challenging portion, which is in some willows and was flooded by the creek. Pass through a closed gate with minor signage and ascend slightly steeper terrain to the left (west) side of the valley and onto a flat meadow area near timberline. Continue north for 0.5 mile and follow the trail as it

Chihuahua Lake—Torreys and Grays Peaks

steepens and climbs directly to the northwest and then west for a steep 0.25 mile. The lake will appear at 12,280 feet abruptly in a tucked-away cirque with Grays and Torreys Peaks behind you to your east.

THE LOOP AND HIGH-RIDGE TRAVERSE

2. Torreys Peak (14,267 feet) west ridge with traverse south to Grays Peak (14,270 feet). After enjoying a break at Chihuahua Lake, retrace your steps down and east to the steepest portions of the trail for 0.25 mile and then leave the trail on some grassy terrain, headed north. Aim for the 12,750-foot connecting saddle between Grizzly Peak and Torreys Peak. It's a very broad and grassy saddle and in the summer, a favorite place for mountain goats to congregate. From the saddle, climb a moderately steep mile to the east on Torreys Peak's west ridge. Sometimes you can find a small goat trail that makes the 1,200 feet of elevation gain to the upper ridge a bit easier. The route is intertwined between grass and scree. Once you get to 14,000 feet on the west ridge, the ridge levels out, and your final 250 feet to the summit of Torreys is very scenic and enjoyable. If it's a warm summer day, you may hear people on the top already unless you are very early. From the top of Torreys, continue for another mile and drop down to the 13,900-foot connecting saddle on an easy trail, which will lead you south and back up to the top of Grays, the highest spot on the Continental Divide in the US. Finally, to complete the loop, drop

Most early mornings provide great sunlight and stunning reflections.

Torreys and Grays nearby can be a super fun loop when the goats are around.

directly off the top of Grays and follow a faint game trail to the south and angle to the southwest. Descend on loose rocks and scree for 0.5 mile to the 13,600-foot level on "South Grays." Then travel south into the basin south of Grays Peak. Once into the grassy slopes and lower basin at 12,500 feet, travel west and follow the basin back out toward Chihuahua Creek. If you can read your map and have good routefinding skills, there is a trail that will pick up near timberline, and you can easily follow it to the end of the four-wheel-drive road and the gate for the start of the Chihuahua Lake Trail. Take a left and head south down the road to the trailhead.

DR. JON'S EXTRA CREDIT

A. Traverse to Loveland Pass from Chihuahua Lake (Class 2). This little adventure requires a car shuttle or leaving a car at the top of Loveland Pass before launching. If the weather is good, descend a few hundred feet from the lake in the direction you came up via the trail, take a short northwest descent to the basin you came up, and then continue to the 12,750-foot saddle between Torreys Peak and Grizzly Peak. From the saddle, travel west along Grizzly's east ridge to the top of 13,427-foot Grizzly Peak. Continue north along ridges for 2.5 miles to Loveland Pass. This scenic ridge traverse is also great starting at Loveland Pass, arriving at Chihuahua Lake, and finishing at the Peru Creek/Chihuahua Gulch Trailhead for a total distance of about 8 miles.

B. Ice Skating on Chihuahua Lake (Class 2). In late October and into November most years, you can take advantage of the cold fall nights and sunny fall days to have an amazing experience skating Chihuahua Lake. Start early and soak up the sunshine!

CHIHUAHUA LAKE —TORREYS AND GRAYS PEAKS

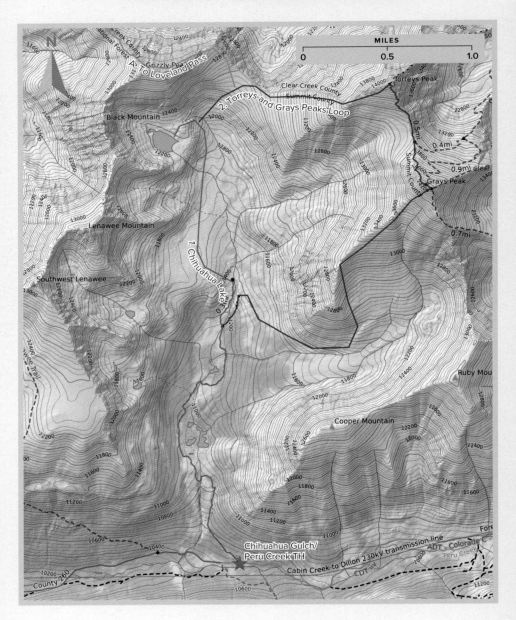

TENMILE/MOSQUITO RANGE

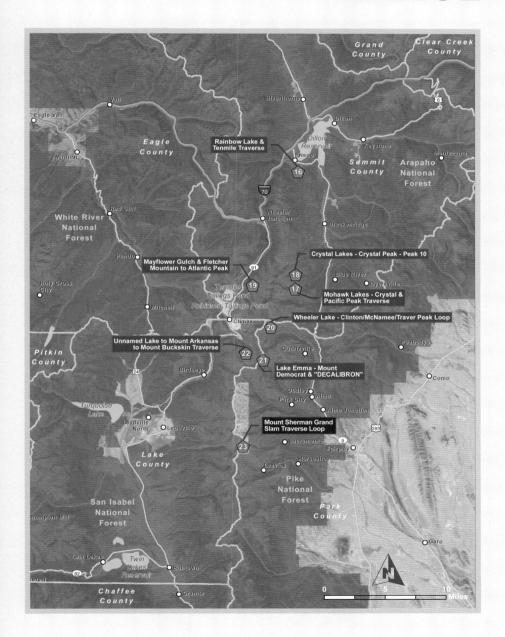

RAINBOW LAKE—TENMILE TRAVERSE FROM FRISCO TO BRECKENRIDGE

16

Elevation Gain	150 feet for Rainbow Lake; 1,400 feet for Mount Royal; 3,500 feet for Peak 1 (12,580 feet); 8,500 feet for the full Tenmile Traverse to Breckenridge
Round-Trip Distance	1.2 miles for Rainbow Lake; 3.5 miles for Mount Royal; 6.6 miles for Peak 1; 19.2 miles one-way to Breckenridge for Tenmile Traverse to Peak 10
Trailhead	Rainbow Lake/Mount Royal (9,080 feet)
Difficulty Ratings	Class 1–2 trail and Class 2–4 off trail on tundra and scree
Optimal Season	June to October
Maps	Trails Illustrated #109; White River National Forest

COMMENT: The Tenmile Traverse is one of Colorado's classic high-ridge traverses. You can start early in Frisco and grab lunch in Breckenridge before using a car shuttle to return to Frisco. The first part of the traverse can get a bit spicy but never too technical. Views of the Gore Range, Front Range, and Sawatch Range in addition to Dillon Reservoir make for an amazing backdrop as you make your way from north to south.

Rainbow Lake.

Fall colors en route to Rainbow Lake. *Photo by Erin Snow*

GETTING THERE
Rainbow Lake/Mount Royal Trailhead (9,080 feet). Take Exit 201 from I-70, and follow Main Street into town. Take a right (south) on Second Avenue, travel 4 blocks, and look for another right turn crossing the bike path into a dirt parking lot.

THE LAKE
1. Rainbow Lake (9,250 feet). This rolling hike through aspens and pine forest is the perfect way to start your day or take the family for an easy hike in a beautiful setting. Upon leaving the parking lot, pass some willows, emerge onto a boardwalk to the south, and then ascend through pine trees. After 0.3 mile, the trail levels out through aspen forest and then drops down a hill before a gradual incline for the final 0.3 mile in meadows and aspens. Fall colors here are stunning.

THE HIGH-RIDGE TRAVERSE
2. Tenmile Traverse. Always start early (3:00–5:00 a.m.), especially once monsoon season is in full swing. Realistically, I prefer to do this route after September 1 to minimize the potential for thunderstorms. There is nothing like being on this ridge on a crisp fall day with not a cloud in the sky. Follow the Rainbow Lakes Trail south for 0.25 mile through willows and across a boardwalk. Next, you will come to

a trail junction for Mount Royal and Masontown. Take a right turn and head into the woods. Follow the trail as it gains elevation. At your first trail junction after less than 0.5 mile, go left (south), and after a short flatter distance, you will come to another trail junction. Take a sharp right and follow the signs to Masontown. The trail ascends into the pine forest again, and at another flat spot, yet another trail junction will lead you to the Mount Royal Trail. Head west on the Mount Royal Trail, climbing to the base of a prominent avalanche chute. Cross the bottom of the chute and follow the trail as it ascends and contours up the basin. At mile 2.2, you will meet a signed trail junction. To the right is Mount Royal, and you can take a quick side excursion to Mount Royal, but continue left following the signs to Mount Victoria. The trail steepens through the upper reaches of the pine forests, gains the ridge, climbs over Mount Victoria, passes a radio tower, and emerges above tree line before reaching Peak 1 (12,580 feet).

Assess the weather and your time before continuing, as the traverse from Peak 1 through Peaks 2, 3, and 4 gets progressively harder. From Peak 1 to Peak 2, you can follow a sparse climbers' trail on Class 2 terrain. The most challenging portions of the traverse are from Peaks 2 to 3 and then some from 3 to 4. Staying on the ridge crest without a rope isn't always possible but realize that if you choose to take on too much Class 4 terrain, you aren't on the best route.

Once you reach Peak 4, the route across the ridge gets grassier and very easy. You will basically be crossing rolling hills and terrain on a very scenic ridge that has

Looking north from Crystal Peak to Peak 10 (right) and the entire Tenmile Traverse extending to the left.

Gorgeous high ridgelines are what the Tenmile Traverse delivers. *Photo by Chris Tomer*

you working your way toward the top of Breckenridge ski area. The travel is fairly easy through Peak 7, but once you choose to commit to Peaks 8, 9, and 10, you will be going up and down a lot and actually have a challenging hike up rocks and scree on sparse climbers' trails for the last 1,000 feet of elevation gain to the summit of Peak 10.

There are numerous ways to shorten this adventure and still reach Breckenridge. One possibility is to descend from Peak 7 down through the resort to the Grand Lodge on Peak 7 and a car shuttle. From Peak 10, you can follow the east ridge down to a hiking trail that eventually works its way back to Breckenridge. Or, you can also find some old four-wheel-drive roads that lead toward the ski resort and descend back to town.

DR. JON'S EXTRA CREDIT
A. Weston Pass. From the Summit of Peak 10, go for the gusto and climb thirteener Crystal Peak along the ridgeline. Some hearty souls and purists have actually followed the ridgeline across the Tenmile Range as far as Weston Pass on the south side of the Mosquito Range. I did a two-night backpack with a complete traverse of this line crossing over a dozen thirteeners and several fourteeners in the fall of 2006, reaching Weston Pass after nearly 50 miles of high ridges and old mining trails. Create your own adventure and enjoy!

RAINBOW LAKE—TENMILE TRAVERSE FROM FRISCO TO BRECKENRIDGE (NORTH)

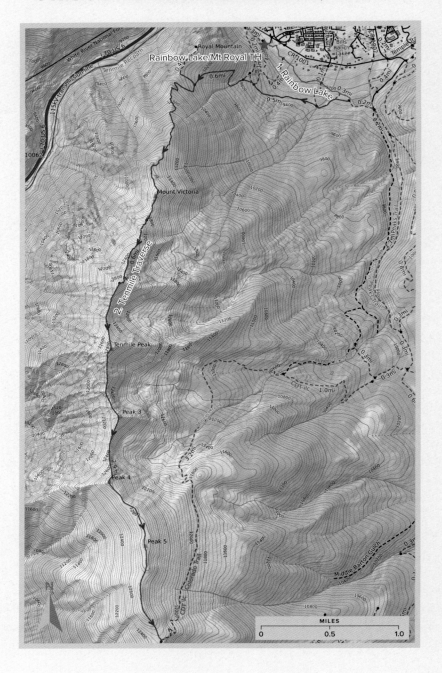

RAINBOW LAKE—TENMILE TRAVERSE FROM FRISCO TO BRECKENRIDGE (SOUTH)

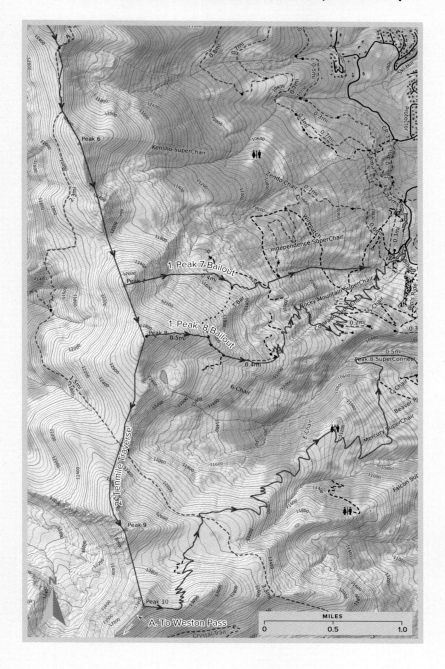

MOHAWK LAKES —CRYSTAL AND PACIFIC PEAKS TRAVERSE

17

Elevation Gain	1,400 feet for Lower Mohawk Lake; 1,850 feet for Upper Mohawk Lake; 3,551 feet for Pacific Peak; 4,300 feet for Crystal to Pacific Loop
Round-Trip Distance	6 miles to Mohawk Lake; 7 miles to Upper Mohawk Lake; 11 miles to Pacific Peak; 14 miles for Crystal to Pacific Peak Loop
Trailhead	Mohawk Lakes/Spruce Creek Road (10,400 feet)
Difficulty Ratings	Class 1–2 on trail to lakes; above the lakes is Class 2–2+ off-trail tundra, scree, and rocky ridgelines for Pacific Peak and Crystal Peak
Optimal Season	June through October
Maps	Trails Illustrated #109; White River National Forest

COMMENT: Mohawk Lakes are a relatively easy and fun hike into a deep glacial valley near Breckenridge. You can venture farther west into the basin and also tackle two Centennial thirteeners: Crystal and Pacific Peaks, which are always far less crowded than neighboring Quandary but offer even better, more isolated views.

View of Pacific Peak and the Upper Mohawk Lakes from the top of Crystal Peak.

Left: Lower Mohawk Lake shimmers in the morning light. *Photo by John Fielder* **Right:** Mohawk Lake.

GETTING THERE

Mohawk Lakes/Spruce Creek Trailhead (10,400 feet). From the Boreas Pass Road junction at the south end of Breckenridge (the final traffic light on the south end of town), travel south on Colorado Highway 9 for 1.7 miles to Spruce Creek Road. Turn right (west) onto Spruce Creek Road. Pass through a housing development, and you will reach the winter trailhead parking after 1.2 miles. The trailhead is marked for the Mohawk Lakes Trail. After the snow melts in the spring, four-wheel-drive vehicles can travel another 1.8 miles (if the gate is open), reaching the water diversion dam at 11,100 feet.

THE LAKES

1. Mohawk Lakes (11,800 feet) (Class 1). The Mohawk Lakes Trail travels from the winter parking area up the four-wheel-drive Spruce Creek Road and passes the water diversion dam at the end of the road. From here, stay left at a trail junction at mile 1.6 (Wheeler Trail) near the end of the water diversion dam. Just before reaching Continental Falls, about 2.5 miles above the water diversion dam, pass some old log mining buildings and proceed left (southwest) after intersecting with the Mayflower Lakes Trail. Continue up the basin on the trail to the left of the falls. There are plenty of mine buildings en route to the upper basin. Continue for another 0.5 mile past several more cascades in the creek, arriving at Lower Mohawk Lake at mile 3. You will see that the lake is located in a gorgeous basin with Mount Helen in the background. After passing Lower Mohawk Lake, take the trail up for another 0.5 mile and 500 feet to reach the even more spectacular and larger Upper Mohawk Lake.

Left: Steep grassy slopes on the north aspects of Crystal with the rock glacier (middle) and the connecting north ridge to Pacific Peak on the ridge to the right. **Right:** The highest Mohawk Lake, above 12,000 feet.

THE LOOP AND HIGH-RIDGE TRAVERSE

2. Crystal Peak (13,852 feet) and Pacific Peak (13,951 feet) (Class 2). Once up on gentler terrain, the upper basin greets you with Upper Mohawk Lake at 12,100 feet. Continue walking up the flat basin and leaving the timberline for 1.3 miles to reach the end of the upper basin while traveling past the highest Mohawk Lake at 12,600 feet. You will pass three Upper Mohawk Lakes in total to get to this point from 12,300 feet to 12,600 feet. Standing in the basin, the sharp-looking Pacific Peak will be to your left and Crystal Peak will be to your right (north). From above the highest lake, locate a destroyed mining building and its wooden ruins. From here, there are basically two options: (1) Ascend grass and scree directly west to the 13,200-foot connecting saddle between Crystal and Pacific. Scramble south along the ridgeline (Class 2+) to the summit of Pacific Peak. (2) From the basin, travel north on grassy benches to the rocky southeast slopes of Crystal, ascend Crystal, and then follow the ridgeline south to Pacific Peak as described above. Continue the loop by taking the east ridge of Pacific Peak and descending via the Hawaii Chutes (Class 2+) back into the Mohawk Lakes basin and eventually back to the lakes and trailhead.

DR. JON'S EXTRA CREDIT

A. Pacific Peak's north couloir (Class 4). The challenge is obvious. Snow conditions for this climb will be best in June and July. Make sure you brought crampons and an ice ax. Ascend the couloir toward the large and prominent cornice on the north ridge. On the ascent, pass a prominent rock tower on your left. After that, turn left into the upper portion of the couloir. The steepest and narrowest sections are in this area at about 13,400 feet. Climb the couloir to the summit, which is just to the east of the top of the chute. Descend via another route.

MOHAWK LAKES
—CRYSTAL AND PACIFIC PEAKS TRAVERSE

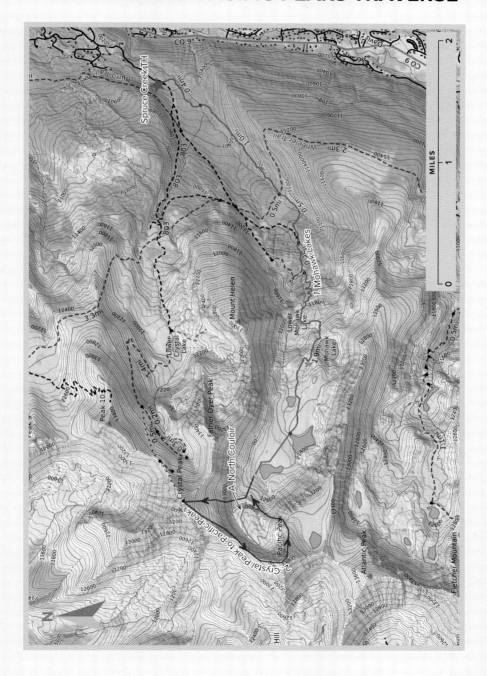

CRYSTAL LAKES —CRYSTAL PEAK —PEAK 10

18

Elevation Gain	1,200 feet for Lower Crystal Lake; 2,500 feet for Upper Crystal Lake; 3,450 feet for Crystal Peak; 3,950 feet for Crystal to Peak 10 Traverse
Round-Trip Distance	5.5 miles to Lower Crystal Lake; 8.5 miles to Upper Crystal Lake; 10 miles to Crystal Peak; 12 miles for Crystal Peak to Peak 10 Loop
Trailhead	Spruce Creek (10,400 feet)
Difficulty Ratings	Class 1–2 trail and Class 2 off trail on tundra and scree
Optimal Season	June to October
Maps	Trails Illustrated #109; White River National Forest

COMMENT: Crystal Lake basin is a beautiful place for an excursion to a high-mountain lake with relatively few people. Francie's Cabin in the lower basin also makes this a place you might want to bring friends, stay a couple of nights, swim in some lakes, and stand on top of some peaks. This is true Colorado through and through.

Crystal Lake.

Crystal Peak summit.

GETTING THERE

Spruce Creek Trailhead (10,400 feet). From the Boreas Pass Road junction at the south end of Breckenridge (the final traffic light on the south end of town), travel south on Colorado Highway 9 for 1.7 miles to Spruce Creek Road. Turn right (west) onto Spruce Creek Road. Pass through a housing development, and you will reach the winter trailhead parking after 1.2 miles.

THE LAKES

1. Lower Crystal Lake (11,600 feet) and Upper Crystal Lake (12,900 feet) (Class 1–2). Both lakes are located in the heart of Crystal basin. From the Spruce Creek Trailhead, follow the Spruce Creek Trail for 2.2 miles through pine forest until you reach a trail junction for Francie's Cabin. From the junction, continue straight (west) for another 0.8 mile, and you will enter high mountain meadows and wild-flowers and reach the lake after 3 miles. From the lower lake to the upper lake, follow an old four-wheel-drive mining road that is mainly a single-track use trail. The trail rises to the north then switches back to the west to gain the southern slopes of Peak 10 while climbing farther west into the basin toward Crystal Peak. Follow this trail for 1.5 miles and gain over 1,000 feet to reach the cirque at the base of Crystal Peak's east face. Upper Crystal Lake will appear abruptly, tucked into this glacial cirque.

THE LOOP AND HIGH-RIDGE TRAVERSE

2. Peak 10 (13,619 feet) and Crystal Peak (13,852 feet) (Class 1–2). From Upper Crystal Lake, look to the west-northwest in a small flat area and locate a use trail that climbs grassy slopes to the 13,390-foot connecting saddle between Crystal Peak and Peak 10. Ascend the trail and follow Crystal's northeast ridgeline to the summit. Crystal's summit has amazing views of the Gore Range, Sawatch, east to the Front Range, and even all the way southeast to Pikes Peak and south to the Sangre

Above: Sunset on Peak 10 in early winter brings vibrant colors.
Left: Upper Crystal Lake with Father Dyer Peak behind.

de Cristos on a clear day. Descend the same route you came up, and if you are feeling ambitious, continue to the northwest on the moderately rugged ridgeline from the Crystal/Peak 10 saddle to the summit of the 13,619-foot Peak 10. You can make this a complete loop by following Peak 10's eastern ridge to the east and passing a prominent radio tower on boulders, which then gives way to grassy tundra. Descend to a trail 1 mile east of Peak 10. This is the main trail that can be followed back southeast toward Francie's Cabin and to the Spruce Creek Trail to return to the trailhead.

DR. JON'S EXTRA CREDIT

A. Consider a stay for a couple of nights at Francie's Cabin. Go to huts.org to book in advance. While staying at this hut, you can spend more time at the lakes or explore the ridgelines and basins in the area in addition to the ones described here.

CRYSTAL LAKES—CRYSTAL PEAK—PEAK 10

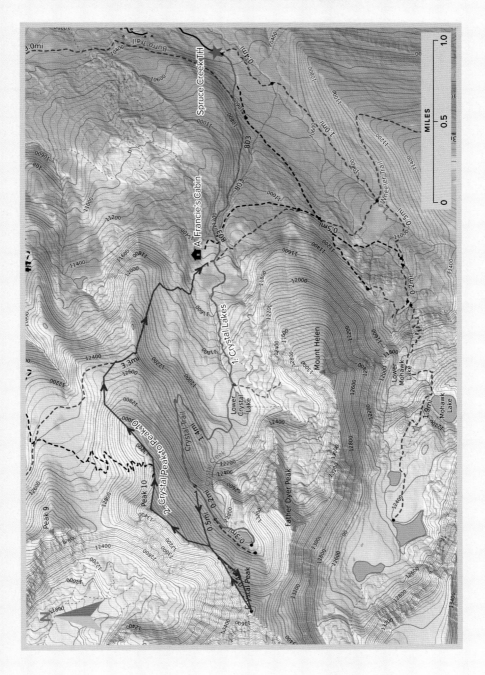

MAYFLOWER GULCH —DRIFT PEAK TO FLETCHER MOUNTAIN TO ATLANTIC PEAK TRAVERSE

19

Elevation Gain	2,850 feet for Atlantic Peak only; 3,320 feet for Drift Peak to Fletcher to Atlantic Peak Loop
Round-Trip Distance	7 miles to Atlantic Peak only; 9.5 miles for Drift to Fletcher to Atlantic Peak Loop
Trailhead	Mayflower Gulch (11,000 feet)
Difficulty Ratings	Class 1–2 on four-wheel-drive roads and use trails; Class 2–3 off trails on tundra, scree, and rocky outcroppings as well as jagged ridgelines
Optimal Season	June through October
Maps	Trails Illustrated #109; White River National Forest

COMMENT: The stunning basins below Atlantic Peak, Drift Peak, and Fletcher Mountain are perhaps two of the most easily accessible areas for an outing in the Colorado Rockies outside the Front Range. While this is one of the only entries

From the summit of Drift looking north across to Fletcher to the traverse to Atlantic.

Above: The old cabins at Mayflower Gulch.
Right: Sunrise framed in Mayflower Gulch.

in this book without a lake as a destination, the stunning beauty of the dramatic peaks in this basin will explain why they have been included here. Most people will simply hike to the old, abandoned cabins for a photo op in the upper basin above tree line, while others can try either one of the challenging peaks or traverses described here.

GETTING THERE

Mayflower Gulch (11,000 feet). This trailhead is right off Colorado Highway 91 and is open year-round. From 75 miles west of Denver, take Exit 195 at Copper Mountain and travel 6 miles south on Colorado Highway 91. The trailhead is on the east side of the highway in a large, paved parking area, which is plowed in winter. If approaching from Leadville to the south, the trailhead is 4 miles north of the top of Fremont Pass. In late spring, it is possible to take the forest road for 1.5 miles up to abandoned cabins near the old Boston Mine at 11,600 feet.

THE HIGH-RIDGE TRAVERSES

1. Atlantic Peak's west ridge (13,841 feet) (Class 2). This climb ascends the prominent west ridgeline of Atlantic Peak. Start at the Mayflower Gulch Trailhead and go up the often-busy road for about 1 mile toward the southeast. (Sometimes it's possible to leave the road before traveling a mile and turn northeast to head up Pacific Creek Basin.) Before heading into the trees and up the basin, you will have to cross Mayflower Creek and contend with many large willows. As of 2017, there was actually a pretty good use trail marked with cairns near tree line within view of the old Boston Mine ruins. The use trail climbs steeply among sparse trees and leaves timberline behind through a narrow valley (which is easiest on the west and northwest side of Pacific Creek) leading to a broad valley at the base of Pacific Peak to the northeast, and Atlantic Peak to the southeast. From 12,200 feet, the basin is still narrow, and you should traverse to the east (right) to gain the prominent west ridgeline. From here, you will follow the west ridge as it climbs for about 1,700 feet to reach Atlantic's broad, flat summit. The ridge is easy at first and gets steeper as you get higher. Stay on the crest for the best footing.

2. Drift Peak (13,900 feet) to Fletcher Mountain (13,951) (Class 2+). The more difficult peak of the two, Fletcher Mountain's south ridge is a bit more challenging than Atlantic's as described, and you need to climb up and over the west ridge of Drift Peak, a soft-ranked thirteener subsummit of Fletcher at 13,900 feet. If you don't want to commit to this peak's difficulties, consider just hiking to the mine ruins at tree line and enjoying the sunshine. Once you have passed the mine buildings, travel higher in the basin on an old four-wheel-drive road for a couple hundred

Left: Drift Peak; the west ridge is visible. **Right:** The rugged upper west ridge of Drift.

Looking back down Mayflower Gulch from Drift.

yards. Then look to your right (south) and locate an old, faint use trail that was once a mining trail and follow it into a shallow basin toward Drift's west ridge crest. Ascend talus, large boulders, and moraines to a prominent point of the ridgeline. From here, the climbing gets steeper (Class 2+) on the more challenging portions of the ridge. In a few cases, it will be easier to bypass the sharpest parts of the ridge on the left (north side). At 13,700 feet, there is a nice shallow saddle for a great view and resting point, and then scramble up solid boulders and rock slabs for 200 feet to the summit of Drift. From the top of Drift, a sharp but solid granite ridgeline takes you up only an additional 50 feet for 0.5 mile to Fletcher's summit.

DR. JON'S EXTRA CREDIT
A. Loop of Drift to Fletcher to Atlantic (Class 3). I recommend doing this loop in counterclockwise order because you won't have to downclimb Drift's steep west ridge. Follow option 2 above to the summit of Fletcher Mountain. From here, take the approximately 1-mile ridgeline north to the summit of Atlantic. There is an occasional Class 3 move on the ridgeline on the southern portions of the ridge, and the ridgeline gets easier as you get closer to the top of Atlantic Peak. Descend Atlantic Peak by way of its west ridge route as described in option 1 above. If it's a bluebird day without thunderstorms, feel free to explore the extra mile north of Atlantic and climb to the summit of Pacific Peak as well!

MAYFLOWER GULCH —DRIFT PEAK TO FLETCHER MOUNTAIN TO ATLANTIC PEAK TRAVERSE

WHEELER LAKE —CLINTON/MCNAMEE/ TRAVER PEAKS LOOP

20

Elevation Gain	1,218 feet for Wheeler Lake; 3,300 feet for Clinton Peak to Traver Peak Loop
Round-Trip Distance	7 miles to Wheeler Lake; 10.5 miles to Clinton to McNamee to Traver Peaks Loop
Trailhead	Montgomery Reservoir (10,950 feet)
Difficulty Ratings	Class 1–2 on four-wheel-drive road to lake; Class 2 on tundra and rocky ridgelines above lake
Optimal Season	June to October
Maps	Trails Illustrated #109 and #1302; Pike National Forest

COMMENT: This little off-the-beaten-path adventure allows you to not only visit a gorgeous lake, but you get to travel on some high ridges to collect three 13,000-foot peaks where you are likely to be all alone in the Rockies. There may be some off-road vehicles or ATVs on the approach to Wheeler Lake, but once you leave the lake to travel to Clinton Peak and the traverse to McNamee and Traver Peaks, you should have it all to yourself.

Spectacular morning reflection hiking along the banks of Wheeler Lake.

Wheeler Lake.

GETTING THERE

Montgomery Reservoir Trailhead (10,950 feet). This trailhead is located south of Breckenridge and south of Hoosier Pass along Colorado Highway 9. Less than a mile south of the pass, take CR 4 west from Colorado Highway 9. Follow CR 4 for 1.8 miles to the trailhead near a water shed and concrete wall next to the reservoir. After you leave Highway 9, at 0.3 mile, stay straight and at 0.8 mile, go right on the higher road. At 1.5 miles, reach the parking area, cross a small bridge, and travel around the reservoir.

THE LAKE

1. Wheeler Lake (Class 1). This relatively easy hike along a four-wheel-drive road leaves the reservoir and the pine trees, and emerges into willows, wildflowers, and tundra. At mile 3, the road ascends steeply above the timber toward the lake for the final 0.5 mile. After 3.5 miles, you will reach a gorgeous high alpine lake tucked into a shallow mountain basin. At the far end of the lake, see if you can locate an old abandoned early 1900s car for a fun photo with your friends.

THE LOOP AND HIGH-RIDGE TRAVERSE

2. South Slopes Clinton Peak (13,857 feet) to McNamee and Traver Peaks Loop (Class 2). From Wheeler Lake, you can follow the shallow creek basin to the southwest for 0.75 mile to reach an even smaller pond/lake at just above 13,200 feet. From here, Clinton Peak is directly to your north. Follow the rocky south slope for 600 feet to reach the summit of Clinton. While standing atop Clinton Peak, McNamee is 0.5 mile to the southwest along the gentle Class 2 ridgeline. There are some social trails and goat trails along the ridgeline, which drops to a mere 13,700 feet

Left: Coming up the valley with peaks (right to left) Wheeler, Clinton, McNamee, and Traver.
Right: Traver Peak (center) approaching from the east.

before ascending to the top of McNamee (13,780 feet). Cables and other old mining relics are found near the summit. Next continue southeast for less than a half mile to the 13,852-foot summit of Traver Peak. The last 200 feet of Traver's northwest ridge become steep and rocky with boulders near the remnants of an old tower. Finally, after collecting your third thirteener summit of the morning, you have to descend northeast from Traver along the ridgeline back toward Wheeler Lake, following the stream back to the lake.

DR. JON'S EXTRA CREDIT
A. Wheeler Peak to Hoosier Pass (Class 2+). This is a classic Colorado high traverse. Consider doing the above-described traverse in reverse order, collecting Traver, McNamee, and Clinton Peaks from Wheeler Lake, and then traversing to the east on the ridge from Clinton to the summit of 13,690-foot Wheeler Peak. You can either leave a car or a bike on the summit of Hoosier Pass another 3 miles to the east to allow you to return to your vehicle at Montgomery Reservoir.

> Note: Portions of these routes pass through private land and mining claims, which may or may not be open to public use. Please check with local land managers to determine accessibility, and respect all closure and no trespassing signs.

WHEELER LAKE
—CLINTON/MCNAMEE/TRAVER PEAKS LOOP

LAKE EMMA —MOUNT DEMOCRAT AND "DECALIBRON"

21

Please note that the DeCaLiBron area is a patchwork of public and private land. Access may be limited in some areas, and users should respect all closures and private property boundaries. Stay on designated trails and confirm current regulations before visiting this area as access may change.

Elevation Gain	1,400 feet for Lake Emma; 2,148 feet for Mount Democrat, 3,148 feet for the full DeCaLiBron Loop
Round-Trip Distance	2 miles for Lake Emma; 4.5 miles for Mount Democrat; 7.5 miles for the DeCaLiBron Loop
Trailhead	Kite Lake or below depending on seasonal road snow coverage (12,000 down to 11,000 feet)
Difficulty Rating	Class 1–2 on trails; please stay on designated trails to avoid trespass
Optimal Season	June through October
Maps	Trails Illustrated #109 and #1302; Pike National Forest

COMMENT: Democrat is a high peak in the Tenmile/Mosquito Range with easy access to two beautiful lakes: Kite Lake and Lake Emma. Most people will be using this trailhead to hike the "DeCaLiBron," a loop of four fourteeners (7.5 miles round-trip and 3,700 feet) that can easily be done in a day. Lake Emma is a stunning and more isolated choice away from the popular fourteeners, but there is something for everyone here.

The peaks of Mount Democrat, Lincoln, and Bross are private property and many segments of the DeCaLiBron loop cross through private mining claims. As of this book's publication, the owner of Mounts Democrat and Lincoln has generously granted access to the peaks, provided hikers stay on the designated trail, follow Leave No Trace principles, and avoid the summit of Mount Bross, which is closed to public access. Be sure to check with the Forest Service South Park Ranger District about the status of the trail and peak access.

Lake Emma from above; you can see east out to Fairplay and South Park.

GETTING THERE

Kite Lake Trailhead (12,000 feet). This trailhead is privately owned and maintained by a partnership with the US Forest Service and Town of Alma. A $2 to $10 fee is charged through self-issued parking permits. In past years, the fees have fluctuated. From the center of Alma, travel west and then north on Park County 8, which is a dirt road. Follow the signs to Kite Lake for 6 miles. You can reach the center of Alma from Colorado Highway 9 either from the north, 6 miles south from Hoosier Pass, or from the south, 6 miles on Colorado Highway 9 north from US Highway 285 in Fairplay. The last mile of this road can be too rough for small vehicles; four-wheel-drive is recommended. It's possible to park near the Sweet Home Mine 1.4 miles below Kite Lake and travel the extra distance on foot. The Kite Lake Road is closed to vehicles in winter and spring to minimize road damage. Contact the US Forest Service South Park Ranger District for current road information.

THE LAKES

1. Lake Emma (13,400 feet) (Class 1–2). You can spend time at Kite Lake to celebrate your day or even go for a dip if it's a warm afternoon, but start by following the Lake Emma Trail southwest and then west from Kite Lake as it ascends through the tundra and rocky shelves along a small creek. Cross the outflow creek of Lake Emma and follow the trail north for the final 0.25 mile as it steepens and arrives at the lake abruptly. Lake Emma is tucked into a glacial cirque below the southeast face

Left: The traverse from Democrat to Cameron is on an easy trail. **Right:** Mount Lincoln from Cameron; you can see how flat the terrain is.

of Mount Democrat. Visit the lake early in the morning for sunrise reflections. As of this publication, the route to Lake Emma crosses through private property and is not an authorized trail.

THE LOOPS AND HIGH-RIDGE TRAVERSE

2. Mount Democrat (14,148 feet) (Class 2). Leave the parking area, cross the creek that flows out of Kite lake, and then pass by Kite Lake by traveling north on the lake's eastern edge. Ascend an easy trail as it switches back for a mile up into a sweeping basin on the eastern side of Mount Democrat. After several switchbacks you will climb gentle slopes of talus and scree on a well-defined trail to the 13,380-foot connecting saddle between Democrat and Cameron. Turn left (west), and ascend large boulders on a climbers' trail that crosses and zigzags across the southeast face of Democrat. At 13,900 feet, leave the southeast face, arrive on a small broad false summit and then travel west for 300 yards to the top of Mount Democrat. Return back to the trailhead at Kite Lake the same way you came up, or continue on to the DeCaLiBron Loop. (See "Dr. Jon's Extra Credit" below.)

DR. JON'S EXTRA CREDIT

A. DeCaLiBron Loop (Class 2). This is a classic Colorado fourteener peakbagger's day. Start from the Kite Lake Trailhead and aim for the 13,380-foot connecting saddle between Democrat and Cameron, which is to your north-northwest. Turn left (west) and follow the ridgeline trail as described above for 0.5 mile to the summit of Democrat. Retrace the trail back to the Democrat-Cameron saddle, travel east over Cameron, farther east to Lincoln, and then south past Mount Bross (note that the summit of Mount Bross is private property and is closed to public access) before returning down a steep trail back to Kite Lake for a total of 7.5 miles and 3,700 feet of elevation gain.

Lake Emma—Mount Democrat and "DeCaLiBron"

LAKE EMMA—MOUNT DEMOCRAT AND "DECALIBRON"

UNNAMED LAKE TO MOUNT ARKANSAS TO MOUNT BUCKSKIN TRAVERSE

22

Elevation Gain	1,200 feet for the unnamed lake in upper Arkansas Basin; 2,865 feet for the summit of Mount Arkansas; 3,500 feet for Mount Arkansas Traverse to Mount Buckskin
Round-Trip Distance	5.5 miles to the unnamed upper Arkansas Basin lake; 8 miles to Mount Arkansas summit; 10 miles for Arkansas to Mount Buckskin Traverse Loop
Trailhead	Fremont Pass (11,000 feet)
Difficulty Ratings	Class 1–2 four-wheel-drive road and off-trail hiking; Class 3 scrambling ridge traverse, steep snow-climbing for Mount Arkansas
Optimal Season	June through October
Maps	Trails Illustrated #109; Pike National Forest

COMMENT: The headwaters of the Arkansas River form a long and gradual basin, formerly covered by glaciers. These gentle slopes are ideal for a headwaters' basin tour and hiking through summer wildflowers, while the surrounding peaks, Buckskin, Arkansas, and Democrat, offer unlimited climbing options from their summits and connecting ridges. This zone is very isolated, mainly due to its few trails and lack of fourteener access to Mount Democrat, so enjoy the solitude of this place.

The wildflowers greet you on the way to Mount Buckskin.

GETTING THERE

Fremont Pass (11,000 feet). This trailhead is right off Colorado Highway 91 and is open year-round. From 75 miles west of Denver, take Exit 195 at Copper Mountain and travel 10 miles south on Colorado Highway 91 to the top of Fremont Pass near the Climax Mine. The trailhead is 0.75 mile from here on the south side of the pass on the downhill and east side of the sharp curve on the highway. If approaching from Leadville to the south, the trailhead is 12 miles north of Leadville on Colorado Highway 91. In summer, it is possible to take the forest road that heads east from the highway 1.5 miles up to a road closure and trail junction. In the winter, the east side of the road is plowed enough for a handful of cars to park, and I've never seen more than three cars parked here at any time.

THE LAKE

1. Unnamed upper Arkansas Basin lake (12,200 feet) (Class 1–2). From the trailhead at Colorado Highway 91, follow the four-wheel-drive road east and then southeast as it follows the broad basin above timberline. After 1.5 miles, you will come to the end of the four-wheel-drive road and will leave the trees behind. Continue south (right) climbing past krummholz trees and grassy areas as well as a few willows. You will gain access to a shallow basin, and at 12,200 feet, a sizeable unnamed lake will appear in front of you.

THE LOOP AND HIGH-RIDGE TRAVERSE

2. Mount Arkansas north couloir (13,795 feet) traverse to Mount Buckskin (13,865 feet) via west ridge (Class 2–3 in steep snow). From the south end of the unnamed lake, ascend grassy and relatively flat slopes for 0.5 mile into the upper basin below Mount Arkansas's north face at 12,500 feet. In June and July, make sure you brought your ice ax and crampons. Climb the couloir for nearly 1,200 feet of sustained 45–50 degrees. Once reaching the top of the couloir, it is a short 100-foot scramble (Class 2+) on stable rock and talus to the summit of Mount Arkansas. From the top, traverse the ridgeline to the east toward Mount Buckskin. On the way, you will also traverse over the top of 13,619-foot Mount Tweto. Tweto is merely a minor bump on the ridge as you traverse. On the way past Tweto, you will descend 475 feet of easy Class 2 terrain on rocks, and there is a small user trail sometimes visible on the ridgeline and on the southern aspect of the ridgeline. From the 13,325-foot connecting saddle between Tweto and Buckskin, stay to the right side (south) on the west ridge and follow it east for 450 feet and 0.5 mile to the summit. Some sections are part game trail, part rocky boulders. When returning to the trailhead, descend to this connecting saddle between Buckskin and Arkansas, and follow loose scree and

Left: Parking along the four-wheel-drive road in Arkansas Basin. **Right:** High on the ridgeline between Arkansas and Buckskin.

use trails for 750 feet down into the flat grassy basin. It's possible to circle around the upper Buckskin basin by following the creek and user trails to reconnect with the four-wheel-drive road near 12,000 feet and return to the trailhead.

DR. JON'S EXTRA CREDIT

A. North Loop (Class 2+). Due to several decades-long land issues, staying high on the ridge from Mount Buckskin to Mount Democrat in this area is no longer possible. Instead, if you climb Mount Buckskin (option 2 above), return to your vehicle in the upper basin trailhead and consider an alternative "North Loop" that bypasses Democrat altogether. Leave the upper 4WD parking and ascend directly north for 1,600 feet on grassy benches followed by rocks and scree to find the 13,200-foot connecting saddle between Mount Democrat and Traver Peak. Once in the saddle, Democrat will be to your east and the rocky Traver to McNamee to Clinton ridge (see entry 20) will get you to the top of Clinton. There is a grassy chute/gully on McNamee's southwest aspect that will help you return to your vehicle parked at Colorado Highway 91 or at the upper 4WD trailhead as indicated on the map. An optional out-and-back to Clinton can make this loop more scenic, or perhaps consider a visit to Wheeler Lake as well (see entry 20).

> Note: Portions of these routes pass through private land and mining claims, which may or may not be open to public use. Please check with local land managers to determine accessibility, and respect all closure and no trespassing signs.

UNNAMED LAKE TO MOUNT ARKANSAS TO MOUNT BUCKSKIN TRAVERSE

MOUNT SHERMAN GRAND SLAM TRAVERSE LOOP

23

Elevation Gain	2,900 feet for Dyer to Gemini to Sherman Loop; 5,600 feet for Dyer to Gemini to Sherman to Sheridan to Peerless to Horseshoe Loop
Round-Trip Distance	6.5 miles for Dyer to Gemini to Sherman Loop; 10 miles for Dyer to Gemini to Sherman to Sheridan to Peerless to Horseshoe Loop
Trailhead	Iowa Gulch (11,200 feet)
Difficulty Ratings	Class 1–2 on four-wheel-drive roads, old mining roads, and climbers' trails, as well as Class 2 on tundra and rocky ridgelines above tree line
Optimal Season	June to October
Maps	Trails Illustrated #110 and #149; Pike National Forest

COMMENT: While this incredible adventure loop doesn't visit any lakes directly, it allows you to collect up to six summits over 13,348 feet, and five summits all above 13,748 feet, including fourteener Mount Sherman. By parking at Iowa Gulch, you can also choose to do a shorter or longer version of this peakbagging adventure near Leadville with views to the Sawatch, Front Range, and even to the Elk and Sangre de Cristo Ranges on a super clear day. Keep an eye out for columbines in the summer near the trailhead and in the lower valley portion below Mount Sherman; they are often in abundance here.

Columbines greet you below Mount Sherman.

A beautiful fall day near the summit of Dyer Peak; the Sawatch Range is on the far horizon.

GETTING THERE

Iowa Gulch at Asarco (11,200 feet). This trailhead is accessed from the west side of the mountain range and to the east of the town of Leadville. From the central part of Leadville, follow US Highway 24 for 0.3 mile. Before US Highway 24 takes a sharp right turn, turn left onto Monroe Street and follow it up the hill for 0.3 mile. Next turn right (south and then southeast) onto Lake County Road 2. Follow Lake County Road 2 for 3.4 miles as it climbs to an obvious turnout. This road is plowed all winter long. At the turnout, the winter parking is on Lake County 2, while the narrower dirt road continues to the left on a road shelf. Lake County 2 drops to the right and down to the Asarco mine. Take the left fork, which you can skin up in the winter. The road will melt out by late May.

THE LOOPS AND HIGH-RIDGE TRAVERSES

1. South slopes Dyer Peak (13,855 feet) traverse to Gemini (13,951 feet) and Mount Sherman (14,036 feet) (Class 2). From the upper reaches of the road in Iowa Gulch, follow the old mining road northwest for a few hundred yards as you climb north into the upper basin. The steep west face of Sherman will be visible to your right (east). Ascend grassy then rocky slopes to the summit of 13,855-foot Dyer Peak. Next look to traverse the rocky ridge to the east to Gemini and Sherman. Partway down the 1-mile ridgeline to Gemini, you will pass under a sizeable electrical line. Then from the 13,380-foot connecting saddle, follow a use trail to the east, eventually scrambling up large boulders to the top of Gemini. From Gemini, follow an easy ridge for 0.5 mile to Sherman's summit, your high point for the day. The summit is super flat with South Park and Pikes Peak visible to the east and southeast.

Left: Mount Sherman's southwest ridge is a popular winter fourteener climb. **Right:** Centennial Horseshoe Mountain's northwest ridge; Sheridan and Sherman are to the north.

From the top of Sherman, descend the south ridge of Sherman to the southwest and then south for 1 mile to the 13,140-foot connecting saddle between Mount Sherman and Mount Sheridan. From here, it is possible to find a significant trail leading down into Iowa Basin and looping back to your car for 1.3 miles.

2. Grand Slam Traverse, adding Sheridan (13,748 feet), Peerless (13,348 feet), and Horseshoe Mountain (13,898 feet) Loop (Class 2). Follow the above description to reach the 13,140-foot connecting saddle between Mount Sherman and Mount Sheridan. Instead of dropping into Iowa Basin and heading back to the car, make your way up the northeast slope of Mount Sheridan and then continue north along the long ridgeline across some climbers' trails and some old mining roads to the summit of the lower Peerless Mountain. Finally, continue another 0.75 mile farther south to the rounded gentle summit of Horseshoe Mountain, one of Colorado's Centennials. This high-ridge traverse is very simple and easy to follow and provides great views. Returning to your vehicle in Iowa Gulch is simple. Backtrack down and across Peerless. Once you are several hundred yards north, follow a faint mining trail as it skirts to the east side of Mount Sheridan and back to the 13,140-foot connecting saddle between Sherman and Sheridan. From this saddle, it's an easy 1.3 miles back down into Iowa Gulch and the trailhead.

DR. JON'S EXTRA CREDIT

A. Finnback Knob (13,069 feet) and the Emma and Marceline Yurts (Class 2+). Consider an overnight stay at the well-kept Emma or Marceline Yurts to the west of Finnback Knob. You can access the six peaks described here in this entry near Horseshoe Mountain by climbing up and over Finnback Knob. Visit leadvillebackcountry.com to book one of these great yurts.

MOUNT SHERMAN GRAND SLAM TRAVERSE LOOP

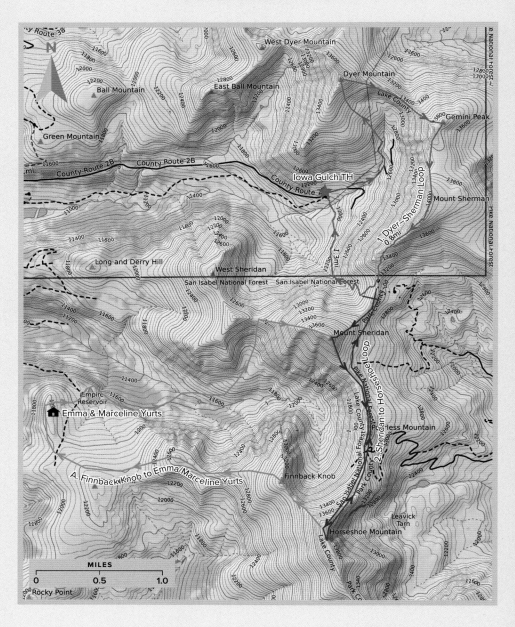

...

CHAPTER 4

GORE RANGE/ VAIL VALLEY

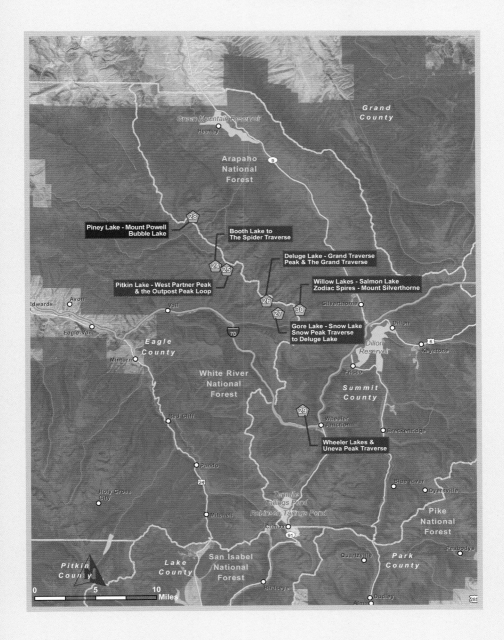

Green Mountain Reservoir

Heeney

Grand County

Arapaho National Forest

9

28

Piney Lake - Mount Powell Bubble Lake

Booth Lake to The Spider Traverse

Deluge Lake - Grand Traverse Peak & The Grand Traverse

24 25

Pitkin Lake - West Partner Peak & the Outpost Peak Loop

Edwards

Avon

Vail

Eagle-Vail

26

Willow Lakes - Salmon Lake Zodiac Spires - Mount Silverthorne

Silverthorne

27 30

Dillon

70

Gore Lake - Snow Lake Snow Peak Traverse to Deluge Lake

Dillon Reservoir

6

Keystone

Eagle County

Minturn

White River National Forest

Frisco

Summit County

Red Cliff

29

Wheeler Junction

Breckenridge

Wheeler Lakes & Uneva Peak Traverse

Pando

Holy Cross City

24

Mitchell

Blue River

Dyersville

Termite Tailings Pond
Robinson Tailings Pond

Climax

Pike National Forest

91

Pitkin County

Lake County

San Isabel National Forest

Birdseye

Quartzville

Park County

Peabodys

Dudley
Alma

285

0   5   10
Miles

BOOTH FALLS —BOOTH LAKE TO THE FLY AND SPIDER TRAVERSE

24

Elevation Gain	1,500 for Booth Falls; 3,035 feet for Booth Lake; 4,435 feet for the Spider Traverse via the Fly
Round-Trip Distance	4.4 miles for Booth Falls; 10.2 miles for Booth Lake; 12.5 for the Spider Traverse
Trailhead	Booth Falls (8,440 feet)
Difficulty Ratings	Class 1–2 on trails to Booth Lake; Class 2–3 off-trail scrambling on the Fly and Spider
Optimal Season	June through October
Maps	Trails Illustrated #108 and #149; White River National Forest

COMMENT: The Gore Range is arguably the best range in the state for moderately technical scrambles combined with lack of crowds. While the first 2 miles of this trail won't generally avoid the masses, what will give you solitude is getting up super early to hike the 5 miles to Booth Lake and beyond. Keep an eye out for mountain goats in this upper basin and on the ridgelines; this is their domain.

Climbing to the Fly with Booth Lake below.

GETTING THERE

Booth Falls Trailhead (8,440 feet).
Take Exit 180 (East Vail) from I-70. Follow the North Frontage Road west for
1 mile, passing Vail Mountain School
(VMS) on your right. Immediately after
passing the school, take a right on Booth
Creek Road. Follow this road for one-
eighth mile to a small paved parking area.
This trailhead gets busy, so go early and
do not park near VMS, otherwise you'll
get ticketed or towed. As of 2021, the
town of Vail has closed this trailhead to
private vehicles and encourages hikers to
take the town bus or get dropped off at the
trailhead, so plan ahead.

Traversing to the Spider.

THE LAKES

**1. Booth Lake (11,475 feet) (Class
1–2).** Follow a gorgeous trail with a mod-
erate grade through a series of aspen, then meadows, then aspens and meadows
again before a set of switchbacks bring you to Booth Falls at mile 2.2. From the falls,
ascend through the pine forest and eventually some higher sparse meadows before
climbing the final half mile through some rock shelves to Booth Lake. There is a cool
island in the center of the lake to remind you that you are in the right place.

THE LOOPS AND HIGH-RIDGE TRAVERSE

**2. Southwest face of the Fly (12,580 feet) to the south ridge of the Spi-
der (12,692 feet) (Class 3).** From Booth Lake, you can see the fly to your north.
Ascend a broad bowl first by staying in the center of the face. Once you bypass some
cliffs on your left, get up onto the grassy face at 12,200 feet and ascend the ledges
to the north to reach the final ridge. The final Class 3 ridge is a fun scramble to the
summit of the Fly (12,580 feet). If for some reason you climbed more to the left when
leaving Booth Lake, you will top out on the ridgeline earlier for a bit more of a solid
rock Class 3–4 scrambling variation. From the summit of the Fly, descend the left
(west side) of the mountain to reach the 12,295-foot connecting saddle between the
two peaks. Follow this ridgeline north to the summit of the Spider. Most of the ridge
is Class 2+ with an occasional Class 3 move near some boulders midway up and also

Left: Descending the Spider with West Partner Peak across the valley to the right. **Right:** Booth Lake.

near the summit. Everything to the east side of the ridge drops off as the cliffs are deeply glacially cut there. From the summit, you get awesome views of the entire Ripsaw ridgeline in the Gore Range as well as Upper Piney Lake to the east and an unnamed lake to the west, Mount Powell to the north, and West Partner Peak to the east. Descend the same route.

DR. JON'S EXTRA CREDIT

A. West Partner Peak Loop (13,041 feet) (Class 3–4). This is a classic Gore Range peakbagger's day. From the Spider, descend partway across the traverse from the Fly. As you are headed south, there are a couple of places to drop from toward a small pond with a series of benches in the upper basin at 11,400 feet. From these benches, traverse toward the southeast, reaching a broad obvious saddle between the Fly and West Partner Peak at 12,050 feet. From this saddle, ascend a more jagged ridgeline and look to the south to see another small unnamed lake in the Upper Booth Lake basin. You can drop down for a visit to this lake, or you can stay on the ridgeline to West Partner Peak's summit. Returning to the basin by way of this 12,050-foot saddle and then getting back into the Booth Creek drainage near the unnamed lake are relatively easy to the south from this saddle. To the north of this saddle, you will see Upper Piney Lake way down in the drainage. Booth Lake to Fly to Spider to West Partner Peak and down is 14.5 miles and 6,085 feet of elevation gain.

BOOTH FALLS—BOOTH LAKE TO THE FLY AND SPIDER TRAVERSE

PITKIN LAKE —WEST PARTNER PEAK AND THE OUTPOST PEAK LOOP

25

Elevation Gain	2,900 feet for Pitkin Lake; 5,000 feet for West Partner Peak to Outpost Peak Traverse; 5,155 feet for Partner Traverse
Round-Trip Distance	10 miles for Pitkin Lake; 13.2 for the West Partner Peak to Outpost Peak Traverse Loop; 12.9 miles for Partner Traverse
Trailhead	Pitkin Lake (8,480 feet)
Difficulty Ratings	Class 1–2 on trails to Booth Lake; Class 2–3 off-trail scrambling on the high ridges
Optimal Season	June through October
Maps	Trails Illustrated #108 and #149; White River National Forest

COMMENT: Pitkin Lake is yet another fun tucked-away gem in the Gore Range. Both traverse options described here from West Partner Peak are isolated and scenic, and will test your routefinding and scrambling skills.

GETTING THERE

Pitkin Lake Trailhead (8,480 feet). Take Exit 180 (East Vail) from I-70. Follow the North Frontage Road east for 0.5 mile, passing some condos and arriving at a small paved parking area that is marked right next to the interstate.

Glass on Pitkin Lake.

Can you find this lake, to the west of West Partner Peak? It's not far from Booth Lake.

THE LAKES

1. Pitkin Lake (11,390 feet) (Class 1–2). Follow a gorgeous trail with a moderate grade through a series of aspen, then meadows, and then a meadow recently cleared by a large avalanche. From the avalanche zone, ascend through the pine forest and some higher sparse meadows before climbing the final half mile through some rock outcroppings to Pitkin Lake. The lake is at the upper end of the valley tucked into a glacial cirque and has plenty of fish in the outlet creek as well as the lake.

THE LOOPS AND HIGH-RIDGE TRAVERSE

2. West Partner Peak (13,041 feet) traverse south ridge to Outpost Peak (12,362 feet) (Class 3). Leave Pitkin Lake and hike up the basin above the lake traveling north. Once 200 to 300 feet above the lake, you have two choices: (1) climb the face of the basin directly to the summit of 13,041-foot West Partner Peak, or (2) traverse left (west) on some very distinct grassy benches to gain the south ridgeline and get to the 12,180-foot connecting saddle of the south ridge of West Partner Peak and Outpost Peak farther south. You can climb this ridge to the summit. Most of the safest ledges along the ridge are actually on the west side of the ridge as you ascend. Once on West Partner Peak, return south to this saddle carefully down some solid easy Class 3 rock and continue for 1 mile south on a relatively flat but scenic

Above: The dramatic ridgeline connecting to East Partner Peak. **Left:** Traversing with Upper Piney Lake below.

ridgeline to the summit of Outpost Peak. Descend back to the Pitkin Lake drainage to the trail via the grassy northeast face of Outpost Peak.

DR. JON'S EXTRA CREDIT

A. West Partner Peak to East Partner Peak Loop (13,041 feet to 13,057 feet) (Class 3–4). Once you summit West Partner Peak, consider traversing to Peak V, also known as East Partner Peak: the Partner Traverse. Study your maps, launch early, and get ready for a fun day on the spine of the Gore Range.

B. Pitkin Lake to West Partner Peak descent to Booth Lake and Booth Falls (Class 3–4). This awesome car-to-car loop is 12.3 miles and gets you some amazing views and allows you to see two separate drainages. Get picked up at Vail Mountain School and start from Pitkin Lake Trailhead.

PITKIN LAKE—WEST PARTNER PEAK AND THE OUTPOST PEAK LOOP

DELUGE LAKE—GRAND TRAVERSE PEAK AND THE GRAND TRAVERSE

26

Elevation Gain	3,100 feet for Deluge Lake; 4,400 feet for Grand Traverse Peak; 4,900 feet for Grand Traverse to North Traverse Peak and down into Big Horn drainage to Big Horn Trailhead
Round-Trip Distance	9 miles for Deluge Lake; 11 miles for Grand Traverse Peak; 19 miles Grand Traverse Peak across Grand Traverse to North Traverse Peak with descent into Big Horn Basin (a car shuttle is needed at Big Horn Trailhead)
Trailheads	Gore Creek (8,700 feet) and Big Horn (8,600 feet)
Difficulty Ratings	Class 1–2 hike both on trails and across tundra/scattered alpine forest ecozone with no trails; Class 3–4 on the Grand Traverse Loop
Optimal Season	June 15 through October
Maps	Trails Illustrated #108 and #149; White River National Forest

COMMENT: This is the iconic view of the Gore Range from the shops on Gore Creek Drive in Vail Village. You get to climb Grand Traverse Peak and be in someone else's postcard photo from afar, so smile and have fun!

Grand Traverse Peak reflected in Deluge Lake in the early morning.

Left: Columbines along the high ridges of the Gore Range. **Right:** Deluge Lake with Snow Peak behind.

GETTING THERE

Gore Creek Trailhead (8,700 feet). Take Interstate 70 to Exit 180 for East Vail. Travel east on Big Horn Road for 2.3 miles and cross underneath the large interstate bridges to reach the parking area on the left for the trailhead.

Big Horn Trailhead (8,600 feet). If doing a vehicle shuttle for the Grand Traverse Loop, leave a car at the Big Horn Trailhead in East Vail. Travel east on Big Horn Road from the East Vail Exit for 0.75 mile, turn left (north) on Columbine Drive, pass under a single-lane interstate tunnel, and arrive at the Big Horn Trailhead.

THE LAKE

1. Gore Creek Trail to Deluge Lake (11,760 feet) (Class 1–2). Follow the Gore Creek Trail initially for 200 yards east as it leaves the trailhead into an aspen grove and meets the Deluge Lake Trail junction. Take the left fork of the trail at the signed junction and follow the Deluge Lake Trail for nearly 4.5 miles to Deluge Lake. The trail climbs steeply through aspen forest initially, and the first mile of the trail is the toughest as you ascend into the Deluge basin. You'll hike in a deep dark pine forest for an additional mile before emerging into some meadows and the high alpine along a creek that leads you to even higher meadows and peaks that surround Deluge Lake.

THE LOOP AND HIGH-RIDGE TRAVERSE

2. Grand Traverse Peak (13,041 feet), Grand Traverse to North Traverse Peak (13,057 feet) Loop (Class 4). From Deluge Lake, follow the use trail from the north side of the lake up a steep, grassy gully for several hundred feet to a saddle

Left: Scouting out the route from the Grand Traverse looking south. **Right:** The east and northeast sides of the ridge were deeply carved out by glaciers.

to gain a ridgeline. Grand Traverse Peak's east ridge becomes gentle as it rolls up the ridge crest on a minor use trail through some boulders. You'll top out on Grand Traverse Peak with views down to Vail ski area, the Vail Valley, Holy Cross, and Mount Elbert to the south and a sea of peaks in other directions. Take care, as you can choose to descend the same route you came and head back to the Gore Creek Trailhead or proceed across the Grand Traverse. To get to North Traverse Peak, you will have to traverse 0.75 mile northwest then north. Carefully descend a Class 3 ledge system off of the top of Grand Traverse Peak initially to the west. At 350 feet below the summit, you can find a minor use trail that stays on the left side (Vail Valley side) of the ridgeline a hundred feet or so below the crest and traverses the ridge's most difficult portions. As you get closer to North Traverse Peak, the rock quality improves and becomes enjoyable Class 3 and 4. Top out on North Traverse Peak, enjoy the view, and then continue north for 0.5 mile descending to a prominent grassy saddle (12,350 feet) at the head of the Big Horn Creek Valley. Descend the Big Horn Creek for 6 miles back to the Big Horn Trailhead. One prominent stop is an old cabin 2 miles down into the basin at 10,810 feet.

DR. JON'S EXTRA CREDIT

A. Keller Mountain, southwest ridge (13,085 feet) (Class 2+). Upon reaching the grassy saddle at 12,350 feet north of North Traverse Peak at the head of the Big Horn drainage, ascend a rocky and grassy ridgeline to the northeast for 1 mile and 750 vertical feet to the summit of Keller Mountain. This summit puts you deep in the heart of the Gore Range.

DELUGE LAKE—GRAND TRAVERSE PEAK AND THE GRAND TRAVERSE

GORE LAKE —SNOW LAKE —SNOW PEAK TRAVERSE TO DELUGE LAKE

27

Elevation Gain	2,700 feet for Gore Lake; 3,300 feet for Snow Lake; 4,000 feet for Snow Pass Loop to Deluge Lake
Round-Trip Distance	11.6 miles for Gore Lake; 13.6 miles for Snow Lake; 13.1 miles for Gore Lake to Snow Lake to Snow Pass and Deluge Lake Loop
Trailhead	Gore Creek (East Vail) (8,700 feet)
Difficulty Rating	Class 1–2 hike both on trails and across tundra/scattered alpine forest ecozone with no trails
Optimal Season	June 15 through October
Maps	Trails Illustrated #108 and #149; White River National Forest

COMMENT: This is Gore Range's signature loop. You visit three high mountain lakes, get up above the timberline to see some jagged peaks, and experience the Gore Range's ruggedness without the route being too difficult. Also, from Snow Pass, Mount of the Holy Cross will greet you way off in the distance to the south. These lakes are stunning, and on this tour in addition to the wildflowers in midsummer, it's possible to cross paths with mountain goats, bighorn sheep, bears, marmots, and more.

Gore Lake.

Snow Lake and Snow Peak partially frozen in June; Snow Pass is to the right.

GETTING THERE

Gore Creek Trailhead (8,700 feet). Take Interstate 70 to Exit 180 for East Vail. Travel east on Big Horn Road for 2.3 miles and cross underneath the large interstate bridges to reach the parking area on the left for the trailhead.

THE LAKES

1. Gore Creek Trail to Gore Lake (11,400 feet) to Snow Lake (11,950 feet) (Class 1–2). Follow the Gore Creek Trail east as it slowly climbs up the Gore Creek Valley for 4.1 miles. You will travel along the creek at times with a couple of small creek crossings in the first 2.5 miles. The trail is easy to follow and not very steep most of the way. Gore Creek will always be on your right as you ascend. At mile 3 or 4 you will leave some of the meadows and enter a deeper forest before emerging into a meadow near some great campsites at 10,200 feet. The Gore Creek Trail will continue into the valley, and you will see a marked trail junction with a memorial to some early Gore Range pioneers. At this junction, follow the Gore Lake Trail to the left (north) as it climbs steeply into the pine forest alongside a gorgeous cascade. After 500 vertical feet in 0.6 mile, the trail again levels out in some sparse alpine meadows and bogs as you pass amazing wildflowers. For the final 0.5 mile to the lake, the trail gets a bit steeper and turns to the northwest and west and finally emerges at Gore Lake. The best campsites are on some flat treed areas on the lake's north side above and away from the lake in the direction of Snow Lake. After your break or overnight

A scenic tarn along the way from Gore Lake to Snow Lake.

camp at Gore Lake, continue north from Gore Lake. To reach Snow Lake, there is no trail to follow, but you can ascend some grassy wildflower meadows and sparse trees along an alpine bench without losing elevation to follow the actual creek basin to Snow Lake. When you get 200 yards or so to the north of Gore Lake, start to contour the basin by doing an ascending traverse of grassy and flowering benches for 0.25 mile to the north and then northwest. Once you pass a bit of a flat ledge with cliffs on your left, look north to see a relatively easy uphill traverse to a small saddle and gap in the cliffs. Ascend a minor grassy gully on a broken game trail and reach a small lake/pond at 11,900 feet. To reach the separate basin, continue up for another 75 vertical feet through a small flat pass and then turn left (west) into the east-to-west-oriented basin, going around a small stand of pine trees and heading into Snow Lake basin. From this little ridgeline/pass, you will see Snow Lake tucked into the basin a half-mile distant. Continue to the lake, and it's possible to find a small use trail on the north side of the creek that will take you to the north side of Snow Lake at nearly 12,000 feet.

THE LOOP AND HIGH-RIDGE TRAVERSE

2. Snow Pass (12,550 feet) to Deluge Lake (11,750 feet) Loop (Class 2).
From Snow Lake, follow the use trail from the north side of the lake across a small scree field initially as it climbs west on some grassy portions for 500 feet to gain the pass. From the top, you will be able to see Holy Cross to the south on the horizon and Grand Traverse Peak above Deluge Lake to the northwest. From Snow Pass,

Above: Hiking above Snow Lake to Snow Pass.
Right: Headed over the pass to descend into Deluge Lake drainage.

descend to the northwest on a climbers' trail into the basin, pass Deluge Lake on its south side, and you can also follow the very nice Deluge Lake Trail into the basin as it travels southwest for 4 miles back to the Gore Creek Trailhead.

DR. JON'S EXTRA CREDIT

A. Snow Peak, north ridge (13,024 feet) (Class 2–3). Upon reaching Snow Pass, ascend broken ledges and solid rock to the south for 0.4 mile and 500 vertical feet to the summit of Snow Peak.

B. Gore Lake, Snow Peak to Snow Pass (Class 3). The south ridge of Snow Peak is slightly more challenging than the route mentioned above, but you can instead climb out of the basin from Gore Lake, reach Gore Pass to the west of Gore Lake, then traverse the south ridge to the summit of Snow Peak, descend the north ridge of Snow Peak, and head down to Deluge or Snow Lake.

C. Bonus peaks to attempt from Snow Lake (Class 3–4). Willow Peak (13,357 feet) and Red Peak (13,189 feet) as well as Mount Valhalla (13,195 feet).

D. Red Buffalo Pass and Eccles Pass, East Vail to Frisco car-to-car (Class 1–2). Do your own research, but from the East Vail side, you can hike the Gore Creek Trail to Red Buffalo Pass for 6.5 miles, then over Eccles Pass toward Frisco: 13.1 miles leads you to your car at Meadow Creek Trailhead (Trail #33). You can take Exit 203 Frisco on I-70, for a longer version of this traverse (14.5 miles), which will take you to the North Tenmile Trail (#37) where you can arrive to a car parked at I-70 Frisco Exit 201.

GORE LAKE—SNOW LAKE—SNOW PEAK TRAVERSE TO DELUGE LAKE

PINEY LAKE —MOUNT POWELL —BUBBLE LAKE

28

Elevation Gain	3,600 feet for Bubble Lake; 4,130 feet for Mount Powell
Round-Trip Distance	13 miles for Bubble Lake; 12 miles for Mount Powell
Trailhead	Piney Lake (9,450 feet)
Difficulty Rating	Class 1–2+ hike both on trails and across tundra/scattered alpine forest ecozone with no trails
Optimal Season	July through October
Maps	Trails Illustrated #107, #108, and #149; White River National Forest

COMMENT: Ranked 198 out of 200, Mount Powell barely qualifies as one of Colorado's two hundred highest, or Bicentennial, peaks. But this highest peak in the Gore Range has incredible views and mystique in a wild and isolated setting. Bubble Lake is one of the most idyllic places in all of Colorado and one of my personal favorites in this entire guidebook. You can be out with your party on the peak or spend a night at Bubble Lake and won't see another soul because the Gore Range is devoid of fourteeners. Consider combining the two objectives here: camp at Bubble Lake and climb Mount Powell; you will return home longing to go back!

Bubble Lake glistening brilliantly in the afternoon sunshine.

Bubble Lake looks inviting.

GETTING THERE

Piney Lake Trailhead (9,450 feet). The trailhead is located about 11 miles north of Vail on Red Sandstone Road. Take Interstate 70 Exit 176 from Vail Pass. From the main Vail exit roundabouts, travel on North Frontage Road west along I-70. After 0.5 mile, you will cross under the pedestrian bridge that spans I-70. About 200 yards after crossing under the bridge, take a right on Red Sandstone Road. This road is paved at the beginning. After two switchbacks, take a left before the third switchback onto FSR 700, which is dirt. Follow the winding road for 11 miles to Piney River Ranch. Even though the ranch is private at the lake, there is public parking at the trailhead. Park near the gate to access Piney Lake and the trail beyond.

THE LAKES

1. Piney Lake Trail to Kneeknocker Pass to Bubble Lake (11,275 feet) (Class 1–2+). Start at Piney Lake and follow the Piney Lake Trail northeast as it contours and climbs gently up through grassy slopes and through some aspen trees, which can be quite stunning in mid-September. You will hike the Upper Piney Lake Trail along the vast Piney River and basin for 3.25 miles. The trail is very flat, and after the first 1.5 miles, you'll enter trees, where the trail switches back but elevation gain is minimal. In the aspens at mile 3, you will descend 150 feet to return to the creek level by navigating some large boulders and granite slabs along the river, then take a sharp left turn near a well-marked cairn near the river, and continue northeast into a steeper basin. The main trail continues right (east) toward Upper Piney Lake. (See "Dr. Jon's Extra Credit" below.) Take the left branch, follow the creek up, crossing it twice near the 10,500-foot level, and reach sparse tees and a flat area just below tree line in a gorgeous basin at 11,200 feet. Mount Powell's southwest face will be directly ahead to the northeast of you when you leave timberline and get to 11,350 feet in the basin, with a clear view of a climbers' trail that heads east over Kneeknocker Pass, and you will be standing next to a creek where you can look directly up at the pass.

The nearly 1,000-foot gain from the bottom of the basin up the climbers' trail is steep and somewhat loose, so use caution, but climb 0.25 mile to the 12,250-foot saddle between Peak C to the south and Mount Powell to the north. Continue east into the drainage basin for another 1.3 miles to arrive at Bubble Lake.

THE HIGH-RIDGE TRAVERSE

2. Mount Powell's 13,580-foot southwest couloir/southwest ledges (Class 2+). This is a spectacular climb. Follow the description above to reach timberline in the basin below the southwest face of Mount Powell. At about 11,350 feet, take a sharp left turn (north) in the relatively flat basin (not toward Kneeknocker Pass)

The hike begins from Piney Lake; Mount Powell and Peak C as well as Kneeknocker Pass are to the left on the skyline.

Left: Summit of Mount Powell, the highest peak in the Gore Range; Upper Bubble Lake is visible to the left of Peak C. **Right:** Several couloirs and ledges on the southwest face of Mount Powell keep the climb interesting.

and after 0.25 mile, look for an obvious couloir on the central face of Powell. Head north toward Cataract Pass. Before you get to the pass, look northeast at Mount Powell. There are two couloirs here; choose the left (northernmost) couloir. At about 11,800 feet, enter the couloir and angle northeast again, climbing for 1,000 feet. The southwest face opens up above the narrow sections, and you can gain the broad and obvious shoulder of Powell's west ridge at about 13,000 feet. From the shoulder, wrap around to the north and into a west-facing bowl of Powell, doing an ascending traverse for 400 feet to gain the flat area near the summit. Travel east for 250 yards and up another 180 feet, and the summit is yours.

DR. JON'S EXTRA CREDIT

A. Mount Powell traverse options (Class 2–3). Leave the summit of Mount Powell and continue your journey to Bubble Lake. The first option for descent is the east ridge of Mount Powell; the second is the south couloir, which descends to the east of Kneeknocker Pass. Both will get you to Bubble Lake; just be smart with the weather and your navigation.

B. Upper Piney Lake Trail (Class 2). Instead of ascending the basin from the Piney River to climb to Mount Powell or Bubble Lake, stay right along the Piney River near the Piney River Falls, and follow the trail along the river basin for 4 miles to Upper Piney Lake.

PINEY LAKE—MOUNT POWELL
—BUBBLE LAKE

WHEELER LAKES AND UNEVA PEAK TRAVERSE

29

Elevation Gain	1,325 feet for Wheeler Lakes; 2,747 feet for Uneva Peak
Round-Trip Distance	7.2 miles for Wheeler Lakes; 13.7 miles for Uneva Peak
Trailhead	Wheeler Junction/Copper Mountain (9,775 feet)
Difficulty Rating	Class 1–2 hike both on trails and across tundra/scattered alpine forest ecozone with no trails
Optimal Season	July through October
Maps	Trails Illustrated #108 and #149; White River National Forest

COMMENT: The Eagle's Nest Wilderness and the southern portion of the Gore Range host some beautiful views and an easy trail to a high-ridge traverse, including a visit to some small lakes. Hike through this area in mid- to late July, and the flowers are some of the best around. During fall hikes, keep an eye out for elk and bear, which frequent the meadows. Go early in the morning, and you will be rewarded with solitude.

GETTING THERE
Wheeler Junction/Copper Mountain Trailhead (9,775 feet). Take I-70 from Denver to Exit 195 Copper Mountain. From Vail, go east over Vail Pass on I-70. Just

Wheeler Lake.

Left: The gentle southern ridgelines of Uneva Peak. **Right:** Columbines bursting in July.

to the east of the westbound off-ramp, there is a small dirt alcove close to the road to park vehicles. In recent years, some no-parking signs have been installed here, so it's actually best to park an additional half mile to the west on a scenic overlook rest stop, accessible only to westbound I-70 drivers. Pull off to the small rest area and look for the signed trailhead. The alternative on busy weekends is to take Exit 190 (Colorado Highway 91) to the first parking lot for the Copper Mountain ski resort just south of the first stoplight. You can walk from the lot for 0.4 mile on the west side of Colorado Highway 91, cross the interstate on the bridge, and arrive at the trailhead.

THE LAKES

1. Wheeler Lakes (11,100 feet) (Class 1–2). Follow the Gore Range Trail west as it contours and climbs gently up through grassy slopes and through some aspen trees, which can be quite stunning in mid-September. The Copper Mountain ski resort will be visible to the south. After the first mile and a couple of switchbacks, you will pass the Eagle's Nest Wilderness boundary sign. Continue through subalpine forest and meadows in the second mile of the trail. At mile 2.9, take a right (north) and follow the Wheeler Lakes Spur Trail. In 0.2 mile, the first Wheeler Lake appears on the right, and you can continue for another 0.2 mile to the second Wheeler Lake to the left. Both lakes are great places to have lunch and relax. On the northeastern edge of the lakes, you can reach a viewpoint that peers back down to the northeast toward Officer's Gulch and the Tenmile Canyon—some great views! There is also a rocky outcropping to the west just above the first Wheeler Lake, which is a good place to enjoy a nice view of the lake and of the Tenmile Range as well as Jacques Peak.

Looking back down the ridgeline toward Copper Mountain ski resort.

THE HIGH-RIDGE TRAVERSE

2. Uneva Peak (12,522 feet) south slopes/ridgeline (Class 2). Start at the Wheeler Junction/Copper Mountain trailhead and follow the previous description for 2.9 miles on the Gore Range Trail west then north to the Wheeler Lakes spur junction at 11,050 feet. Instead of going to Wheeler Lakes, follow the Gore Range Trail west and then northwest for an additional 2.2 miles through forest and meadows. In the first mile, you will pass some small tarns, weaving through several small meadows. The trail will turn north and then northeast for a short distance. At 11,600 feet in a small pass/saddle, when the trail continues north (mile 4.5), leave the trail, travel west and northwest along a small ridgeline to then get above the timber. Once above timber line, ascend north along a rolling ridgeline crossing two small rolling false summits for 1.5 miles to Uneva Peak. The last 0.4 mile of the ridge turns slightly northwest and gets a bit rocky, and you can also follow a faint climbers' trail most of the way.

DR. JON'S EXTRA CREDIT

A. Backpacking the Gore Range Trail (Class 2). Consider making this corner of the Gore Range an overnight backpacking excursion. You can camp at Wheeler Lakes or travel several miles farther into the Eagle's Nest Wilderness on the Gore Range Trail. There are two more small lakes beyond 5 miles on the Gore Range Trail. The first is called Lost Lake (0.5 mile past where you leave the trail to follow the ridgelines to Uneva Peak), and a second is a secluded lake on the southeastern flanks of Uneva Peak. Lots to explore here, and you won't see anyone during certain times of the year.

WHEELER LAKES AND
UNEVA PEAK TRAVERSE

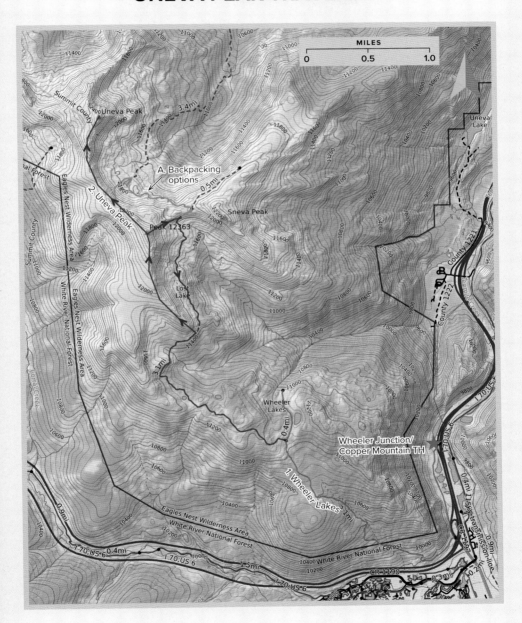

WILLOW LAKES
—SALMON LAKE
—ZODIAC SPIRES
—MOUNT SILVERTHORNE 30

Elevation Gain	2,470 feet for Upper Willow Lake; 2,215 feet for Salmon Lake; 4,400 feet for Mount Silverthorne; 6,050 feet for the Zodiac Traverse (south to north) with Mount Silverthorne
Round-Trip Distance	13.2 miles for Willow Lake; 10.3 miles for Salmon Lake; 13 miles for Mount Silverthorne and East Thorne Loop Traverse; 15 miles for the south-to-north Zodiac Traverse with Mount Silverthorne exit
Trailhead	Willowbrook (8,980 feet)
Difficulty Ratings	Class 1–2 hike both on trails and across tundra/scattered alpine forest ecozone with no trails; Class 3–5 for any high-ridge traverses
Optimal Season	July through October
Maps	Trails Illustrated #108 and #149; White River National Forest

COMMENT: The Zodiac Spires are a nice destination and a stunning ridgeline tucked away in the Gore Range. Definitely take the day to hike all the way up to Upper Willow Lake and enjoy the beauty away from the crowds. There is something for everyone here. Easier peaks to climb include Mount Silverthorne (13,357 feet at Willow Benchmark) and Red Peak B (13,189 feet). You can also test yourself with the technical Zodiac Traverse.

GETTING THERE
Willowbrook Trailhead (8,980 feet). This trailhead is located at the top of the Willowbrook neighborhood north of Silverthorne. Use Exit 205 Silverthorne off I-70. Travel north on Colorado Highway 9 for 2 miles and turn left (west) on Willowbrook Road. Overnight parking is prohibited at this trailhead by the town of Silverthorne, but numerous times I have seen and heard of people getting dropped off here for an overnight backpacking trip.

THE LAKES
1. Upper Willow Lake (11,400 feet) (Class 1–2). Leave the Willowbrook neighborhood and travel through a dense pine forest for a majority of this trail. This trail

Zodiac Spires guard Upper Willow Lake.

should be called the "Willowberry Trail," as mountain huckleberry, raspberries, and strawberries peak in mid-August and are found everywhere along the trail. Immediately out of the parking lot, take the north (right) fork of the ditch trail and leave the subdivision passing some homes. Follow the North Willow Creek Trail at a sign junction, turn left, and start in aspens. Pass a junction with the Gore Range Trail (#60) at mile 1.5 and continue west on the Gore Range Trail by staying straight. You will enjoy a rolling trail through pine and blown-down timber until reaching another trail junction at mile 3. Follow the Willow Lake Trail (#36) to your left at this split. The trail incline gets steeper between miles 3 and 4. At mile 4.5, you will reach a junction with a small spur trail that leads to Salmon Lake (see below). Continue on the left branch for another 1.5 miles to reach the uppermost Willow Lake. Several of the Willow Lakes dot this upper basin for the final mile of trail to your left and make for a stunning setting. Zodiac Spires will greet you as a stellar backdrop to the west once you reach the final lake.

2. Salmon Lake (11,195 feet) (Class 2). This short spur trail (#36.1) about a mile shy of the Willow Lakes gets you into a beautiful lake basin where you can also access Mount Silverthorne to the west. Consider camping here if you are doing any of the high peaks or traverses in the area. The early morning reflection on this lake is amazing.

THE LOOP AND HIGH-RIDGE TRAVERSES

3. Mount Silverthorne (13,357 feet) to East Thorn (13,333 feet) (Class 2–3). From the west side of Salmon Lake, follow a faint use trail as it parallels North

Left: Mountain huckleberry along the trail in August. **Right:** Upper Willow Lake.

Willow Creek. At 12,000, feet, continue west up a narrow grassy gully. Ascend some ledges to the southwest between 12,200 and 12,400 feet to gain access to Mount Silverthorne's northeast bowl. Hike up the bowl to 13,000 feet and then follow grassy and rocky terrain to the gentler broad summit plateau and eventually to the top of Mount Silverthorne. From this Willow Benchmark summit, traverse along easy ridgeline for 0.4 mile to the top of East Thorn. The final 150 feet on the ridge gets narrow but never too technical (easy Class 3).

4. Red Peak B (13,189 feet) (Class 2). From Upper Willow Lake, follow the creek basin south for 0.75 mile to the summit of Red Peak. The grassy basin gives way to some easy grassy ramps and rocky scree near the summit, but never exceeds Class 2 if you stay on route.

DR. JON'S EXTRA CREDIT

A. Zodiac Traverse (Class 5). The Zodiac Traverse is quite challenging, and you should carry a rope as well as some slings and a small rack of cams/nuts #0.3–1 if you want to stay directly on the crest. My advice is that it is a bit easier and more logical to do this traverse from south to north and go all the way to Mount Silverthorne and then descend to Salmon Lake to make your way home. The traverse of the Zodiac Spires includes nine named towers, from south to north: Cancer, Capricorn, the Gemini Twins, Taurus, Scorpio, Libra Sagittarius, and Aries. Follow the Red Peak description above to the summit of Red Peak. From Red Peak, travel 0.3 mile south-

Left: Salmon Lake and the gateway to Mount Silverthorne.
Above: The turnoff to Salmon Lake.

west along the ridge and then turn north along the ridgeline for another 0.3 mile on Class 2 talus to access the Zodiac Spires. Just south of Upper Willow Lake, if you are crafty and do not want to climb all the way to Red Peak, you can climb steep talus just south of Cancer to ascend out of the basin to begin the traverse.

To begin the spires, you can climb Cancer's south face (Class 4). It is possible to downclimb the northern side of Cancer a short distance until reaching a cliff. To get off Cancer, rappel 55 feet. Usually there is webbing around a boulder here off the east side to a ledge. Once off rappel, follow the ledge back to the ridge.

Next, scramble up Capricorn (Class 4) and downclimb for 15 feet until you reach another cliff. You can either rappel 30 feet or downclimb the 30 feet in very exposed Class 4 to a small ledge with webbing around a boulder. Next you must rappel west 80 feet, on a free hanging rappel, where you will land on the ridge.

A fun part of the traverse is next as you scramble up the twin summits of South Gemini Twin (Class 3 and 4). To get down, drop into the north chimney between the subsummits, or you can rappel up to 50 feet. After this rappel, scamper up a gully on North Gemini Twin and turn left to find an excellent 15-foot dihedral on the north side (Class 5.4). Use this dihedral to climb up and then get down the other side. This is likely the most fun pure climbing of the entire traverse, so enjoy it.

Taurus's face looks pretty intimidating at first, but it stays Class 4. There is a rappel of about 75 feet on the north, but strong climbers can simply downclimb it rather than rappel. Next, scramble up the east side of Scorpio and fold around to the

You'll see the Zodiac Spires and Mount Silverthorne as well as East Thorne as you ascend the valley.

north face. Climb the northwest aspect, hook a left to the summit (Class 5.6 for 25 feet plus 15 feet of easier low Class 5, the toughest of the route for the day), and you must rappel down for just shy of 50 feet.

Scramble up and over Libra, walk the knife edge, and climb the mini tower "Libra Prime" (Class 5.0, loose blocks) or bypass it on the right if you don't feel like doing it.

Finally, the challenges of the last two spires are much easier. Ascend Class 2–3 up Sagittarius, and from the top, you can rappel 40 feet on the north side. The existing station, usually with webbing, is just below the summit between the twin summits.

Lastly, ascend Class 2–3 up and over Aries, and you're done with the technicalities of the nine Zodiac Spires.

Willow Benchmark (Mount Silverthorne) can be climbed at Class 2 followed by a Class 3 to 4 gully up to the summit plateau. Go left for Silverthorne or right for East Thorne (Class 3 as described in the "The Loop and High-Ridge Traverses" above). If adding on Silverthorne and descending to the west, consider tacking on Zodiac View via the southwest flanks of Silverthorne (Class 2). Zodiac's grassy flanks will be welcome. You can descend the grassy drainage west of Zodiac View where you will pass some high-altitude tarns and intersect the Gore Lake Trail down to Gore Creek and East Vail. But if you parked at Willowbrook, descend to Salmon Lake and beyond on the North Willow Lake Trail.

WILLOW LAKES—SALMON LAKE
—ZODIAC SPIRES—MOUNT SILVERTHORNE

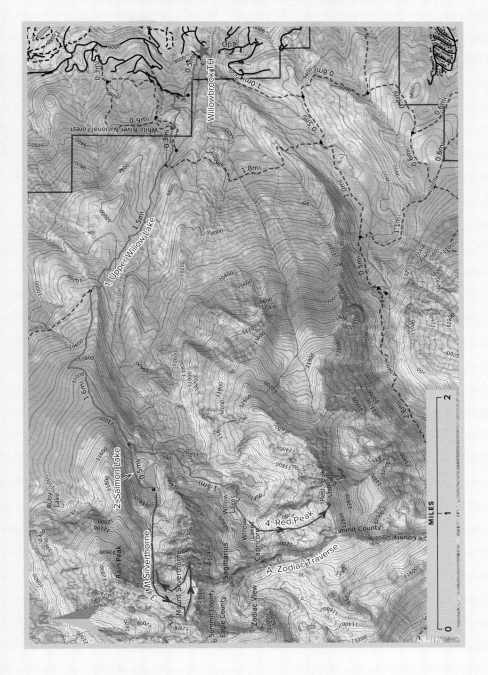

CHAPTER 5

STEAMBOAT AREA/PARK RANGE/RAHWAH/FLAT TOPS

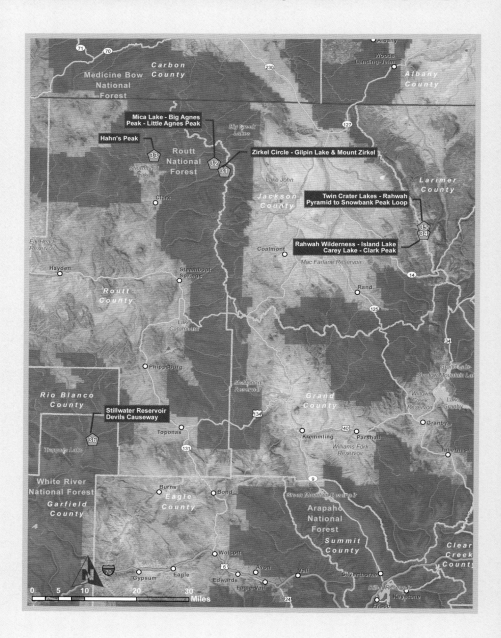

ZIRKEL CIRCLE: GILPIN LAKE AND MOUNT ZIRKEL —FLATTOP MOUNTAIN

31

Elevation Gain	2,700 feet for Gilpin Lake and Zirkel Circle; 4,200 feet for Mount Zirkel
Round-Trip Distance	11 miles for the loop; 18 miles for Mount Zirkel
Trailhead	Slavonia (8,400 feet)
Difficulty Rating	Class 1–2 hike both on trails and across tundra/scattered alpine forest ecozone with no trails
Optimal Season	July through October
Maps	Trails Illustrated #116 and #1304; Medicine Bow and Routt National Forests

COMMENT: The Mount Zirkel Wilderness is probably one of Colorado's most underrated wilderness areas. While the highest peak (Mount Zirkel) is only 12,191 feet, the beauty here is stellar. Glacier lilies abound in the alpine basins, and the

Gilpin Lake from Gilpin saddle; Mount Zirkel is to the right.

Left: Mount Zirkel dominates over the valley. **Right:** Entering the wilderness.

scenery is world-class. Because the Zirkels are so far away from the rest of the state, the area stays relatively uncrowded (unless it's a weekend). Consider a hike of Mount Zirkel, Flattop Mountain, or combine a backpacking trip to really enjoy the area and see some wildlife.

GETTING THERE

Slavonia Trailhead (8,400 feet). From Steamboat Springs, travel 1 mile from the west end of town on US Highway 40 to the stoplight for County Road 129 (Elk River Road). Follow CR 129 for 20 miles (paved), passing through the little town of Clark.

June brings out the glacier lilies.

Just beyond Clark, turn right (northeast) and follow County Road 60 (Seedhouse Road/FSR 400) for 15 miles as it turns to dirt, arriving at the trailhead.

THE LAKES LOOP

1. Zirkel Circle counterclockwise: Gold Creek Lake to Gilpin Lake (10,350 feet) Loop (Class 1–2). Leave the parking area through some willows and aspen forest. At 0.2 mile, the trail splits. Turn right and follow the Gold Creek Lake Trail (#1150). Pass some gorgeous columbines and enjoy a cruiser trail through a mixed pine and aspen forest, a series of waterfalls, and excellent creekside scenery between miles 1 and 2 on the

Left: Gilpin Lake with Gilpin saddle above. **Right:** Gold Lake is a nice stop on the Zirkel Circle.

trail. At mile 1.8, you will cross to the river's south side on a sturdy log. There is lots of timber deadfall right after the crossing, so stay right, and at 2.5 miles, you will pass a rocky outcropping with a beautiful view where you will notice that you are getting up out of the valley. It is about 3 miles to Gold Creek Lake, which can be a nice place to take a dip on the northern edge of a rocky outcropping. After the lake, in some sparse evergreens, meet a junction with the Wyoming Trail (#1101). Continue left on the Gold Creek Lake Trail (#1150) at 3.5 miles and then arrive at a water crossing at 3.65 miles that requires some good river-crossing skills using logs or rocks, or just take your shoes off and walk across.

A quarter mile upstream from the crossing, there are several large logs that provide some easy crossings, but you have to look for them. Glacier lilies dominate in late June and early July as the snow melts out. At 9,800 feet (mile 4), you come to a meadow and the trail starts to climb left (north) toward Gilpin Lake. At mile 5.2 on Trail #1150, there is a junction with Red Dirt Pass Trail #1142 as well as the Gilpin Lake Trail (#1161). At this point the trail splits, and you should continue up north (left) on #1161 toward the pass. Follow the trail as it switches back up steep terrain and the views keep getting better and better. Keep going up, and you'll reach the pass after about eight or ten switchbacks, 5.75 miles from the trailhead. The views to the north are sweeping with Big Agnes, looking down to Lake Gilpin and Mount Zirkel to the north.

Then continue on down the trail as it switches back down into the basin of the beautiful Lake Gilpin. The trail traverses to the east end of the lake, which is in a deep glacially cut basin 7 miles in. The north side of the lake provides some excellent rocks to sit on and enjoy the views and have lunch.

Once you leave the lake on descent, about a mile below the lake, there is another narrow log crossing at 8 miles to consider. The remainder of the 3 miles back to

Zirkel Circle: Gilpin Lake and Mount Zirkel—Flattop Mountain

A calm setting on Gilpin Lake: true Colorado.

your car are very nice through the woods and meadows with two creek crossings on logs on the way out.

THE HIGH-RIDGE TRAVERSE

2. Mount Zirkel (12,191 feet) south slopes/ridgeline (Class 2). Start at the Slovenia Trailhead and follow the previous description for 5.2 miles on the Gold Creek Lake Trail (#1150) to the junction with the Gilpin Creek Trail #1161. Instead of traveling up to the pass and over to Gilpin Lake, at this junction, continue right on the Gold Creek Lake Trail #1150. In 1 more mile, meet another trail junction and follow the trail straight (left) as it becomes the Red Dirt Pass Trail (#1142). Near the 11,550-foot pass, you will see the Slavonia Mine (mile 7). From Red Dirt Pass, take a left and ascend from the saddle to the flat ridgeline plateau in a west-northwest direction. In recent years, the climbers' trail has improved some in this area, but most of your route simply follows the ridgeline west, then northwest, and then north for 2 miles to the summit.

DR. JON'S EXTRA CREDIT

A. Red Dirt Pass Traverse to Flattop Mountain (12,118 feet) (Class 2). After ascending Red Dirt Pass via the Red Dirt Pass Trail (#1142) route, travel along the open and viewsome ridgeline southeast and then south for nearly 3 miles to the top of Flattop Mountain (12,118 feet). This summit is the third highest in the Park Range here in the Zirkel Wilderness and worth the isolated side trip for solitude. You can view the stark western aspect of Flattop Mountain from Gold Creek Lake.

CLASSIC COLORADO HIKES

ZIRKEL CIRCLE: GILPIN LAKE AND MOUNT ZIRKEL—FLATTOP MOUNTAIN

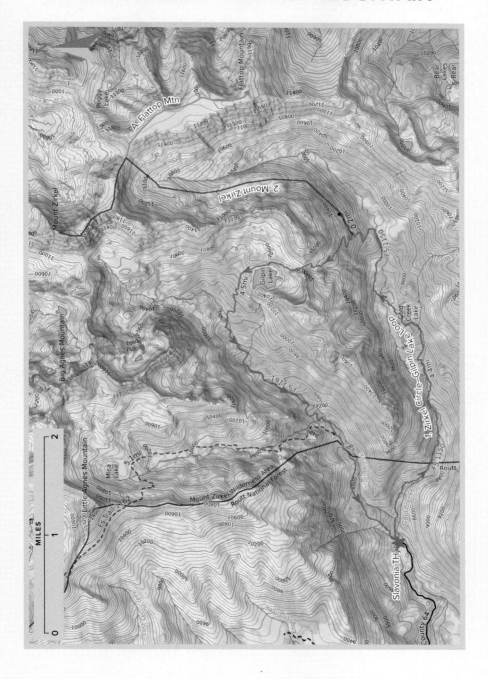

MICA LAKE
—BIG AGNES PEAK
—LITTLE AGNES PEAK

32

Elevation Gain	2,028 feet for Mica Lake; 3,700 feet for Big Agnes Mountain
Round-Trip Distance	8.4 miles for Mica Lake; 11.5 miles Big Agnes Mountain
Trailhead	Slavonia (8,400 feet)
Difficulty Ratings	Class 1–3 hike both on trails and across tundra/scattered alpine forest ecozone with no trails; some Class 3 scrambling for a few small moves to access the summit of Big Agnes
Optimal Season	July through October
Maps	Trails Illustrated #116 and #1304; Medicine Bow and Routt National Forests

COMMENT: The Mount Zirkel Wilderness is probably one of Colorado's most underrated wilderness areas. Zirkel Circle (previous entry) gets all the attention, so consider visiting Mica Lake and perhaps even a climb of Big Agnes Peak, which is one of the three highest peaks in this area. Raymond Ave, the author of *Backcountry Adventure Guide to the Mount Zirkel Wilderness,* states: "According to *The Historical Guide to Routt County,* Big Agnes Mountain was named by Robert McIntosh, who prospected the area for gold in 1875. It didn't really say who Agnes was. *The*

The Big Agnes summit pinnacle is not the highest point. *Photo by Amy Charity*

Historical Guide to Routt County said that Mount Zirkel was named for a trapper who lived near the mountain, but in fact, it was named for Ferdinand Zirkel, who (according to documents from the US Geologic Survey) conducted petrographic analysis on some rock samples collected on a geologic exploration in the area in the late 1800s."

GETTING THERE

Slavonia Trailhead (8,400 feet). From Steamboat Springs, travel 1 mile from the west end of town on US Highway 40 to the stoplight for County Road 129 (Elk River Road). Follow CR 129 for 20 miles (paved), passing through the little town of Clark. Just beyond Clark, turn right (northeast) and follow County Road 60 (Seedhouse Road/FSR 400) for 14 miles as it turns to dirt, arriving at the trailhead.

THE LAKE

1. Mica Lake (10,428 feet) (Class 1–2). Leave the parking area through some willows and aspen forest. At 0.2 mile, the trail splits. Turn left and follow the Gilpin Creek Trail (#1161). At mile 1.5, you will reach a junction with the Mica Lake Trail (#1162). Turn left and head north into a shallow valley of pine and wildflowers. At times, this trail follows the remnants of the Old Seedhouse Road, which you can see clearly as you hike. The trail gradually climbs out of the Gilpin Creek canyon into the Mica basin and near sparse timber to the broad cirque and Mica Lake.

Top: Mica Lake with Little Agnes Peak. *Photo by Amy Charity* **Bottom:** Green waters of Mica Lake. *Photo by Amy Charity*

Mica Lake—Big Agnes Peak—Little Agnes Peak

Top: Frozen Lakes in the northern cirques hold ice and snow for most of the summer. *Photo by Amy Charity* **Bottom:** Stunning wildflowers. *Photo by Amy Charity*

THE HIGH-RIDGE TRAVERSE

2. Big Agnes Mountain (12,059 feet), southwest slopes (Class 2–3). Start at the Slovenia Trailhead and follow the previous description for 1.5 miles on the Gilpin Lake Trail (#1161) to the junction with the Mica Lake Trail #1162. Hike 2.7 miles to Mica Lake at 10,428 feet and consider the weather and route for Big Agnes Mountain. Travel up easy grassy slopes for 1 mile and about 1,600 vertical feet toward the northeast to reach the final sections of Big Agnes and the rocky twin summits of the peak. A few Class 3 moves are required right near the summit.

DR. JON'S EXTRA CREDIT

A. Big Agnes Mountain Traverse to Little Agnes Mountain (11,497 feet) (Class 2+–3). After ascending Big Agnes Mountain, you can stay high on the ridgeline and head west-southwest from Big Agnes to climb Little Agnes Mountain. The ridgeline is mainly Class 2 with an occasional Class 3 move. A broad saddle that separates the two peaks rises only 417 feet, so this makes for a nice scenic tour adding an extra mile to your trip.

MICA LAKE—BIG AGNES PEAK —LITTLE AGNES PEAK

HAHN'S PEAK FIRE LOOKOUT

33

Elevation Gain	1,500 feet for Hahn's Peak
Round-Trip Distance	3.6 miles for Hahn's Peak
Trailhead	Hahn's Peak (9,300 feet)
Difficulty Rating	Class 1–2 hike mainly on trails and four-wheel-drive roads
Optimal Season	May 15 through November 1
Maps	Trails Illustrated #116 and #1304; Routt National Forest

COMMENT: Hahn's Peak is a really fun hike. The old, eroded volcanic cinder cone is extinct, and the historic summit fire lookout is an awesome place to enjoy views from Wyoming south to Steamboat Lake, Steamboat Springs, and beyond. The fire lookout on top of Hahn's Peak was originally built in 1912 and restored in 2013. You can read about the history on a sign mounted inside the lookout.

GETTING THERE

Hahn's Peak Trailhead (8,400 feet). From Steamboat Springs, travel 1 mile from the west end of town on US Highway 40 to the stoplight for County Road 129 (Elk

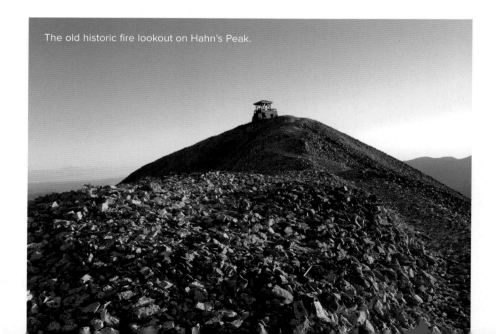

The old historic fire lookout on Hahn's Peak.

The refurbished lookout is a great place to relax and enjoy the amazing views.

River Road). Follow CR 129 for 29 miles (paved), passing through the small town of Clark and on to the little settlement of Columbine. Just beyond mile marker 29, turn right (east) and follow Forest Road 490 (dirt) for 1 mile to the Prospector Trailhead. At the trailhead, bear left (Forest Road 418) for an additional half mile to Hahn's Peak Trailhead. Forest Road 418 is dramatically rough, requiring four-wheel-drive vehicles; park at the Prospector Trailhead if you have a smaller passenger car.

THE LAKE
1. Hahn's Peak Lake (Class 1). This is a fun place to meet your family and friends for lunch after your hike. Both Hahn's Peak Lake and Steamboat Reservoir are great places for a relaxing afternoon of fishing or swimming after you view them from above at the summit fire lookout.

THE HIGH-RIDGE TRAVERSE
2. Hahn's Peak (10,839 feet), west slopes to north ridge (Class 1–2). Start at the Hahn's Peak Trailhead and follow the four-wheel-drive road west then north as it gets steep and rough for the first 0.25 mile. At 0.5 mile, you will see a sign for Hahn's Peak #1158. Turn right and follow the single-track trail as it switches back up the west slopes of the peak to timberline and several great viewpoints. Once above the trees and on the talus, follow the rocky ridges to the south for the final 400 feet to reach the summit of Hahn's Peak. Early on after your first mile on the trail, the summit fire lookout will be visible, and you'll be able to see it get larger and larger as you ascend.

Above: Fall colors are great for a sunset hike at the end of September. **Left:** The trails are broad, as horses brought people and supplies to the summit a century ago.

DR. JON'S EXTRA CREDIT

A. Take a dip in nearby Steamboat Reservoir (Class 1). After your hike of Hahn's Peak, stop for a refreshing swim at the nearby Steamboat Reservoir. It's a local state park, so an entry fee is required. Then if you are really serious about catching a great sunset, go up the peak for a second time in a day for a stellar light show at sunset.

B. Super Hahn's (mountain bike) (Class 2). Ride from either Columbine or nearby Clark on your mountain bike. Ride as far as you can up the four-wheel-drive road or even higher, and then climb to the summit. Some people have ridden to the top and back down. The area has many different four-wheel-drive roads and single-track trails to consider; just use caution and don't go over your handlebars!

C. Prospector Trail. Park at the Prospector Trailhead and explore the Prospector Trail and the aspens in the fall throughout the lower reaches of Hahn's Peak.

HAHN'S PEAK FIRE LOOKOUT

RAHWAH WILDERNESS: ISLAND LAKE—CAREY LAKE—CLARK PEAK

34

Elevation Gain	2,700 feet for Island Lake, Carey Lakes, and Timber Lake; 4,550 feet for Clark Peak
Round-Trip Distance	14.5 miles for Island Lake and Carey Lake; 18.5 miles with Clark Peak back to Island Lake; 19 miles with Timber Lake visit from Clark Peak Summit
Trailhead	West Branch (8,575 feet)
Difficulty Rating	Class 1–2 hike both on trails and across tundra/scattered alpine forest ecozone with no trails
Optimal Season	July through October
Maps	Trails Illustrated #112 and #1304; Arapaho and Roosevelt National Forests

COMMENT: The Rahwah Wilderness, located on the southern edge of the Medicine Bow Mountains, was one of the original five wilderness areas created by the Wilderness Act of 1964. "Rahwah" is a Native American term meaning "wild place." The Colorado Wilderness Act of 1980 increased the Rahwah Wilderness

Looking south to Carey Lake and Island Lake.

Left: Island Lake with Peak 12,364' above. **Right:** Carey Lake with Island Lake Peak (left) and Rahwah Pyramid (right).

from 25,000 acres to the current 73,868 acres of today, and it is indeed a special wild place due to its isolated location in Colorado as well as a lack of mountains above 13,000 feet. Campfires are permitted throughout the wilderness, just not above 10,800 feet, so consider using a stove while backpacking to minimize your impact in this "wild place."

GETTING THERE

West Branch Trailhead (8,575 feet). Take US Highway 287 north from Fort Collins to Colorado Highway 14 (Poudre Canyon). Travel Colorado Highway 14 west 52 miles toward Cameron Pass to Laramie River Road. Do not pass the turn for Chambers Lake off of Colorado Highway 14, otherwise, you have gone too far. Turn right (north) on Laramie River Road; the turn is 7 miles east of Cameron Pass. Travel north on Laramie River Road for 6.7 miles (smooth dirt) to the West Branch Trailhead, which appears immediately after Tunnel Campground on your left (west).

THE LAKES LOOP

1. Carey Lake to Island Lake to Timber Lake Loop (11,150 feet) (Class 1–2). Cross a bridge near the Tunnel Campground and follow the West Branch Trail as a dirt road for the first 0.25 mile then Trail #960 for 2 miles as it climbs southwest through a pine forest. At 2.6 miles, you will reach a trail junction with the Camp Lake Trail (#968). Stay on the West Branch Trail as it follows the broad valley through several open areas of less dense trees heading southwest. The West Branch Trail will intersect with the Rahwah Trail (#961) at mile 3.5 (right, north) after a loggy creek crossing and the Blue Lake Trail (#959) at mile 4.7 (left, south). At about 7 miles, you will emerge out of the trees in a gorgeous basin at 11,000 feet after having climbed some switchbacks along a beautiful cascading creek. Carey Lake will be 0.25 mile to

Left: Clark Peak to the south. **Right:** Cameron Peak.

your right (north), and you can travel to Island Lake 0.25 mile to your south, both approximately 7.2 miles from the trailhead and above tree line. To continue on to Timber Lake, leave the east end of Island Lake and walk around the east end of a massive rock glacier or pile of talus debris while descending through sparse trees (no trails here) to the southeast for 1 mile to the west end of Timber Lake. To complete the loop for the day, you can return the same way you came (retrace your steps) or simply travel north for 0.75 mile along the timberline, grassy valley, and rocky meadow outcroppings to the West Branch Trail (#960) at 10,900 feet to the northeast of Island Lake. Return 6.5 miles to the West Branch Trailhead.

THE HIGH-RIDGE TRAVERSE
2. Clark Peak (12,951 feet), south slopes/ridgeline (Class 2). Start at the West Branch Trailhead and follow the previous description for 7 miles on the West Branch Trail southwest to Island Lake at 11,150 feet. From the east end of Island Lake, descend southwest for 1 mile to Timber Lake. From the west end of Timber Lake, ascend grassy slopes to the southwest alongside a medium-sized rock glacier. You will be getting above Timber Lake and will lose sight of Island Lake to your north as you gain elevation to access Clark Peak. At 11,400 feet, you will be directly south of Island Lake and also south of some small tarns in the basin. Turn south and hike along the north ridge of Clark Peak toward Peak 12,654'. Once over Peak 12,654', the north ridgeline is very steep to the west and should be avoided, while slopes to your east (left) as you ascend are grassy and gentler, leading you the correct way. Travel 0.5 mile to the 12,951-foot summit of Clark Peak. This is the highest peak between here and the Colorado-Wyoming border to the north, so enjoy the spectacular views!

A nice place for a rest along the shores of Island Lake.

DR. JON'S EXTRA CREDIT

A. Clark Peak Traverse of northeast ridge (12,951 feet) (Class 2+). After ascending Clark Peak via the north and northwest ridge route, travel along the scenic ridgeline between Clark Peak and Cameron Peak (12,057 feet). Leave Clark Peak's summit and descend the northeast ridge for 1 mile. Timber Lake and Island Lake will be far below you and down to the northwest. Avoid the northwest aspects of the ridgeline as it is very steep. While hiking northeast on the ridge, you will also see Hang Lake and Blue Lake below and to your east. At a broad point on the ridgeline at 11,500 feet, you can descend directly east toward Cameron Peak to reach a saddle at 10,900 feet where you will find the Blue Lake Trail (#959). This trail will connect you to the north with the West Branch Trail (#960) and loop you either back to your campsite near Island Lake or Timber Lake or can take you back to the West Branch Trailhead. If time and weather allow, feel free to visit Blue Lake to the south or climb Cameron Peak to the east before returning to the north.

B. Rahwah Wilderness/Island Lake backpacking (Class 2). Island Lake is an amazing place to set up camp for the first night of a backpacking adventure. Consider turning your trip into two, three, or four nights in this amazing, secluded wilderness area. On subsequent nights, you can explore Rahwah Lakes up Rahwah Trail (#961) or venture up Camp Lake Trail (#968). The jagged ridgeline to the west from Island Lake including a long linkup of the spine from Peak 12,364' to Island Lake Peak to Rahwah Pyramid also looks intriguing! Don't forget your fishing rod as there are so many lakes to fish for trout!

RAHWAH WILDERNESS:
ISLAND LAKE—CAREY LAKE—CLARK PEAK

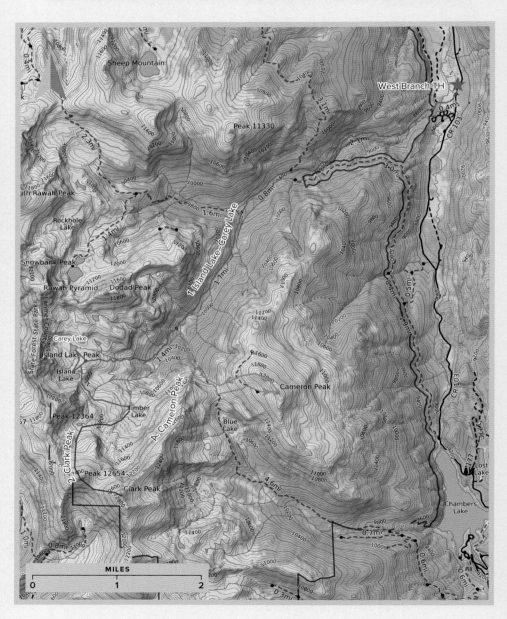

TWIN CRATER LAKES —RAHWAH PYRAMID TO SNOWBANK PEAK LOOP

35

Elevation Gain	2,575 feet for Twin Crater Lakes (upper lake); 4,550 feet for Rahwah Pyramid
Round-Trip Distance	12.4 miles for Twin Crater Lakes; 15.5 miles for Rahwah Pyramid back to Twin Crater Lakes; 16 miles for the loop traverse with Rahwah Pyramid and Snowbank Peak
Trailhead	West Branch (8,575 feet)
Difficulty Ratings	Class 1–2 hike both on trails and across tundra/scattered alpine forest ecozone with no trails; Class 2+ on the easiest routes on the peaks
Optimal Season	July through October
Maps	Trails Illustrated #112 and #1304; Arapaho and Roosevelt National Forests

COMMENT: The Rahwah Wilderness, located on the southern edge of the Medicine Bow Mountains, was one of the original five wilderness areas created by the Wilderness Act of 1964. "Rahwah" is a Native American term meaning "wild place." Indeed, this place is wild. Twin Crater Lakes is a great place for a fun backpacking trip and

Early morning reflection on Upper Twin Crater Lake with Rahwah Pyramid (left) and Snowbank Peak (right center).

Left: Entering the wilderness. **Right:** Approaching Rahwah Pyramid from the valley.

climbing the two peaks. Rahwah Pyramid and Snowbank Peak can be launched from this basin and enjoyed likely without seeing another soul along the high ridgelines.

GETTING THERE

West Branch Trailhead (8,575 feet). Take US Highway 287 north from Fort Collins to Colorado Highway 14 (Poudre Canyon). Travel Colorado Highway 14 west 52 miles over Cameron Pass to Laramie River Road. Do not pass Chambers Lake, or you have gone too far. Travel north on Laramie River Road for 8 miles to the West Branch Trailhead, which appears immediately after Tunnel Campground on your left (west).

THE LAKES

1. Twin Crater Lakes (11,050 feet) (Class 1–2). Cross a bridge near the Tunnel Campground and follow the West Branch Trail (#960) for 2 miles as it climbs southwest through an aspen forest that slowly transitions to a pine forest and uses several gentle switchbacks along the way. At 2.7 miles, you will reach a trail junction with the Camp Lake Trail (#968). Stay on the West Branch Trail (straight) as it follows the broad valley through several open areas of less dense trees heading southwest. The West Branch Trail will intersect with the Rahwah Trail (#961) at mile 3.5 (right, north). Follow the Rahwah Trail north through plenty of deadfall and one significant log stream crossing for 2 miles to a junction with the Twin Crater Lakes Trail. Turn left (west) and follow this trail to the upper basin, arriving at the lakes in a stunning glacial cirque in another 1.7 miles. The final 0.5 mile to the lakes crosses a spectacular meadow after another creek crossing, then gets steep with great meadow views, and then arrives at the lakes abruptly. Return the same way for 6.7 miles to the West Branch Trailhead.

Left: Above the lakes headed to the saddle near Dodad Peak. **Right:** The steep Rahwah Pyramid's south face.

THE LOOP AND HIGH-RIDGE TRAVERSE

2. Rahwah Pyramid (12,448 feet) Traverse of north ridge to Snowbank Peak Loop (12,535 feet) (Class 2+). Start at the northwest end of upper Twin Crater Lake on a flat grassy area. When looking to the northwest, there is an obvious curved gully that provides the best passage onto the upper bowl-shaped basin at 12,000 feet between Snowbank and Rahwah Pyramid. Take the gully for 800 feet to access a grassy and flatter basin, and then curve west and then south on easy grassy slopes to the summit of Rahwah Pyramid. Then, you can hike easy slopes of grass and wildflowers to the top of Snowbank Peak and complete this mini loop by returning down the rocky and loose gully. Use caution on the descent.

DR. JON'S EXTRA CREDIT

A. Rahwah Traverse to South and North Rahwah Peaks (Class 2+). After ascending Snowbank Peak via the south ridge/slopes route, it's possible to continue north along the ridgeline for several miles and climb twelvers South Rahwah and North Rahwah Peaks. Just east of these peaks, several Rahwah lakes exist (numbered 1–4) and are super fun to explore. You can catch the Rahwah Trail in this area to make it a loop back to the West Branch Trailhead.

B. Rockhole Lake (11,250 feet) (Class 2). This lake is up on a shelf above 11,200 feet north of Twin Crater Lakes. Find it and you will be rewarded.

C. Twin Crater Lakes Pass to Island Lake and Carey Lake Loop (Class 2). South of Twin Crater Lakes, you can climb up and over a col to access Island Lake and Carey Lakes 1 mile farther to the south. This is a gorgeous way to do a nice long 16-mile loop, collecting visits to at least six lakes in the process. From Island and Carey Lakes, find the West Branch of the Laramie River Trail to loop back to the trailhead. (See entry #34.)

TWIN CRATER LAKES—RAHWAH PYRAMID TO SNOWBANK PEAK LOOP

STILLWATER RESERVOIR —DEVILS CAUSEWAY —TRAPPERS LAKE

36

Elevation Gain	1,600 feet for the Devils Causeway Loop
Round-Trip Distance	6.2 miles for Devils Causeway; 10.7 miles for the Devils Causeway counterclockwise loop
Trailhead	Stillwater Reservoir (10,290 feet)
Difficulty Rating	Class 1–2+ hike mainly on trails and short portion of jagged ridgeline
Optimal Season	June 1 through November 1
Maps	Trails Illustrated #150 and #1304; Routt National Forest

COMMENT: Devils Causeway is an iconic land bridge located in the Flat Tops Wilderness, a 235,000-acre wilderness area (Colorado's second largest), wild and isolated, north of Glenwood Springs and south of Steamboat Springs. At its narrowest point, the land bridge is only 3 feet wide and can be challenging to get across, especially if it's windy. On either side of the land bridge, a 4-mile ridgeline hosts 70- to 100-foot cliffs and does not allow for an easy exit from your loop hike, so carefully plan your day by leaving the trailhead early.

Devils Causeway looking west.

Flat Top Mountain is on the horizon, upper right.

GETTING THERE

Stillwater Reservoir Trailhead (10,290 feet). From Steamboat Springs, travel south for 21 miles on Colorado 131 from the south end of town via US Highway 40 to the town of Oak Creek. From Oak Creek, follow Colorado Highway 131 south for 9 miles (paved), passing through the little town of Phippsburg. In Yampa, turn right (southwest) and follow County Road 7 for 7 miles (paved) to the junction of Forest Service Road 900. Continue onto FSR 900 (dirt) and drive 9 miles passing Yamcolo Reservoir and Upper Stillwater Reservoir to the parking area where the road dead-ends with a bathroom located on the northeast side of the reservoir near the dam.

THE LAKES

1.   Stillwater Reservoir (10,268 feet) to Devils Causeway, or Trappers Lake (Class 1). You can visit both of these lakes before, after, or separate from hiking the Devils Causeway Loop (described in the next section). If you are looking for a shorter day hike, consider just hiking to Devils Causeway out-and-back.. Along the loop, you will get to also view several other lakes from above (Mosquito Lake, Steer Lake, Skillet Lake, and Little Causeway Lake). From the western reaches of Devils Causeway on your loop hike (see below), you will have a nice view of Trappers Lake. When finishing the Devils Causeway, instead of turning east on the Chinese Wall Trail (#1803) to travel back to your vehicle at Stillwater Reservoir, you can travel west on the Chinese Wall Trail for 4 miles and visit Trappers Lake, which is just to the west of Little Trappers Lake (just off the map). The alternative to Devils Causeway is to take the trails in the valley from west to east (East Fork Trail #1119, Bear River Trail #1120, and Chinese Wall Trail #1803) from Stillwater Reservoir to Trappers Lake for 8 miles (16 miles round-trip).

THE LOOP AND HIGH-RIDGE TRAVERSE

2. Devils Causeway Loop counterclockwise (11,812 feet) (Class 1–2+). Start at the Stillwater Reservoir Trailhead and follow the East Fork Trail (#1119) as it skirts around the north side of the reservoir. At 0.75 mile from the trailhead, you'll arrive at the Bear River Trail (#1120) junction. Stay to the right and continue along the East Fork Trail through pine and meadows to proceed up to the Devils Causeway, passing into the Flat Tops Wilderness at mile 1.1.

At 1.6 to 1.7 miles, the trail passes Little Causeway Lake, on your left and traverses across an open slope above the lake. Looking straight ahead (northwest) at this point, you'll see the Devils Causeway. Toward the left, looking west, you'll see the Chinese Wall. The introduction of the hike is now over, and the real traversing of the ridge is about to begin as you enter a large bowl in order to eventually gain the ridgeline. Over the course of the next 1.3 miles and three significant switchbacks, you'll climb almost 1,000 feet—while crossing talus slopes—to reach the Devils Causeway ridgeline. At 2.8 miles, you will reach the divide between the Bear River and East Fork watersheds. Turn left at this point on the ridge (leaving trail #1119 to join the Devils Causeway Trail) to make a short steep climb for 0.25 mile to arrive at Devils Causeway.

Left: Little Causeway Lake, Devils Causeway on the ridgeline. **Right:** Switchbacks up the bowl to the saddle.

Flat Top Mountain in the distance above Stillwater Reservoir. *Photo by Zack Wilson*

Use caution crossing the causeway, which can be extremely dangerous. The narrowest portion has steep drops on both sides for about 75 yards. I advise crossing in the calm of an early morning when winds are light and storms are absent. Many people are reduced to crossing it on their hands and knees or even on their butts, but with careful footing and balance, you can just walk across it.

If you're able to make it across the Causeway, you'll have the option of completing this great one-way loop hike. The Devils Causeway Trail will dead-end into the Chinese Wall Trail (#1803) in an additional 1.3 miles. From this junction, you'll turn left onto the Chinese Wall Trail and hike 2.3 miles to reach the Bear River Trail (#1120) where you'll make another left turn. From here, travel another 4 miles back to the Stillwater Reservoir.

DR. JON'S EXTRA CREDIT

A. Flat Top Mountain (12,361 feet) (Class 2). After your hike of Devils Causeway Loop, consider venturing over to the south of Stillwater Reservoir to the top of Flat Top Mountain, which is the highest point in the Flat Tops Wilderness. From here, you will command a view from Steamboat Springs to Aspen and the Elk Range and over to Vail and the Gore Range. The easiest way to this flat summit is by taking the west ridge of Flat Top Mountain, which is the standard route. From Stillwater Reservoir, the North Derby Trail can be followed south for 2.1 miles to the saddle between Flat Top Mountain and Peak 11,815'. From there, the sparse trail and route across the tundra travels 2.2 miles east along the gentle and beautiful ridge to the summit of Flat Top Mountain. The route is 8.75 miles round-trip with 2,250 feet of elevation gain.

STILLWATER RESERVOIR
—DEVILS CAUSEWAY—TRAPPERS LAKE

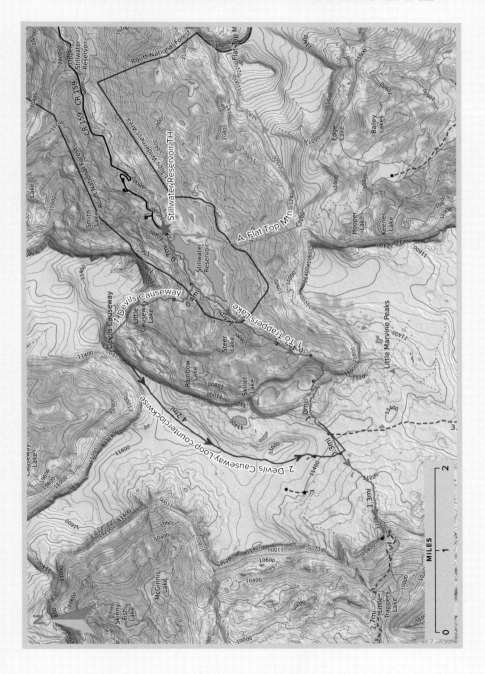

CHAPTER 6

SAWATCH RANGE

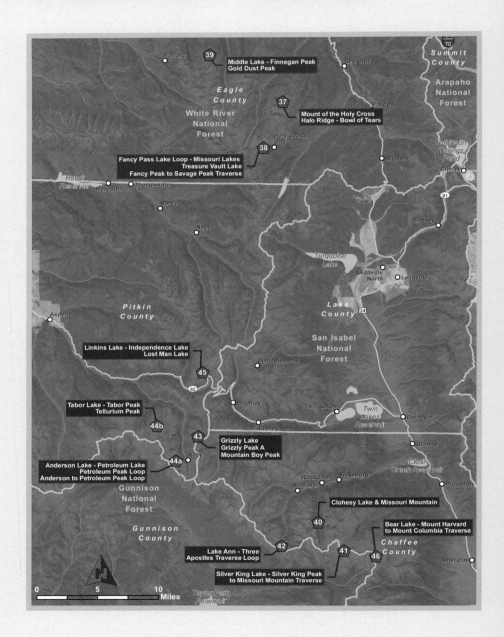

Middle Lake - Finnegan Peak
Gold Dust Peak

Mount of the Holy Cross
Halo Ridge - Bowl of Tears

Fancy Pass Lake Loop - Missouri Lakes
Treasure Vault Lake
Fancy Peak to Savage Peak Traverse

Linkins Lake - Independence Lake
Lost Man Lake

Tabor Lake - Tabor Peak
Tellurium Peak

Grizzly Lake
Grizzly Peak A
Mountain Boy Peak

Anderson Lake - Petroleum Lake
Petroleum Peak Loop
Anderson to Petroleum Peak Loop

Clohesy Lake & Missouri Mountain

Bear Lake - Mount Harvard
to Mount Columbia Traverse

Lake Ann - Three
Apostles Traverse Loop

Silver King Lake - Silver King Peak
to Missouri Mountain Traverse

MOUNT OF THE HOLY CROSS —HALO RIDGE —BOWL OF TEARS

37

Elevation Gain	2,680 feet for Bowl of Tears; 4,685 feet for Mount of the Holy Cross; 5,440 feet for Halo Ridge to Notch Mountain Traverse and Loop
Round-Trip Distance	12 miles for Holy Cross on standard Holy Cross Trail; 10 miles to Bowl of Tears; 13 miles with Holy Cross summit plus Halo Ridge Loop to Notch Mountain
Trailheads	Halfmoon (10,320 feet); Fall Creek Trailhead to access Notch Mountain is located here too
Difficulty Ratings	Class 1–2 hike both on trails and across tundra/scattered alpine forest ecozone with no trails; Class 2–3 climbing with steep snow for the Holy Cross Couloir; Class 2 off-trail on boulders for the high ridges
Optimal Season	June through October
Maps	Trails Illustrated #126; White River National Forest

COMMENT: Mount of the Holy Cross is a Colorado classic. The legendary cross is visible from the top of the Vail Mountain ski area and from the west portals of the Interstate 70 Eisenhower Tunnel. Many have seen the Cross, but few have climbed or even skied this uniquely challenging objective. Travel to the top of Notch Mountain in mid- to late June and view the cross up close; it's breathtaking!

The entire Halo Ridge route (left) and the standard north ridge (right) seen from Notch Mountain.

Holy Cross with Bowl of Tears lower left.

GETTING THERE

Halfmoon Trailhead (10,320 feet). From Vail, travel west on I-70 for 5 miles to Exit 171. Take US Highway 24 east for 5 miles, passing through the town of Minturn to Tigiwon Road #107. Turn right onto Tigiwon Road and follow the road as it switches back several times for 8.5 miles to the Halfmoon Trailhead, where there is ample parking as well as a campground. The road usually opens by mid-June. For winter and spring access, consider using snowmobiles to get to the summer trailhead.

THE LAKES

1. Bowl of Tears (12,000 feet) (Class 2). Start from the Halfmoon Trailhead and hike 1.7 miles to reach Halfmoon Pass at 11,640 feet. From the pass, there are a couple of options. Some hearty souls have managed to traverse basically to the west and southwest along the slopes of Notch Mountain to find their way into the basin near Lake Patricia and eventually to the Bowl of Tears at 12,000 feet. However, it's best to follow the summer trail corridor and descend nearly 1,000 feet into the East Cross Creek basin. Once down to East Cross Creek, cross the creek and leave the main trail on a faint use trail that climbs through some thicker trees initially and up a narrow grassy gully on the creek's west side. Once above some cliff bands in the

Left: Climbing the Cross Couloir in June. **Right:** Near the summit of Holy Cross.

basin, the terrain flattens out, and you can ascend a boulder-strewn basin to Lake Patricia and then through a series of rock slabs and grassy benches to reach the Bowl of Tears. Once you arrive at the Bowl of Tears, you will realize the effort was worth it!

THE HIGH-RIDGE TRAVERSE

2. Cross Couloir to Halo Ridge (Class 2–3). From the Bowl of Tears, climb 800 feet of snow slopes angling to the north to get into the lower third of the Cross Couloir. Aim for a notch at 12,800 feet above the cliffs that guard the bottom of the couloir. (When skiing the Holy Cross, make sure to exit the couloir at this notch.) Once in the couloir, climb for 1,200 feet to the summit. After July 1, the snow in the couloir gets very thin, and it's best to avoid this route by then. The couloir barely exceeds 40 degrees at the steepest parts, but be aware of any cornices at the top of the couloir. Exit the couloir and walk north for less than 100 feet to reach the true summit. While enjoying the views from the summit of Holy Cross, you can see the entire Holy Cross Ridge in a panorama to the west, southwest, south, southeast, and east all the way over to Notch Mountain. If the weather is good and it is still early in the day, proceed to traverse counterclockwise from the Holy Cross Ridge summit (a Centennial thir-

A memorable summit with the author's mom, sister, and brother-in-law on Mom's sixtieth birthday!

Left: Traversing the Halo Ridge loop. **Right:** Bowl of Tears far below; the ridge route to Notch Mountain is visible at right.

teener), over several subsummits, and arriving at the Notch Mountain shelter at 13,100 feet. Descend the Notch Mountain Trail on switchbacks to reach the Fall Creek Trail and return to the trailhead.

DR. JON'S EXTRA CREDIT

A. Complete loop traverse: Mount of the Holy Cross, Halo Ridge, and Notch Mountain (Class 1–2). Instead of proceeding to the Bowl of Tears from the East Cross Creek, continue on the Mount of the Holy Cross Trail and up the northeast ridge of Holy Cross to the summit. Once above timberline, there are some well-constructed large cairns to guide the way, and only the last 300 feet from the top of the Angelican Couloir to the summit require some boulder hopping. Leave the summit and continue on the traverse to Holy Cross Ridge (13,831 feet) and Notch Mountain (13,200 feet) as described above.

B. Notch Mountain via Fall Creek Trail and the Notch Mountain Trail. This separate 10-mile round-trip trail, gaining 2,900 vertical feet, is a nice alternative to the often-crowded Halfmoon Pass Holy Cross Trail, and you get a very nice view of the Cross Couloir from the Notch Mountain shelter. Plus, when you hike the Holy Cross Trail over Halfmoon Pass, you actually don't even get to see the cross when you climb the peak. Follow Fall Creek Trail (#2001) for 2 miles before it meets the Notch Mountain Trail. Take Notch Mountain Trail as is switches back over twenty times to reach the Notch Mountain shelter and enjoy the cross from this special vantage point. If desired, careful routefinding from the Notch Mountain shelter to the west toward the cross can take you down to the banks of the Bowl of Tears, but beware of the cliff band partway down into the basin.

MOUNT OF THE HOLY CROSS
—HALO RIDGE—BOWL OF TEARS

Halfmoon TH

1.6mi

White River National Forest
Holy Cross Wilderness

B. Notch Mtn to Bowl of Tears

3.6mi

1.5mi

Notch Mountain

A. North Ridge to Halo Ridge

1. Bowl of Tears

Lake Patricia

Mount of the Holy Cross

Bowl of Tears

Peak 13248

2. Cross Couloir to Halo Ridge

Cross Ridge

2.1mi

Tuhare Lakes

Holy Cross Ridge–Middle Peak

Tuhare Lakes

Lake Constantine

Seven Sisters Lakes

Seven Sisters Lakes

0.3mi

MILES

0   0.5   1.0

FANCY PASS LAKE LOOP —MISSOURI LAKES —TREASURE VAULT LAKE —FANCY PEAK TO SAVAGE PEAK TRAVERSE

38

Elevation Gain	2,750 feet for the Fancy Pass to Fancy Lake to Missouri Pass to Missouri Lakes Loop; 3,200 feet for Fancy Peak; 4,850 feet for the traverse to Savage Peak
Round-Trip Distance	9 miles for Fancy Pass to Missouri Lakes Loop; 10 miles for Fancy Peak loop; 14 miles for Fancy Peak to Savage Peak Traverse Loop
Trailhead	Missouri Lakes/Fancy Pass (10,015 feet)
Difficulty Rating	Class 1–3 hike, mainly on trails and short portion of jagged ridgeline
Optimal Season	June 1 through November 1
Maps	Trails Illustrated #126; White River National Forest

COMMENT: This corner of the Holy Cross Wilderness makes you feel far away from the rest of the world. Situated south of Mount of the Holy Cross and in the northern Sawatch, the Fancy Pass to Missouri Lakes Loop is a popular must-see easy day loop with some fun lakes and peaks to explore. In midsummer, the wild-

Fancy Lake.

Left: Treasure Vault Lake and Blodgett Lake (farther away) seen from Fancy Pass. **Right:** A look back at the southern aspects of Fancy Peak from Missouri Pass.

flowers are amazing, and you can also come here in the late fall to ice skate if the conditions are right!

GETTING THERE

Fancy Pass/Missouri Lakes Trailhead (10,015 feet). Travel west on I-70 from Vail to Exit 171 for Minturn, Leadville, and US Hwy 24. Exit here and turn right (southeast) onto US Highway 24. Proceed south for 12.5 miles over Battle Mountain Pass to Homestake Road #703. Turn right and proceed past the Gold Park Campground to mile 8.5. Turn right onto Missouri Lakes Road #704 and continue 3 miles on this dirt road to a T junction and some large black water pipes at 10,000 feet. The trailhead is on the right. Missouri Lakes Trailhead is on the left; you will use both for the loop.

THE LAKES AND LOOP

1. Fancy Lake (11,540 feet), Treasure Vault Lake (11675 feet), Missouri Lakes (11,500 feet) (Class 1). This spectacular 9-mile tour crosses two high passes and gives you plenty of lakes to see along the way. From the Fancy Lake Trailhead, follow Trail #2006 and hike through the thick pine forest as it climbs some rocky terrain and arrives at Fancy Lake after 2.7 miles. Fancy Lake is tucked into a nice glacial-carved cirque, and there are great campsites in the woods near the lake. From Fancy Lake, ascend the trail for 200 yards to a trail junction near a creek. At the trail junction, turn left (west) to then ascend a steep rocky valley and gully for 0.5 mile to the top of 12,390-foot Fancy Pass. From this pass, you can look west into the basin and see two lakes: Treasure Vault and, farther away up on a shelf near a mountain,

Left: Savage Peak above Lower Missouri Lake. **Right:** Lacing up the ice skates in November for a fun skate of Missouri Lake. *Photo by Connor Drumm*

Blodgett Lake. Follow the trail for 0.75 mile as it descends from the pass and arrives at another trail junction right near Treasure Vault Lake. Turn left (south) and ascend 400 feet to the 11,990-foot Missouri Pass. From the top of the pass, you can look south and see the Missouri Lakes. This pass is a great place to take a break and enjoy the view if the weather is good.

From the pass, drop into the Missouri Lakes basin; the two largest lakes will be close to the trail as you descend into the valley. It is 4.5 miles back to the car from the top of the pass, so enjoy the downhill. Once below the lakes, the trail follows the creek and crosses a 2019 avalanche path that destroyed the entire trail, and then the trail descends to some small gorges into the woods before leveling out near the trailhead.

THE LOOP AND HIGH-RIDGE TRAVERSE

2. Fancy Peak (13,192 feet) and Savage Peak (13,139 feet) Traverse (Class 2–3). Start at the Fancy Lake Trailhead and follow the route described above for 3.3 miles to the top of Fancy Pass at 12,390 feet. From the pass, turn north (right) and hike on a faint route that stays just on the west side of the ridge crest. There is a rocky outcrop that you must avoid to keep the difficulty at Class 2; simply stay to the west of the ridge crest. If you can find a faint trail bypassing the outcrop on the left, use it and then regain the ridge around 12,750 feet. Follow the rest of the ridgeline on rocky terrain and some tundra to the summit, which is actually overlooking the Mulhall Lakes to the east. Return to Fancy Pass the same way you came up.

Next, you have a choice: Either way, your goal is to get to Missouri Pass from Fancy Pass. You can certainly take the trail to Treasure Vault Lake and then back

Left: Signs near Treasure Vault Lake mark the route. **Right:** Running at Treasure Vault Lake.

up to Missouri Pass, or better yet, the ridge traverse travels southwest over Peak 12,869' for 1.1 mile down to Missouri Pass. Once on Missouri Pass, ascend to the west and then south quite steeply initially (Class 2+ to 3) for 1.2 miles to Peak 12,898' and another 1.2 miles to the top of Savage Peak. This ridge is fun and scenic. The east and north sides of the ridgeline are very steep looking down into Missouri Lakes, so use caution. To get back to the trailhead, return 2.4 miles back across the ridgeline to Missouri Pass and then back down via Missouri Lakes. This tour of Fancy Pass, the ridgeline, and Savage Peak is a loop of 16.5 miles and 4,850 feet of elevation gain.

DR. JON'S EXTRA CREDIT
A. Blodgett Lake (12,361 feet) (Class 2). From Treasure Vault Lake, you can take the Cross Creek Trail to the west and then hike some grassy slopes for almost a mile to the scenic and isolated lake shores of Blodgett Lake.
B. The Fancy Ice-Skating Loop (Class 2). In late October to as late as the first week of December during a cold and dry fall, consider hiking to Fancy Lake, Treasure Vault Lake, and the Missouri Lakes for an ice skate with your friends in the right conditions.

FANCY PASS LAKE LOOP—MISSOURI LAKES—TREASURE VAULT LAKE—FANCY PEAK TO SAVAGE PEAK TRAVERSE

MIDDLE LAKE—FINNEGAN PEAK—GOLD DUST PEAK TRAVERSE

39

Elevation Gain	3,500 feet for Middle Lake; 5,726 feet for Finnegan Peak; 6,526 feet for Gold Dust Peak Traverse and Loop
Round-Trip Distance	16 miles for Middle Lake; 21 miles with Finnegan Peak and loop back to Middle Lake; 24 miles with Middle Lake visit plus Finnegan Peak and Gold Dust Peak Summit
Trailhead	East Lake Creek (8,520 feet)
Difficulty Ratings	Class 1–2 hike both on trails and across tundra/scattered alpine forest ecozone with no trails; Class 3 and 4 scrambling is required on the Finnegan Peak to Gold Dust Peak Traverse
Optimal Season	July through October
Maps	Trails Illustrated #126; White River National Forest

COMMENT: The far northwest corner of the Holy Cross Wilderness in Eagle County and the northern reaches of the Sawatch Range, also known as the New York Mountains, are as beautiful as they are remote and rarely visited. If you choose to make the effort to visit this place, make a backpacking trip out of it, and you can expect to be rewarded and not see another soul during your entire journey.

The view south to Finnegan and Gold Dust Peaks; New York Lake is in the basin to the right.

GETTING THERE
East Lake Creek Trailhead (8,520 feet). Take I-70 Exit 163 Edwards approximately 115 miles west of Denver and 45 miles east of Glenwood Springs. Take the Edwards access road to the central roundabout in Edwards. Turn right (west), follow US Highway 6 for 0.7 mile to Lake Creek Road, turn left (south), and follow Lake Creek Road for 1.8 miles to West Lake Creek Road. Travel 3.5 miles up West Lake Creek Road, go past the Pilgrim Downs subdivision, and the road turns to dirt. Pass the West Lake Creek four-wheel-drive access road, follow the road to the left, and reach the East Lake Creek Trailhead after 3.5 miles, located in some aspen trees. Make note of the no-camping signs at the trailhead, which is on private property, but an easement has granted access to the trail and national forest beyond. As of 2021, the landowners have placed a camera to deter people from camping at the trailhead.

THE LAKE
1. East Lake Creek Trailhead, Dead Dog Trail to Middle Lake (11,120 feet) (Class 1–2). Leave the parking area as the Dead Dog Trail #2220 gains elevation and switches back through private property and groves of aspen and pine. For the first 0.5 mile, it's important to stay on the trail. At mile 0.75, the trail splits at the junction of the East Lake Creek Trail #1880 and the Dead Dog Trail #2220. Take the right branch through more pine and then old-growth aspen forest. You will pass through wild strawberry fields in July and August. At approximately 3 miles, you will reach a large open meadow surrounded by aspens. The trail descends for 200 yards, turns left (southeast), and leaves the aspen forest, climbing steeply and

Left: Middle Lake down in the basin. **Right:** Lake Thomas is seen as you traverse from Finnegan to Gold Dust Peak.

traversing up through the thick pine forest and a ridgeline near 10,600 feet. The trail will level out after traversing on the east side of a prominent ridgeline with a few excellent views to the northeast and the Gore Range in the distance. Then a series of rolling hills through the forest will bring you to the junction of the Middle Lake Trail (#2223). Take the left (southeast) branch of the trail for another mile up through the thick pine forest to timberline and a spectacular viewpoint of a deep glacial valley and a prominent lodgepole cairn. From here, you can look

Gold Dust Peak's summit pitch is challenging.

to the east and see Middle Lake about 1 mile away down in the deep glacial valley. Follow the trail as it contours south and then southeast and down into the pine forest toward Middle Lake on the far end of the basin. Reach the lake on a fading trail, where there are plenty of great campsites.

THE HIGH-RIDGE TRAVERSE

2. Finnegan Peak (13,346 feet), north slopes/ridgeline (Class 2–3). Start at Middle Lake and walk along the banks of the Middle Creek above the lake and hike up a narrowing basin on some grassy benches that funnel toward the tundra and basin above the lake. After 0.75 mile, you will leave the timber, and careful route-finding will allow you to gain a flatter basin, which leads to a point on the horseshoe ridgeline that keeps the basin you are in enclosed. Aim to the south for the highest point on the ridge. From here, you will have a vantage point to the south of both Finnegan Peak and Thomas Lake to the south and southeast. Hike, traverse, and scramble to the summit of Finnegan Peak (13,346 feet, Class 3).

DR. JON'S EXTRA CREDIT

A. Gold Dust Peak, traverse of north ridge 13,380 feet (Class 4). Consider doing Middle Lake, Finnegan Peak, and Gold Dust Peak as a backpacking trip. Camp at Middle Lake. Then climb Finnegan Peak as described above. After ascending Finnegan Peak, use careful routefinding to traverse to the 13,380-foot Gold Dust Peak. This traverse requires Class 3 and 4 climbing and adds an additional 1.5 miles round-trip to your journey. Return via Finnegan Peak, but traverse across two more subsummits on the ridgeline to the Middle Lake Trail, as shown on the map.

MIDDLE LAKE—FINNEGAN PEAK —GOLD DUST PEAK TRAVERSE

CLOHESY LAKE AND MISSOURI MOUNTAIN

40

Elevation Gain	1,000 feet for Clohesy Lake; 4,100 feet for Missouri Mountain
Round-Trip Distance	6.5 miles for Clohesy Lake; 10.75 miles for Missouri Mountain Loop
Trailhead	Clohesy Lake/Rockdale (9,940 feet)
Difficulty Ratings	Class 1–2 hike, mainly on trails to the lakes and some Class 2+ ridgelines for the traverses
Optimal Season	June 1 through October 15
Maps	Trails Illustrated #129 and #148; San Isabel National Forest

COMMENT: Clohesy Lake is a fun and easy lake to get to. If you are looking for a way to experience some of the Collegiate Peaks, climb fourteener Missouri Mountain or Mount Huron from their nonstandard routes, or stay off the beaten path, this adventure in the Sawatch Range is made for you.

Clohesy Lake.

Just below the summit of Missouri, right after the minor challenges on the north ridge.

GETTING THERE
Clohesy Lake Trailhead (9,940 feet). This trailhead is open by about May 1 most years. Take US Highway 24 south from Leadville for 19.5 miles or north from Buena Vista for 14.5 miles to access the area via Chaffee County Road 390. Turn west onto Chaffee County 390, which is a dirt road, and from this point, travel 7.7 miles to Vicksburg. Go past the Missouri Gulch Trailhead. Next, continue on the four-wheel-drive road for 2.3 miles, and the trailhead is marked on the left (south) side of the road. You can continue down the road toward Clear Creek for a couple hundred yards to the old Rockdale townsite, but if you value your vehicle, parking near the road junction is the best option.

THE LAKE
1. Clohesy Lake (10,974 feet) (Class 1). This trail is initially a rough four-wheel-drive road with a creek crossing. A high-clearance vehicle can save you almost 3 miles here, but you need a good vehicle to follow the four-wheel-drive road south to 10,880 feet into the basin. When parking at Rockdale, follow the four-wheel-drive road for 3.25 miles to Clohesy Lake at nearly 11,000 feet. At 0.25 mile from the lake is an actual trailhead marker in an avalanche debris zone with a locked gate where four-wheel-drive vehicles must park. If you hike the four-wheel-drive road, you will get views to the south to Mount Hope in some meadows that were opened up by avalanche and rockslide paths. There is good camping at the lake.

THE LOOP AND HIGH-RIDGE TRAVERSE
2. Missouri Mountain Traverse Loop (Class 2+). After a visit to Clohesy Lake, venture above the eastern banks of Clohesy Lake, where an unmarked fork breaks off

Left: Pear Lake. **Right:** The saddle between Iowa and Missouri is the place to turn right to make it back to Clohesy Lake.

to the left on a steep trail of loose gravel. This is the way to Missouri Mountain; follow the trail as it ascends quickly and wraps left toward the west ridge. The grade eases in the tundra on the broad basin below Missouri Mountain, and from here, the views open to Huron Peak on the western wall of the basin. For 0.2 mile, a gentle grade gets to 12,000 feet before the climb begins again. You will switchback up grass and tundra to the west ridge crest at 13,000 feet. Continue on this ridge crest for another 0.5 mile to meet up with the standard north ridge route trail at 13,875 feet. You are now 2 miles from Clohesy Lake and 2,000 feet above it. Follow the main trail south for 0.6 mile to the summit. After great views and summit photos, to complete the loop, follow the climbers' trail down the south ridgeline of Missouri to the 13,560-foot connecting saddle between Iowa Peak and Missouri Mountain. From this saddle, you will see the prominent Missouri Mountain Clohesy Lake Trail (#1459). Descend this trail for 2,400 feet to reach the shores of Clohesy Lake. To complete the loop, head north around the lake and back to the four-wheel-drive road in the direction of Rockdale.

DR. JON'S EXTRA CREDIT

A. Pear Lake (12,095 feet) (Class 2). From Clohesy Lake, follow the main trail south to the south shores of the lake. A separate hike follows the entire length of the basin, up and over a 12,500-foot pass, and then down for 400 feet into Pear Lake. This little side adventure is a fun 6-mile round-trip journey from Clohesy Lake with plenty of solitude.

B. Mount Huron (14,003 feet) (Class 2+). From Clohesy Lake, it's possible to find a climbers' trail that switches back and climbs east up very steep terrain to the summit of Huron Peak. This is the more rugged way to summit this fourteener.

CLOHESY LAKE AND MISSOURI MOUNTAIN

SILVER KING LAKE —SILVER KING PEAK —MISSOURI MOUNTAIN MEGA TRAVERSE

41

Elevation Gain	4,100 feet for Silver King Lake; 5,250 feet for Silver King Peak Lake; 6,450 feet for Emerald Peak; 6,900 feet for Iowa Peak
Round-Trip Distance	13 miles for Silver King Lake; 14 miles for Silver King Peak; 14.5 miles for the Silver King to Iowa Peak to Emerald Peak Traverse Loop
Trailhead	Missouri Gulch (9,640 feet)
Difficulty Ratings	Class 1–2 hike, mainly on trails to the lakes, some off-trail tundra travel; some Class 2+ ridgelines for the traverses
Optimal Season	June 1 through October 15
Maps	Trails Illustrated #129 and #148; San Isabel National Forest

COMMENT: Silver King Lake is one of Colorado's hidden gems. Not easy to access, it's at least 8 miles one-way to get to the lake, and that's if you can figure out some secret off-trail routefinding. This high-ridge traverse can allow you some amazing solitude and get you to Centennial and Bicentennial thirteener summits that most

The view down to Emerald and Silver King from Missouri's summit.

Silver King to Emerald to Iowa to Missouri visible along the ridgeline from right to left.

people only get to look at from a distance. Put the extra effort in and you can even add on Missouri to complete what is dubbed the "Missouri Mountain Mega Loop." Take plenty of snacks and water purification and get ready for some amazing views. The routes described here are reserved for those seeking an isolated adventure and who are fit enough to go long miles and long days in the high alpine.

GETTING THERE

Missouri Gulch Trailhead (9,640 feet). This trailhead is open by about April 1 most years. Take US Highway 24 south from Leadville for 19.5 miles or north from Buena Vista for 14.5 miles to access the area via Chaffee County Road 390. Turn west onto Chaffee County 390, which is a dirt road, and from this point, travel 7.7 miles to Vicksburg. The trailhead is well marked on the left (south) side of the road.

THE LAKE

1. **Silver King Lake (12,625 feet) (Class 1–2).** This lake is tucked away deep in the heart of the Sawatch Range. Follow the Missouri Gulch Trail for 2 miles to timberline at 11,400 feet. You will pass the ruins of a small cabin just before breaking out of the trees into the basin. At 2 miles, you will reach the trail junction with the Mount Belford Trail. Continue south (right) and follow the basin south for another 1.5 miles to the base of Missouri Mountain and the Missouri Trail junction at 12,400 feet. Continue left on the main trail and ascend an additional 800 feet in 0.8 mile to 13,200-foot Elkhead Pass. From the pass, if you look to your south, you will see Silver King Mountain and Silver King Lake tucked into the north side of the mountain in the distance. Descend on a good trail into the Pine Creek basin

Missouri Mountain with Silver King, Emerald, and Iowa Peaks in the distance from left to right.

and follow it south for 1.8 miles to a creek crossing at 12,100 feet in the upper basin. Once you cross the creek, the trail will turn left (east). Leave the trail from here, stay southerly for 0.3 mile, and contour above timberline until you reach the Silver King Lake Trail (#1467, Pine Creek Trail) right near a final crossing of Pine Creek to gain the trail. Once back on the trail, hike 1 mile southwest to Silver King Lake at 12,625 feet, located in a spectacular mountain basin. This route covers 6.4 miles to Silver King Lake.

THE LOOP AND HIGH-RIDGE TRAVERSE

2. Emerald Peak (13,904 feet) and Iowa Peak (13,831 feet) Traverse from Silver King Peak (Class 2+). After a visit to Silver King Lake, look south and travel up the nearest ridgeline from the east end of the lake for 0.5 mile to the summit of Silver King Peak. This spiny ridge is steep but does not exceed Class 2 and joins the north ridge 400 feet from the top. From the summit of Silver King Peak, you can see the entire high-ridge traverse over Emerald and Iowa Peaks, and you can view Missouri Mountain. If the weather is good and you are ready for some high ridges, go for it! The 2 miles of ridge to Emerald Peak are the most challenging. Travel west for 300 yards to a subsummit of Silver King Peak, and then turn north and bypass several subsummits on the way. The ridgeline is less steep on the west side, but you can stay on the crest nearly the entire way. The lowest saddle is 12,875 feet after two minor summits (13,600 and 13,400 feet). Continue up to the rocky summit pyramid of 13,904-foot Emerald Peak after passing the final 13,250-foot ridge mini summit.

From Emerald Peak, continue north for 0.75 mile with a straightforward down-and-up grassy saddle on easy slopes to reach the top of 13,831-foot Iowa Peak.

Left: Looking off to Silver King summit. **Right:** Headed to Belford from Missouri and Elkhead Pass.

Dropping off of Iowa Peak, you now have two options: go for Missouri Mountain (see the extra credit below) or return to your camp at Silver King Lake by dropping back to the east and catching the trails in the basin. If this is just a single-push day hike, find the trail back to Elkhead Pass by heading east, then north on the trail to the pass and eventually back to your car at Missouri Gulch Trailhead.

DR. JON'S EXTRA CREDIT

A. Missouri Mountain Mega Traverse Loop (14,067 feet) (Class 2). Due to more traffic in recent years, once you reach the 13,560-foot connecting saddle between Iowa peak and Missouri Mountain, you can find a reasonably worn climbers' trail that comes from Clohesy Lake to the west that will take you up to the north for 500 feet to the summit of Missouri. I would highly recommend adding this on as a grand finish to the traverse work you have done with Silver King.

B. Backpacking at Silver King Lake adding Belford and Oxford (Class 2). Hiking all the way in to Silver King Lake for an overnight backpack, which includes the traverses mentioned here, is a great way to enjoy this part of the Sawatch Range. If you have an extra day, consider tackling Belford and Oxford, two other nearby fourteeners as well. Don't forget to take a swim in Silver King Lake while you are at it!

SILVER KING LAKE—SILVER KING PEAK —MISSOURI MOUNTAIN MEGA TRAVERSE

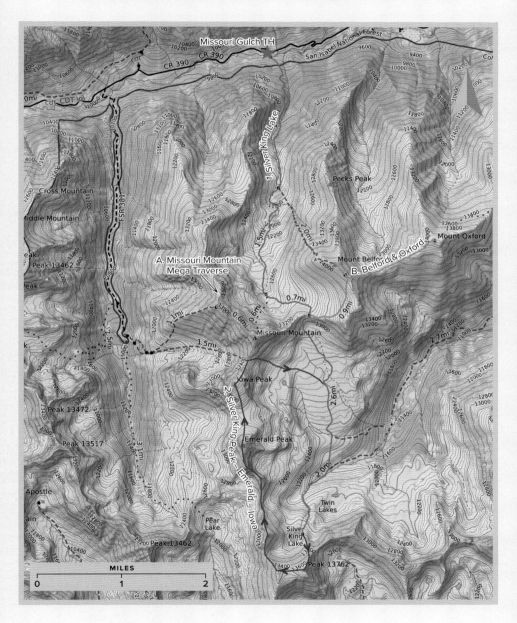

LAKE ANN —THREE APOSTLES TRAVERSE LOOP

42

Elevation Gain	1,350 feet for Lake Ann; 3,150 feet for West Apostle Peak; 4,050 feet for Ice Mountain; 4,460 feet for East Apostle Peak
Round-Trip Distance	6.8 miles for Lake Ann; 12 miles for Ice Mountain and Three Apostles Traverse Loop; 14.5 miles Lake Ann, Three Apostles Traverse, and loop back to lake (if camping at the lake)
Trailheads	South Winfield (10,260 feet); Huron Gate (10,600 feet)
Difficulty Ratings	Class 1–2 hike both on trails and across tundra/scattered alpine forest ecozone with no trails; Class 3 and 4 scrambling is required on the Three Apostles Traverse
Optimal Season	June through October
Maps	Trails Illustrated #129 and #148; San Isabel National Forest

COMMENT: The Three Apostles (Ice Mountain, North Apostle, and West Apostle) are arguably the Sawatch Range's most jagged peaks. Most people view them from the summit of Huron, which is only a few miles to the north. If these gorgeous peaks arouse your curiosity, take some time to visit Lake Ann as well. Staying the night at

Lake Ann tucked up against the Continental Divide.

Left: Approaching the Three Apostles. **Right:** Ice Mountain's small summit.

Lake Ann is a great way to enjoy the beauty of this little corner of the Sawatch Range and to easily access this challenging high-ridge traverse.

GETTING THERE

South Winfield Trailhead (10,260 feet). This trailhead is open by about May 1 most years. Take US Highway 24 south from Leadville for 19.5 miles or north from Buena Vista for 14.5 miles to access the area via Chaffee County Road 390. Turn west onto Chaffee County 390, which is a dirt road, and measure from this point. Travel 11.8 miles to Winfield, which is a clearly marked abandoned town site. The road is closed until late April, but in winter is usually drivable for 4 to 5 miles. From there, a snowmobile or an ambitious slog on skis can take you the rest of the way. Pass west through Winfield and turn left (south), crossing to Clear Creek's south side. Take an immediate right (west) onto South Fork Clear Creek Road (FSR 390.2B). Travel 0.25 mile west on FSR 390.2B to the trailhead. There are plenty of parking and camping spaces here. (Note: not shown on map.)

Huron Gate Trailhead (10,600 feet). Follow the directions for South Winfield Trailhead to South Fork Clear Creek Road (FSR 390.2B). Sometimes by mid-May, you can continue to drive past the South Winfield Trailhead, traveling west then southwest for 2.0 miles to reach a small parking area near a Collegiate Peaks Wilderness gate. This gate is the start of two trails: the trail to Huron Peak (left) and Lake Ann (right). The Lake Ann Trail leads to the Three Apostles, including Ice Mountain.

THE LAKE

1. Lake Ann (11,950 feet) (Class 1). Follow the Lake Ann Trail (right and straight ahead from the gate) south for 0.5 mile to the Collegiate Peaks Wilderness boundary. From the boundary, follow the trail another 0.75 mile through a mix of open

North Apostle's final ridge with the refrigerator couloir of Ice Mountain behind.

meadows and timber to the old Hamilton townsite at 10,820 feet. Here you will find a trail junction; stay left (straight) at the junction and follow the Lake Ann Trail, which at this point is also the Continental Divide Trail and the Colorado Trail. The Lake Ann Trail leaves Hamilton and quickly crosses the south fork of Clear Creek, offering amazing views of the Three Apostles. Prior to some willows in a meadow at mile 1.35, the trail splits: Three Apostles Trail to the left and Lake Ann Trail to the right. After the creek crossing on a good wood bridge (mile 1.4), take a sharp right (southwest-west) on the Lake Ann Trail, continuing up through the conifer forest. There are several viewpoints into a small canyon on your left as you ascend. At mile 2.25, the trail leaves the creek climbing steeply and follows the edge of the forest and willows for 0.5 mile while also crossing another small log bridge at mile 2.85. Descend two switchbacks to one last creek crossing at mile 3, then enter the woods, and climb steeply through the last bit of thick pine forest, finally emerging near timberline, climbing two more switchbacks, and arriving at the lake in a sweeping cirque basin at mile 3.4. The CDT/Colorado Trail will continue up to a saddle to the southwest above the lake.

THE LOOP AND HIGH-RIDGE TRAVERSE

2. Three Apostles Traverse (Class 3–4). Start at Lake Ann and walk along the banks of the lake then above the lake to the south on some grassy benches that funnel toward the tundra and basin above the lake. Soon the basin widens and becomes more rock than grass. Looking at the western ridgeline of West Apostle, aim for a small notch in the ridge, and it's possible to climb some social trails in a narrow gully to reach the ridge at 13,100 feet. Once on the ridge, roughly 1 mile above Lake Ann, turn left (east) and follow more faint social trails over two false summits to finally

Lake Ann is the perfect place to camp to complete the Three Apostles loop.

reach the summit of West Apostle (13,568 feet), 1.6 miles from Lake Ann. It is also possible to follow the Colorado Trail from Lake Ann to the saddle on the ridge to connect this route.

Descend to the 13,050-foot connecting saddle between West Apostle and Ice Mountain. Staying on the southern aspect of this traverse most of the way will keep the descent to the saddle and the basic ascent to Ice Mountain Class 2+ to 3 at the most on predominately grassy clefts and slopes. Only the final 200 yards of the ridge to the top of Ice Mountain gets more technical; still, stay on the south aspect for the safest routefinding. From the top of Ice Mountain, enjoy the views and carefully descend Class 4 gullies to climb toward East Apostle, sometimes called Northeast Apostle. From the connecting saddle between the 13,951-foot Ice Mountain and East Apostle, follow a faint climbers' trail on boulders at times (Class 2) to reach the top of 13,860-foot East Apostle. The descent involves returning to the saddle between Ice Mountain and East Apostle and descending rocks and scree to the north into a bowl and returning to the Three Apostles Trail near timberline.

DR. JON'S EXTRA CREDIT

A. Fall wild ice skating on Lake Ann (Class 1). Pick a cold, crisp fall morning in November or December before the first major snows and take a journey to Lake Ann. This high basin tucked into a cirque with mountains to the south is a prime place for some high-mountain "Wild Ice" skating if you time it just right!

LAKE ANN—THREE APOSTLES TRAVERSE LOOP

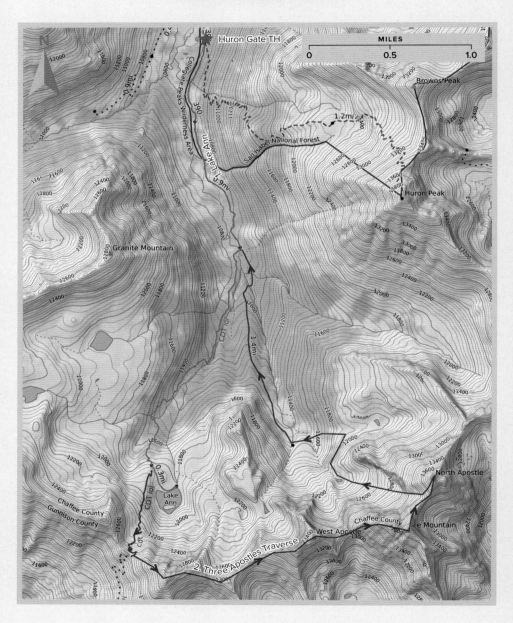

GRIZZLY LAKE —GRIZZLY PEAK A —MOUNTAIN BOY TRAVERSE

43

Elevation Gain	2,000 feet for Grizzly Lake; 3,430 feet for Grizzly Peak A; 4,200 feet for the traverse to Mountain Boy Peak and optionally beyond to Independence Pass
Round-Trip Distance	7 miles for Grizzly Lake; 8.4 miles for Grizzly Peak A; 9.5 miles to Mountain Boy Peak Traverse Loop; 10.5 miles out Independence Pass
Trailhead	Grizzly Reservoir (10,560 feet)
Difficulty Ratings	Class 1–2 hike, mainly on trails to Grizzly Lake and Grizzly Peak and some Class 2+ to 3 jagged ridgelines
Optimal Season	June 1 through November 1
Maps	Trails Illustrated #127 and #148; San Isabel National Forest

COMMENT: Colorado's highest thirteener, Grizzly Peak, is situated on the geographical border between the Elk Range and the Sawatch Range. The peak is truly isolated, and you will see far less traffic hiking to this lake and on the peak compared

Grizzly Lake holds snow and ice into late June due to its location in a north-facing basin.

Left: Beautiful meadows greet you on your hike. **Right:** The connecting ridge between Grizzly and Mountain Boy is visible to the right.

to any of the state's fourteeners. Climb to the top and enjoy endless peaks in all directions.

GETTING THERE

Grizzly Reservoir Trailhead (10,560 feet). This trailhead is typically inaccessible until after Memorial Day because Independence Pass (Colorado Highway 82) may not be open until then. If coming from the east, follow Colorado Highway 82 for 9.7 miles west from the top of Independence Pass. If approaching from the west, travel about 10 miles east from Aspen on Colorado Highway 82. Turn south on Lincoln Creek Road (FSR 106). Travel 6.5 miles up Lincoln Creek Road to the marked trailhead on the left. You will pass the Lincoln Gulch Campground before the first mile on Lincoln Creek Road. You will also pass Grizzly Reservoir and Dam. In the summer of 2021, there was construction that closed the road 3 miles below the trailhead, making this hike longer.

THE LAKE

1. Grizzly Lake (12,500 feet) (Class 1). This is a gorgeous alpine hike through meadows and wildflowers into a spectacular and isolated glacial trough that holds a pristine alpine lake. You'll begin from the Grizzly Lake Trailhead and climb moderate steepness to the east through some pine forest and then weave your way through the alpine on the north side of Grizzly Creek, crossing some avalanche paths in the first 1.5 miles. After that, the trail turns south and aims directly for Grizzly Peak. Cross the creek again into some willows, ascend some rocky outcroppings, and then steeply climb into a large glacial cirque where you will find the lake nestled in the

Panorama of the magnificent valley.

deep end of the valley below Grizzly's north couloir. Enjoy lunch and then head back to the car or continue for a climb of the peak.

THE LOOP AND HIGH-RIDGE TRAVERSE

2. Grizzly Peak A (13,988 feet) and Mountain Boy Peak (13,198 feet) Traverse (Class 2+). After a visit to Grizzly Lake, look south and decide on your route by evaluating the state of the snowpack and what remains on the north side of Grizzly, which is typically a near-permanent snowfield on its northern aspects for most of the year. If it is June or July, an ice ax and crampons are recommended for the route of the north face or north face couloir, which will generally hold excellent snow until August most years.

From Grizzly Lake, angle to your left for 0.2 mile to access the bottom of the broad gully. In April and May, this couloir is a signature ski line off this peak. Climb the gully directly up to the ridge crest for 1,300 feet to reach the 13,800-foot crest of Grizzly Peak A. From the ridge crest, take the Class 2+ ridgeline to the top, but you can stay slightly right (west) of the crest as you ascend the loose rock on a faint climbers' trail for 200 yards.

From the top of Grizzly Peak A, retrace your steps north and arrive back at the ridge crest of the entrance to the north couloir, except just before you get back to the crest, turn right (east) near some prominent gendarmes in order to follow the ridge. From here, it's nearly 3 miles of ridgeline to get to Mountain Boy Peak and 6 miles back to Independence Pass if you choose a vehicle shuttle, so consider the weather and the time. If it's safe to proceed, descend the east ridge through three gendarmes. As you descend, you may have to stay on the east ridge's south (right)

Left: Descending the northeastern col of Grizzly. **Right:** Approaching Grizzly Lake.

side of the gendarmes. After 300 yards of descent and once you get past the rocky features, the ridgeline gets grassy, and you may be able to pick up a faint climbers' trail on the ridge, especially as the ridge begins to turn northeast and then northerly. The ridge will flatten out with a section of looser rock and then gets easier with grass again for several hundred yards before becoming steep yet again and ascending from a 12,569-foot saddle up to nearly 13,200 feet in roughly a mile, reaching the top of Mountain Boy Peak.

From the Top of Mountain Boy Peak, drop west back onto Grizzly Peak basin into a steep but walkable gully (Class 2). You can rejoin the Grizzly Lake Trail roughly 1.3 miles up from the trailhead, making this a nice loop back to your vehicle at Grizzly Reservoir Trailhead.

DR. JON'S EXTRA CREDIT
A. Garfield Peak A (13,780 feet) (Class 3). From the summit of Grizzly Peak A, traverse the southern ridgeline of Grizzly for 0.5 mile to the summit of Garfield Peak A. With some research and careful routefinding, you can make this a loop by descending west into Ruby and the Lincoln Creek basins via the connecting saddle between Grizzly and Garfield. Once down in the basin, find a trail that follows Lincoln Creek north and back to the trailhead.

GRIZZLY LAKE—GRIZZLY PEAK A —MOUNTAIN BOY TRAVERSE

ANDERSON LAKE AND PEAK —PETROLEUM LAKE —PETROLEUM PEAK LOOP

44a

Elevation Gain	627 feet for Anderson Lake; 1,111 feet for Petroleum Lake; 2,450 feet for Anderson Peak only; 3,000 feet for the traverse to Petroleum Peak Loop
Round-Trip Distance	2.4 miles for Anderson Lake; 3.6 miles for Petroleum Lake; 7 miles for the Petroleum Peak Loop
Trailhead	Anderson Lake (11,200 feet)
Difficulty Ratings	Class 1–2 hike, mainly on trails to Anderson Lake and Petroleum Lake and some Class 2+ ridgelines
Optimal Season	June 1 through October 15
Maps	Trails Illustrated #127 and #148; San Isabel National Forest

COMMENT: Tucked away far from the larger peaks in the state, this corner of the border between the Elk Range and Sawatch Range is so beautiful, especially when the wildflowers are popping in July. There are so many lakes here: Anderson and Petroleum, Tabor as well as Truro. This area was heavily glaciated fifteen to twenty

Anderson Lake. *Photo by John Fielder*

Left: Anderson Lake with Anderson Peak behind; access to the northeast ridgeline can be seen at left. *Photo by Carrie Besnette Hauser* **Right:** Sunrise at Petroleum Lake. *Photo by John Fielder*

thousand years ago and the evidence of much larger glacial landscape features exists in these valleys: glacial lakes, tarns, and troughs that have flattened out and created the massive U-shaped valleys and relatively flat high-alpine basins. All are present here for you to explore.

GETTING THERE

Anderson Lake Trailhead (11,200 feet). This trailhead is typically inaccessible until after Memorial Day because Independence Pass (Colorado Highway 82) may not be open until then. If coming from the east, follow Colorado Highway 82 for 9.7 miles west from the top of Independence Pass. If approaching from the west, travel about 10 miles east from Aspen on Colorado Highway 82. Turn south on Lincoln Creek Road (FSR 106). Travel 6.5 miles up Lincoln Creek Road to the marked Grizzly Creek Trailhead on the left. You will pass the Lincoln Gulch Campground before the first mile on Lincoln Creek Road. You will also pass Grizzly Reservoir and Dam. After the Grizzly Reservoir Trailhead, continue on the upper Lincoln Creek Road as it gets even rougher, passing the Portal Campground on the right at 7 miles, and works its way south for an additional 3 miles to a fork in the road. Take the right fork, cross the creek, and arrive at the Anderson Lake Trailhead. After Portal Campground, if you value your vehicle, consider hiking the additional 3 miles and 650 vertical feet to the trailhead. In the summer of 2021, there was construction that closed the road 3 miles below the Grizzly Reservoir Trailhead, making this hike even longer.

THE LAKES

1. Anderson Lake (11,827 feet) and Petroleum Lake (12,306 feet) (Class 1).
This is a gorgeous alpine hike through meadows and wildflowers into a spectacular and isolated glacial trough that holds a pristine alpine lake. Start from the Anderson

Left: Looking south from Tabor/Tellurium Pass; Galena Pass and Petroleum Peak's northern ridge is visible at center. **Right:** From Tabor/Tellurium Pass the connecting ridgeline to Tellurium Peak.

Lake Trailhead, ascending a sparse alpine forest along Anderson Creek, which will be to your south for 0.75 mile until you reach a creek crossing. The trail leaves the glacial trough of the valley, so it is steep at first but levels out once you cross the creek near the confluence of Petroleum and Anderson Creeks and begin to venture above timberline. Continue through willows and strong patches of wildflowers, arriving at the lake after 1.2 miles. About 200 yards before Anderson Lake, you will reach a junction with the trail that forks to the right (north) for Petroleum Lake. If you visit the shores of Anderson Lake, return to this trail junction to next visit Petroleum Lake. Follow the Petroleum Lake Trail for another mile north and then west as it gradually climbs through high-mountain meadows for 500 vertical feet to reach the lake above 12,000 feet. Come in the morning for nice calm reflections in the lake and in your own mind and body.

THE LOOP AND HIGH-RIDGE TRAVERSE

2. Anderson Peak (13,631 feet) and Petroleum Peak (13,505 feet) Traverse (Class 2+). After a visit to Anderson Lake, look south and travel up the basin toward Anderson Peak. As you walk through grass and willows, aim southeast (left) and contour the basin to gain Anderson's gentle northeast pyramid-like ridgeline. Follow the northeast ridge to the summit. The final 200 feet get a bit rockier, but overall, the ridge is very straightforward. If Anderson Peak is all you want to hike for the day, you can return to the lake the same way you came. Anderson Peak alone is 6.4 miles round-trip from the trailhead and 2,500 feet of elevation gain, the route being 1.8 miles from the western shores of Anderson Lake. You can look south and see down into Ruby Lake basin.

If you are feeling ambitious, from the top of Anderson Peak, drop west then north for 0.8 mile on the ridgeline to Peak 13,105', which is roughly halfway to

Grizzly Reservoir is where the road to the Anderson Lake Trailhead gets quite rugged.

13,505-foot Petroleum Peak. Continue on the easy ridgeline, dropping to a minor 12,965-foot saddle, and then head west and north again to reach the top of Petroleum Peak. At times, you may find minor game trails, making progress along the ridgeline easier. There are several ways to drop back to Petroleum Lake, thus completing the loop to return to the trailhead: (1) Petroleum Peak's east spine/ridgeline and aim for the north shoreline of Petroleum Lake (0.8 mile) or (2) loop farther north by staying on the north ridgeline of Petroleum Peak for 0.65 mile to a 12,800-foot saddle, and then turning west and descending near Galena Creek and returning back down to Petroleum Lake.

DR. JON'S EXTRA CREDIT
A. Tellurium Peak (13,300 feet) to Tabor Peak (13,282 feet): The "Double-T" Traverse (Class 3–4). From the summit of Petroleum Peak, instead of returning to Petroleum Lake, traverse the northern ridgeline for 1 mile to the summit of Tellurium Peak. This high ridgeline is ultrascenic. Continue north for another 1.2 miles to the summit of Tabor Peak. Descend the northwest bowl into Tabor Lake and use the Tabor Lake Trail to drop to the Tabor Creek Trail and either head north to a car shuttle parked at Tabor Creek Trailhead or return back south, creating a large loop via the Tabor Creek Trail to Tabor Pass and Petroleum Lake. (See entry #44b for more details.)

B. Tabor Pass to Tabor Lake, one-way traverse (Class 2). Do some map studying and exploring, and you can travel north from Petroleum Lake to Galena Creek and Tabor Pass, hiking toward the north on the Tabor Creek Trail with a visit to Tabor Lake. A car shuttle at the Tabor Creek Trailhead may be required.

ANDERSON LAKE AND PEAK—PETROLEUM LAKE—PETROLEUM PEAK LOOP

TABOR LAKE —TABOR BASIN LAKE —"DOUBLE-T" TRAVERSE LOOP

44b

Elevation Gain	2,200 feet for Tabor Lake; 1,700 feet for Tabor Basin Lake; 5,000 vertical feet for the Double-T Traverse Loop
Round-Trip Distance	7.5 miles for Tabor Lake; 7 miles for Tabor Basin Lake; 12 miles for the "Double T" Traverse Loop
Trailhead	Tabor Creek (10,250 feet)
Difficulty Ratings	Class 1–2 hike, mainly on trails to Tabor Lake and Tabor Basin Lake; some Class 3–4 ridgelines
Optimal Season	June 1 through October 15
Maps	Trails Illustrated #127 and #148; San Isabel National Forest

COMMENT: A fun supplement to visiting Anderson and Petroleum Lakes is exploring Tabor Lake and the Tabor basin, which is an easy and very overlooked place in this part of the western Sawatch. You also don't have to go as far on the particularly rough Lincoln Creek Road, compared to Anderson and Petroleum Lakes, to access

Tabor Basin Lake with the entire ridge traverse from Tabor Peak (right) and Tellurium (left) is visible along the skyline.

Above: The northeastern cirque of Tabor Peak.
Left: Tabor Lake is a rewarding hideaway.

Tabor basin. This area was heavily glaciated fifteen to twenty thousand years ago, and the evidence of much larger glacial landscape features exists in these valleys: glacial lakes, tarns, and troughs that have flattened out and created the massive U-shaped valleys and relatively flat high-alpine basins present here for you to enjoy. Fall is best in these high places because there won't be any afternoon thunderstorms or people to encounter on your adventure.

GETTING THERE

Tabor Creek Trailhead (10,200 feet). This trailhead is typically inaccessible until after Memorial Day because Independence Pass (Colorado Highway 82) may not be open until then. If coming from the east, follow Colorado Highway 82 for 9.7 miles west from the top of Independence Pass. If approaching from the west, travel about 10 miles east from Aspen on Colorado Highway 82. Turn south on Lincoln

Creek Road (FSR 106). Travel 4.2 miles up Lincoln Creek Road to the marked Tabor Creek Trailhead on the right. You will pass the Lincoln Gulch Campground before the first mile on Lincoln Creek Road. You will also pass many established Forest Service campsites (22) on the way as well as a significant avalanche-debris field on a rough road. Tabor Creek Trailhead is right next to the creek off Lincoln Creek Road with several good parking spots.

THE LAKES
1. Tabor Lake (12,315 feet) and Tabor Basin Lake (11,840 feet) (Class 1–2).
This is an amazing hike and exploration that are best done on a holiday weekend when most people are busy clogging up the state's fourteeners. This journey starts from the Tabor Trailhead, and immediately you are faced with a dilemma: how to get across Lincoln Creek. In June or July, wading across the creek can be scary. By August and September, logs downstream from the trailhead often give you a way to cross without fording. Choose your method carefully. Once across Lincoln Creek, the trail ascends steeply for 0.5 mile to a service road and water viaduct. Then the trail continues in pine forest, crosses to the west side of Tabor Creek at 10,725 feet, emerges in a vast glacial valley at 1 mile, and continues to climb through meadows of pine and willow. At 2.8 miles, take a right on a use trail in a flat meadow of sparse willows at 11,700 feet. It switches back to the north on some rocky benches below a prominent rock glacier and then ascends a steeper slope against some cliffs near a waterfall before turning left (southwest) one more time on some grassy ramps to

Left: You must cross Lincoln Creek in order to hike farther up the Tabor basin. **Right:** A small climbers' trail can be found that leads to a hidden Tabor Lake.

Left: Tellurium Peak (right) with Tabor/Tellurium pass at center. **Right:** From Tabor/Tellurium pass, you can climb the west ridge of West Truro to explore more.

arrive at Tabor Lake. If you continue up the valley to the south from the 11,700-foot meadow trail junction, you will ascend gentle slopes to find Tabor Basin Lake tucked in at 11,840 feet in a beautiful place with panoramas of Tabor and Tellurium Peaks.

THE LOOP AND HIGH-RIDGE TRAVERSE

2. Tabor Peak (13,282 feet) to Tellurium Peak (13,200 feet): The Double-T Traverse (Class 3–4). Do this traverse in the opposite direction compared to what is described in entry #44a. From Tabor Lake, leave the west end of the lake, ascending scree for 800 feet to reach the narrow but accommodating north ridgeline of Tabor. From the summit of Tabor, the toughest portion of the just over 1-mile traverse south to Tellurium Peak is to downclimb the south ridge of the peak for several hundred feet. Continue south along this traverse and also climb some spicy towers two-thirds of the way across the ridgeline as you follow the ridge to the top of Tellurium. Give yourself two to four hours for this traverse from peak to peak. From here, the loop gets much easier. Descend gentle slopes to the east of Tellurium to a prominent connecting saddle between West Truro and Tellurium (12,900 feet) with a small tarn just north of the saddle. You may be able to pick up a use trail to descend south back into Tabor basin and to Tabor Basin Lake.

DR. JON'S EXTRA CREDIT

A. West Truro Peak (13,150 feet) (Class 3). Another peak worth visiting in the area is a steep climb of West Truro from the West Truro–Tellurium connecting saddle, and see if you can find Truro Lake. Take a swim in any one of the lakes mentioned here; you won't be disappointed!

TABOR LAKE—TABOR BASIN LAKE —"DOUBLE-T" TRAVERSE LOOP

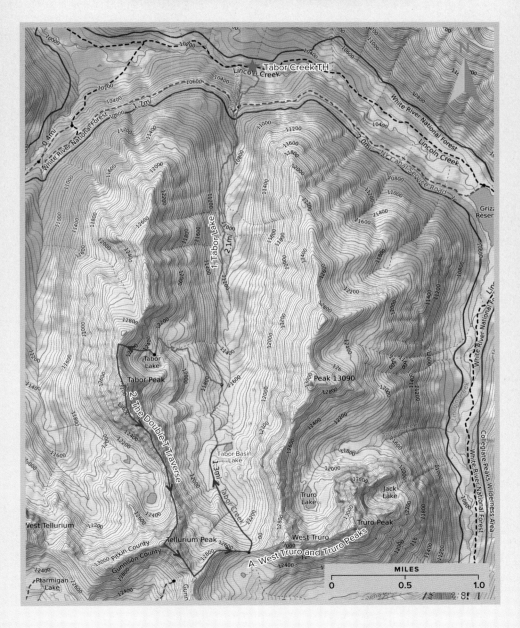

LINKINS LAKE —INDEPENDENCE LAKE —LOST MAN LAKE LOOP AND TWINING PEAK TO INDEPENDENCE PASS

45

Elevation Gain	515 feet for Linkins Lake; 1,000 feet for Independence Lake; 1,400 feet for Lost Man Lake Loop
Round-Trip Distance	1.4 miles for Linkins Lake; 4 miles for Independence Lake; 9 miles for the Lost Man Lake Loop
Trailhead	Linkins Lake/Independence Lake (11,500 feet)
Difficulty Ratings	Class 1–2 hike, mainly on trails to the lakes and some Class 2+ ridgelines for the traverses
Optimal Season	June 1 through October 15
Maps	Trails Illustrated #127 and #148; San Isabel National Forest

COMMENT: An easily accessed and scenic hike with many lakes, the Lost Man Lake Loop delivers. There are so many options in this high-altitude environment with views and wildflowers to boot. Get to the trailhead early to enjoy some high-mountain solitude.

Reflection in Linkins Lake.

Looking south to Independence Lake and Twining Peak. *Photo by Carrie Besnette Hauser*

GETTING THERE

Linkins Lake/Independence Lake Trailhead (11,500 feet). This trailhead is typically inaccessible until after Memorial Day because Independence Pass (Colorado Highway 82) may not be open until then. If coming from the east, follow Colorado Highway 82 for 1.5 miles west from the top of Independence Pass. If approaching from the west, travel about 18 miles east from Aspen on Colorado Highway 82. The trailhead is located on the north side of the first sharp hairpin turn on the west side of Independence Pass at 11,500 feet. In the summer of 2021, the US Forest Service built a brand-new pit toilet in the parking area only 25 feet from the paved road near Independence Creek at the trailhead.

THE LAKES

1. Linkins Lake (11,827 feet) and Independence Lake (12,306 feet) (Class 1). This alpine hike is almost entirely above tree line except at the entrance and exit points to the trailheads. The Lost Man Trailhead side is a bit more in the forest, but starting this car-to-car horseshoe loop from Linkins Lake Trailhead is the way to go. Leave the Linkins Lake Trailhead and hike north through willows and meadows. In the first 200 yards, you will reach a fork in the trail. The left fork takes you up a short switchbacking trail for a little over a mile to Linkins Lake, while the right fork continues up the broad glacial valley and above the timberline for 2 miles to Independence Lake. In early summer (June), this trail can be very muddy with lots of snow and meltwater through the willows on your way to Independence Lake.

Lost Man Lake.
*Photo by Carrie
Besnette Hauser*

THE LOOP

2. Lost Man Lake (12,480 feet) Loop (Class 1). From Independence Lake, continue over the 12,800-foot pass in the high alpine for 1.1 miles to the north to find
Lost Man Lake. The trail isn't too steep above the lake. From Lost Man pass, you will
be able to look back down the valley to the south for a nice view at the 13,988-foot
Grizzly Peak A. Typically in July, the wildflowers will be bursting to life in this entire
basin and near Lost Man Lake, which is tucked high on a glacial shelf with even more
mountains in the background. Complete the car-to-car loop by descending into Lost
Man basin for 6 miles to Lost Man Reservoir and the Lost Man Trailhead. Your final
2 to 3 miles of the trail will be in the pine forest, which can be nice and shady on a
hot summer day.

DR. JON'S EXTRA CREDIT

A. Twining Peak (13,711 feet) to Independence Pass (12,095 feet) (Class 2+).
From the shores of Independence Lake, travel north to Lost Man Pass. Before dropping down to Lost Man Lake, take the ridgeline east and then south over Peak 13,545'
and 13,711-foot Twining Peak. This extension of this fun ridgeline will take you all
the way over to your car at Independence Pass.

B. Lost Man Lake out-and-back (Class 2). If you are unable to create the car
shuttle to do the Lost Man Loop, simply hike to Independence Lake and Lost Man
Lake and then come back. This hike is an awesome 6-mile out-and-back with 1,600
feet of elevation gain, and you'll enjoy views on your descent of the basin that you
didn't necessarily see going up to Independence Lake and beyond. If you are really
ambitious, climb 13,300-foot Geissler Mountain to the west of Lost Man Pass.

LINKINS LAKE—INDEPENDENCE LAKE —LOST MAN LAKE LOOP AND TWINING PEAK TO INDEPENDENCE PASS

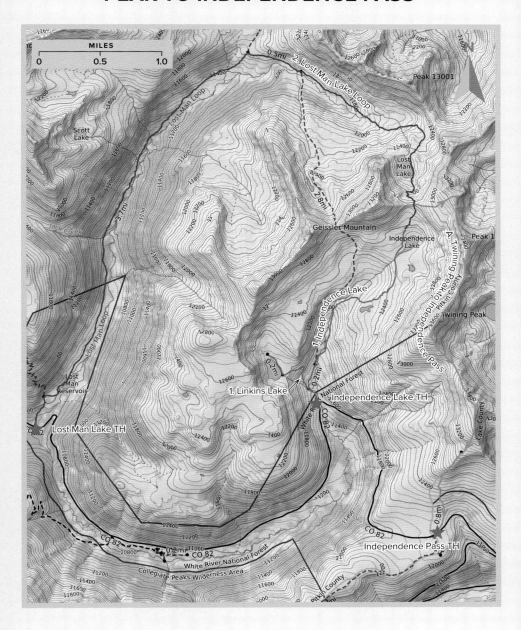

BEAR LAKE —MOUNT HARVARD TO MOUNT COLUMBIA TRAVERSE

46

Elevation Gain	2,550 feet for Bear Lake; 4,600 feet for Mount Harvard; 6,100 feet for the traverse to Mount Columbia Loop
Round-Trip Distance	10.5 miles for Bear Lake; 14 miles for Mount Harvard; 15 miles Mount Harvard to Mount Columbia Traverse Loop
Trailhead	North Cottonwood (9,880 feet)
Difficulty Rating	Class 1–2 hike, mainly on trails and portion of jagged ridgelines as well as off-trail boulder fields
Optimal Season	June 1 through November 1
Maps	Trails Illustrated #129 and #148; San Isabel National Forest

COMMENT: Mount Harvard, Colorado's third highest peak, boasts wild and scenic terrain, including Bear Lake, a gorgeous high-mountain lake far above the trees. Combine this lake visit with a climb of Harvard and even a traverse across to Mount Columbia, and you'll be able to explore a ton of terrain in this central part of the Sawatch Range that is high, scenic, and enjoyable.

Bear Lake is high and gorgeous.

Rolling along the ridgeline on Columbia as the sun sets.

GETTING THERE

North Cottonwood Trailhead (9,880 feet). From the Chaffee County Road 306/ US Highway 24 junction in the center of Buena Vista (at the stoplight), travel 0.4 mile on US Highway 24. Turn west on Chaffee County Road 350 (Crossman Avenue) and measure your distance. Travel west on Chaffee County 350 for 2.1 miles and upon reaching a T junction, turn north (right) onto Chaffee County 361. Chaffee County 361 turns to dirt at mile 2.5 and angles to the northwest. At mile 3, turn left (south) onto Chaffee County 365, which quickly turns to the west, entering the San Isabel National Forest at 5.5 miles. Through the forest, you will pass the Harvard Lakes Trailhead (mile 6.6) and the Colorado Trail. Continue on the road as it narrows and climbs to the North Cottonwood Trail and a circular turnaround area with parking at mile 8.2.

THE LAKE

1.   Bear Lake (12,400 feet) (Class 1). The first several miles of this hike are a long slog through the trees. The trek begins by hiking up the North Cottonwood Trail and crossing to the south side of North Cottonwood Creek on a bridge. Follow the trail for 1.5 miles and then cross the creek again to the north side and reach a trail junction. Take the right (north fork), which leads to Horn Fork Basin and Bear Lake in the direction of Mount Harvard. After another 2 miles, enter the Basin, pass the trail junction for Mount Columbia at mile 3.8, continue straight (left), and break out of the trees and into the meadows above timberline. From here, you can look north and see Harvard's south face. The hiking to timberline in this basin is quite easy. At

Looking northwest to Harvard, you can see the traverse from Harvard along the ridgeline.

mile 5 at 12,350 feet, the trail splits. Turn left (west) and follow the trail now above timberline toward a flattening part of the basin where you will arrive at Bear Lake among tundra, wildflowers, and boulders.

THE LOOP AND HIGH-RIDGE TRAVERSE

2. Mount Harvard (14,421 feet) and Columbia (14,073 feet) traverse (Class 2). After a visit to Bear Lake, follow the Mount Harvard Trail as it ascends to a broad flat area at 12,600 feet. Next head up to gain a shoulder on the northeast side of Peak 13,588'. Stay on the trail on the south side of this shoulder, enter a talus field, and switchback up the rocky terrain for 400 vertical feet to 13,000 feet on the crest of the shoulder in the basin. From here, you have a great view of Harvard's south face. Traverse the upper basin and climb the steep slope below the crest of Harvard's south ridgeline. There are several rock steps, cairns, and an easy-to-follow trail as it switches back and forth to the ridge. Once you gain the ridge, follow it north on a strong trail to the summit block at 14,370 feet. The summit block is the key to making the summit and staying Class 2 on the final pitch. Traverse a crack to the east and walk along narrow ledges to just east of the summit before jumping across large boulders back west and onto the summit for the final 25 feet.

From the summit of Harvard, your day is far from over. If the weather is good, proceed to traverse from Harvard to Columbia. This traverse is nearly 3 miles long and will add 1,500 feet to your day. Most people take two to four hours to complete this traverse; elite hikers and runners that know the terrain and can move quickly can take just one hour. Hike east, descending Harvard down to a prominent notch. Dip down on the east side of the ridge to bypass a rocky outcropping then aim for a

Columbia summit camp.

pointed rock formation at 14,100 feet on the ridge farther beyond. You will pass this rock formation on the right before picking up a faint trail through some talus on the south side of the ridge. Next you will again reach the ridgeline, continue southeast on a trail again toward prominent Peak 13,516', then go farther down to about 13,400 feet and contour around Peak 13,516', then descend down the east-facing ridge of this point. Hike down the ridge and turn right between 12,700 and 12,500 feet whenever it feels right to leave the ridge.

Contour south into the talus near the base of the connecting ridgeline, make your way into a semi-bowl-shaped basin, and cross lots of talus. Now you can look across the basin and see the pyramid-like shape of the northern aspect of Columbia. It's time to go up! Once you get a bit higher and near the ridgeline at 13,000 feet, Columbia's summit will come into view. Next, hike right and to the south around Peak 13,497' and get on the ridge crest. Follow this ridge crest for a little over 500 feet to the summit. From the top, you can use Mount Columbia's south slopes route via the south ridge to get back to your car at the trailhead.

DR. JON'S EXTRA CREDIT
A. Kroenke Lake (11,500 feet) (Class 2). From the trail fork approximately 2 miles from the car, instead of hiking into Horn Fork Basin, consider taking the trail to the west for 2.75 miles and exploring the North Cottonwood Creek basin and a jaunt to Kroenke Lake, which has a cool little island in the middle of the lake.
B. Bear Lake ice skating (Class 1). In late October to as late as the first week of December on a cold and dry fall, Bear Lake is prime for cold nights, high elevation, and glazed ice to skate, if you are willing to hike over 5 miles to find it.

BEAR LAKE—MOUNT HARVARD TO MOUNT COLUMBIA TRAVERSE

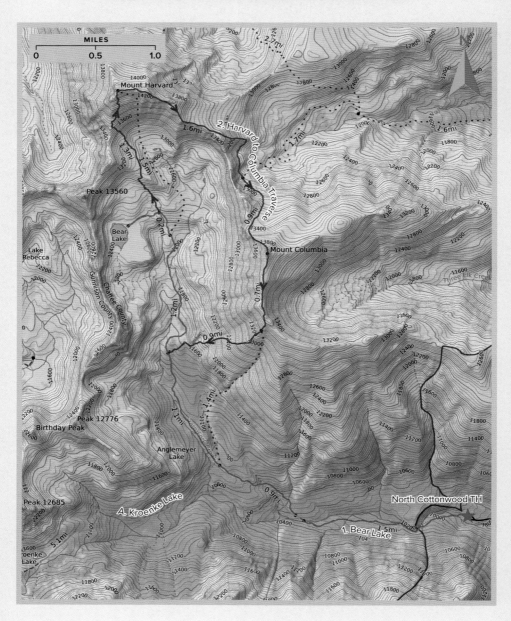

MILES

0   0.5   1.0

Mount Harvard

2.7mi

14000

14200

13800

Peak 13560

2. Harvard to Columbia Traverse

1.6mi

1.7mi

1.6mi

1.3mi

1.5mi

Bear Lake

0.2mi

0.9mi

Lake Rebecca

Mount Columbia

Chaffee County

Gunnison County

0.7mi

Three Elk Creek

0.9mi

1.4mi

Peak 12776

Birthday Peak

2.1mi

Anglemeyer Lake

0.9mi

North Cottonwood TH

Peak 12685

A. Kroenke Lake

1. Bear Lake

1.5mi

5.1mi

Kroenke Lake

CHAPTER 7

ELK RANGE

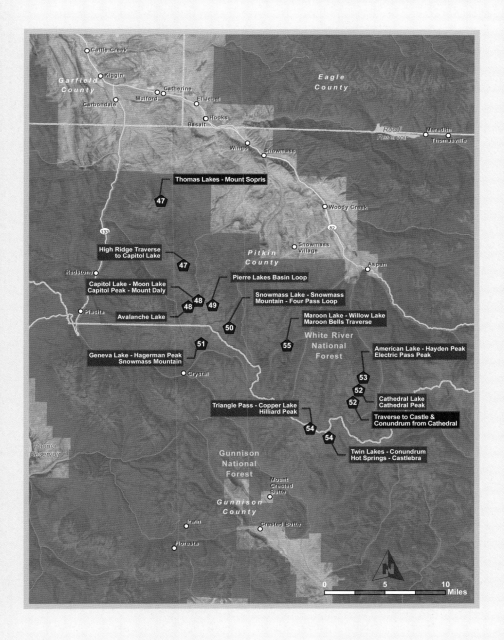

Cattle Creek
Kiggin
Garfield County
Catherine
Mulford
Carbondale
El Jebel
Hooks
Basalt

Eagle County

Roedi Reservoir
Meredith
Thomasville

Wingo
Snowmass

Thomas Lakes - Mount Sopris
47

Woody Creek

133

82

Snowmass Village

Pitkin County

High Ridge Traverse to Capitol Lake
47

Redstone

Aspen

Pierre Lakes Basin Loop

Capitol Lake - Moon Lake
Capitol Peak - Mount Daly
48 **48**

49

Snowmass Lake - Snowmass Mountain - Four Pass Loop

Placita

Avalanche Lake
50

55

Maroon Lake - Willow Lake
Maroon Bells Traverse

White River National Forest

American Lake - Hayden Peak
Electric Pass Peak

Geneva Lake - Hagerman Peak
Snowmass Mountain
51

53

Crystal

52

52

Cathedral Lake
Cathedral Peak

Triangle Pass - Copper Lake
Hilliard Peak

Traverse to Castle &
Conundrum from Cathedral

54

54

Twin Lakes - Conundrum
Hot Springs - Castlebra

Paonia Reservoir

Gunnison National Forest

Mount Crested Butte

Gunnison County

Irwin

Crested Butte

Floresta

N

0   5   10
Miles

THOMAS LAKES —MOUNT SOPRIS —TRAVERSE TO CAPITOL LAKE

47

Elevation Gain	2,100 feet for Thomas Lakes; 4,850 feet for Mount Sopris; 5,900 feet for Capitol Lake Loop Traverse
Round-Trip Distance	8 miles for Thomas Lakes; 14 miles Mount Sopris; 21 miles for the high-ridge traverse to Capitol Lake Loop
Trailhead	Thomas Lakes (8,100 feet) (also referred to as the Dinkle Lake Divide, Prince Creek Divide, or West Sopris Creek Trailhead)
Difficulty Ratings	Class 1–2 hike, mainly on trails to the lakes and some Class 2+ ridgelines for the traverses
Optimal Season	June 1 through October 15
Maps	Trails Illustrated #128 and #143; White River National Forest

COMMENT: Mount Sopris dominates the view from the Roaring Fork Valley near Carbondale and Glenwood Springs. This peak will inspire any person who lays eyes on it to climb its alluring slopes! One of the largest rock glaciers in all of the American West carves out one of the northern valleys from Sopris and can be viewed from the summit.

Upper Thomas Lake; Sopris in the frame.

Left: Approaching Mount Sopris on a bluebird day. **Right:** A fun and very high ridgeline above the surrounding Roaring Fork Valley.

GETTING THERE

Thomas Lakes Trailhead/Dinkle Lake Divide/West Sopris Creek Trailhead (8,100 feet). From the town of Carbondale (west of Aspen and southeast of Glenwood Springs), travel south on Colorado Highway 133 for approximately 1.4 miles. Turn left on Prince Creek Road (which turns to dirt after the first mile) and go 6 miles to a fork in the road. Take a right at the fork and follow it for 2 miles. The trailhead is 0.25 mile before Dinkle Lake. The road generally melts out by the end of April.

THE LAKES

1. West Sopris Creek to Thomas Lakes (10,220 feet) (Class 1). From the trailhead at Dinkle Lake Divide, look for the Forest Service trailhead signs a few hundred feet south of the road; the trail starts up an obvious cut behind these signs and is gradual because it used to be an old wagon road. Sometimes mountaineers in spring snowmobile up the trail corridor to Thomas Lakes and the nearby wilderness boundary. Follow the old roadcut as it makes a long climbing traverse west, then switchbacks, and climbs east to pass around a shoulder at 9,200 feet. Follow the obvious roadcut for a few hundred yards before the trail traverses to the east. In 1.8 miles from the trailhead, you will arrive at a trail junction; follow the signs to Thomas Lakes (right turn) from this first trail junction. Once you've arrived at the shelf above a moderate brush slope (9,600 feet), follow the Thomas Lakes Trail for 2 more miles to reach the lakes. Follow the obvious trail through aspen and conifer to another open area at 10,000 feet. Continue southwest up a small gulch to the vicinity of Lower (northern) Thomas Lake (10,200 feet). The first lake appears through the trees to your right, and you can easily access its shores by some social trails. A five-

Left: Looking south to spot the route for the full high-ridge traverse toward Capitol Peak and Capitol Lake. **Right:** The high ridge extends for nearly 10 miles on moderate terrain.

to ten-minute walk across a flat section of the main trail to the south will bring you to the Upper Thomas Lake (southern lake) surrounded by pine, aspen, and several other deciduous bushes and trees. There is camping in designated sites near both lakes, so please do your part and leave no trace.

THE HIGH-RIDGE TRAVERSE

2. Mount Sopris (12,953 feet), northeast ridge and slopes (Class 2). After a visit to Thomas Lakes, follow the Mount Sopris Trail as it departs the southern lake to the southeast. From the lakes, the trail switches back to gain higher terrain, and as it leaves the timberline after several switchbacks above the lake, there is a prominent wide ridge that rises to the east subsidiary summit of the mountain. The trail will gain the ridge, and the views will get ever more impressive as you get higher. Once on the ridge, hike through a glade to a broad saddle (10,800 feet) near timberline. Above timberline, the terrain steepens, and the trail gets rockier and rougher. The trail sticks to the scrub-covered ridge crest, which leads to a lower-angled area at 11,400 feet where you will be unprotected from wind as you leave the trees for good. Continue up the low-angled terrain to a narrow but rocky trail section of the ridge. Beware of the drop-offs to the south of this ridgeline but stay on the trail and walk to the right (northwest) side of the ridge, next gaining another headwall, which is pretty steep and snow covered until early July. From 11,800 feet to the crest of the ridge at 12,000 feet, take the rocky ridge trail to the left of the headwall (this may require an ice ax in June) and stick with the ridge, which will level out and take you to the east summit (12,085 feet). Follow the ridge from the subsidiary east summit for 0.8 mile west along a broad and rocky ridge to the main summit and Sopris's highest point. There is also a summit farther west, 0.5 mile away, that is nearly as high.

Dropping off the ridge from Capitol/Avalanche Pass to Capitol Lake.

DR. JON'S EXTRA CREDIT

A. Mount Sopris Super Traverse to Capitol Lake (11,500 feet) (Class 2+).
From the summit of Mount Sopris, retrace your steps back east to the crest of the east ridge for 0.8 mile at 12,000 feet. From the prominent eastern ridge point, instead of returning to Thomas Lakes, turn south and descend to timberline aiming for a notable ridgeline that extends through the sparse trees on a spine that continues seemingly forever into the distance in the direction of Capitol Peak. Do some map homework and exploration, and you can follow this ridgeline for 8.5 miles across many 12,000-foot summits on a scenic and high ridge, eventually arriving at Capitol Pass and descending 0.5 mile from Capitol Pass to Capitol Lake. Distances from Thomas Lakes Trailhead to Capitol Lake on this traverse are 15 miles and then an additional 6 miles to get out to Capitol Lake Trailhead from Capitol Lake. The traverse from trailhead to trailhead is 21 miles and 6,000 vertical feet. Leave a car shuttle at Capitol Lake Trailhead for a full day of adventure. The time to do this car-to-car loop traverse varies from twelve to eighteen hours. You can consider an overnight backpack along the way. If you can't do a car shuttle, backpacking or longer options on trails from the Capitol Creek Trailhead allow you to connect the Buzzard Basin and Hay Park Trails to loop back to your car on a mega loop.

B. Mount Sopris, west summit (12,950 feet) (Class 1). If you want an amazing place to meditate, take the super easy ten-minute walk across the ridge from the main summit to the top of Sopris's west summit. The view from this perch is arguably even better than the main summit because of the huge relief down into the Roaring Fork Valley and western Colorado.

C. Thomas Lakes ice skate (Class 1). From late October to early December, "Wild Ice" season can linger, and it can be really amazing to ice skate Thomas Lakes on a cool and sunny late fall day when the ice is smooth and thick.

THOMAS LAKES—MOUNT SOPRIS
—TRAVERSE TO CAPITOL LAKE (NORTH)

THOMAS LAKES—MOUNT SOPRIS —TRAVERSE TO CAPITOL LAKE (SOUTH)

CAPITOL LAKE —MOON LAKE—CAPITOL PEAK—MOUNT DALY —AVALANCHE LAKE

48

Elevation Gain	3,500 feet for Moon Lake; 6,200 feet for Capitol Lake Loop; 5,900 feet for Capitol Peak
Round-Trip Distance	13.5 miles for Moon Lake; 19.5 miles for Capitol Lake Loop; 16.5 miles for Capitol Peak
Trailhead	Snowmass Creek (8,400 feet)
Difficulty Ratings	Class 1–2 hike, mainly on trails and game trails with some Class 2+ ridgelines and challenging Class 3 and 4 for the traverses and peaks
Optimal Season	June 1 through October 15
Maps	Trails Illustrated #128; White River National Forest

COMMENT: Capitol Peak is a slice of Colorado that is unlike any other. While 95 percent of the people who climb Capitol Peak or visit Capitol Lake use the Capitol Lake Trailhead, the routes described here are reserved for the adventurers who want to see this area but aren't afraid of the extra effort and have the ability to hike and travel across a bit more rugged terrain. The basins and lakes in this entry are glacially cut and wild, yet some of the best in Colorado. You really have to understand route-finding and map reading to get deep into this wilderness and back out safely.

Traversing the infamous Knife Edge on Capitol.

Left: Clark Peak and the West Snowmass Creek drainage in fall. **Right:** Capitol Lake is a special place.

GETTING THERE

Snowmass Creek Trailhead (8,400 feet). From the town of Glenwood Springs, take Colorado Highway 82 south for 28 miles to the small town of Snowmass, located at a small gas station and lone stoplight right on Colorado Highway 82. Or travel north on Colorado Highway 82 for 13 miles from Maroon Creek Road on Aspen's north side.

At the stoplight in Snowmass, turn west on Snowmass Creek Road and travel 1.7 miles to a T junction. Turn left and continue up the road for 7.3 miles where the road turns to dirt. You will pass several ranches in a gorgeous mountain valley along the way. At 10.7 miles, cross Snowmass Creek on a bridge; the road is usually plowed to the bridge until it melts out in late April or early May. At 10.9 miles, turn right at another T junction. Proceed to the gate for Snowmass Falls Ranch at 11.3 miles and find a good-sized parking area and a trailhead kiosk.

THE LAKES

1. Moon Lake (11,745 feet) and Capitol Lake (11,500 feet) (Class 2). This is a gorgeous alpine hike through meadows, rugged terrain, and high places. Start from the gate at the Snowmass Trailhead and hike through the aspens and pine on a partial ditch trail for 1.4 miles to a viewpoint of a very large meadow across the Snowmass Creek where you will arrive at a trail junction. Take a horseshoe turn right (north) on the West Snowmass Creek Trail and descend to Snowmass Creek.

Capitol Lake—Moon Lake—Capitol Peak—Mount Daly—Avalanche Lake

Moon Lake and Moon Lake tarn (left) from the summit of Daly with Clark Peak behind.

Ford the creek (be careful in June and July!) and follow the West Snowmass Creek Trail as it ascends, leaves the large meadow, and goes into more aspens. At 2.5 miles, the trail flattens out into a very large meadow with great views of Clark Peak and the upper valley. Cross a small creek and ascend aspens for another 0.5 mile to 10,400 feet in darker pines. Look for a minor trail junction and leave the main West Snowmass Creek Trail, turning left. You may pass a sheep-herding camp in a flat area and then do an ascending traverse through another meadow before the trail gets steeper through yet another pine forest. Basically, you are contouring the larger valley below and heading southwest toward slopes that are under the southeast aspects of Mount Daly. There is one great use trail in particular that traverses the entire valley and gets you to the main chute under Mount Daly's east slopes at 11,400 feet. Once you reach timberline, look southwest and toward a prominent saddle/pass between Mount Daly and a pinnacle-looking, orangish peak feature. A game trail can be followed here for nearly a mile to gain a great viewpoint at 11,900 feet in the upper basin near Moon Lake. In this area, if you are still planning on climbing Capitol Peak or camping, the terrain becomes post-glacial with large boulders, talus, and scree with a few sparse tree stands. Moon Lake is located south of this prominent pass; you just have to read your map to confirm where it is tucked in. Moon Lake is **not** the small lake far below this shelf of orange pinnacles in the trees down in a hole at 11,500 feet in the valley.

From Moon Lake, follow a rugged landscape of boulders and then ascend to a grassy col to your west for 0.6 mile to the 12,500-foot connecting saddle between Capitol Peak and Mount Daly. From here, you have an awesome view down to Capitol Lake and get to decide where your journey can take you.

THE LOOP

2. Capitol Lake Loop (11,500 feet) (Class 2). From the Capitol-Daly saddle, follow the Capitol Peak Trail west for 0.75 mile as it drops 1,000 feet to the shores of Capitol Lake. This lake is a great place to go for a swim and enjoy the towering view of Capitol Peak. To continue the loop, leave Capitol Lake, hiking north on the descending Capitol Creek Trail. Leave the meadows and enter the pine forest for 2.5 miles. You will cross a meadow at 10,100 feet before meeting a trail junction for West Snowmass Creek Trail in sparse pines. Turn right and follow the West Snowmass Creek Trail as it loops back over a pass for 4.5 miles and back to the West Snowmass basin in a familiar meadow that you hiked up earlier in the morning with Clark Peak as the backdrop (or day prior if you did a backpacking adventure). Continue back to the West Snowmass Creek/Snowmass Creek Trails and eventually the trailhead.

THE HIGH-RIDGE TRAVERSE

3. Capitol Peak (14,130 feet) (Class 4). Capitol Peak is arguably Colorado's most difficult and dangerous fourteener. How much fun is climbing this peak from the nonstandard drainage? After a visit to Moon Lake, instead of hiking to the Capitol-Daly saddle, continue west then south, climbing a rocky and very rugged glacial basin for 1.25 miles to reach the top of Colorado's K2 at 13,664 feet. To get to the top of K2, some Class 3 and easy Class 4 moves are required on the east side directly on the ridge spine. From K2, consider your future. You can see the entire northeast ridge from here. Descend some drop-offs to your north to access the ridge proper, and then beyond K2, you will need to cross the 100-foot-long infamous knife edge. The flat section of ridge is on very solid granite rock but drops off 2,000 feet on each side. After carefully crossing the knife edge, follow the ridge for several hundred more yards on easier terrain, and then from a crack/col known as the "Secret Chute," ascend some tougher and steeper Class 3 and 4 pitches of granite along the ridgeline. Everything to the north of the ridgeline spine drops off dangerously, so use caution. This section is getting easier and easier over the years due to massive amounts of fourteener climbers who have been visiting Capitol Peak. You can find fragments of trail corridor in several places that make the climb safer and easier with less loose rock. Stay on the ridge's south side to traverse to a prominent rock rib at 13,800 feet and then ascend directly north and northwest on some granite slabs and solid rock

Left: Capitol takes on a whole new appearance from above 13,000 feet on Daly. **Right:** Sunrise ascending the final pitches of Capitol Peak.

to get to the summit ridge. For the final 50 to 100 feet, you will traverse below the south side of the ridge or get on the ridge proper to climb to the highest point. Well done! Now you have to get down safely.

DR. JON'S EXTRA CREDIT

A. Avalanche Lake (10,702 feet) (Class 2). From the shores of Capitol Lake, hike east for 0.5 mile to the 12,085-foot saddle of Capitol Pass, sometimes called East Avalanche Pass. From the pass, descend for 1,500 feet through some stunning meadows to the west for an additional 1.6 miles to reach the valley floor and a trail junction near Avalanche Creek. Turn left (south) and hike the Avalanche Lake Trail for 0.5 mile to reach Avalanche Lake. This out-and-back from Capitol Lake adds 2,400 feet of elevation and 5 miles to your already big day.

B. Clark Peak (13,561 feet) (Class 3–4). Do some map studying, but there are some fantastic peaks to the south of Moon Lake that have been climbed by very few people. Clark Peak and Peaks 13,040' and 12,903' are all challenging and give you spectacular perches over Pierre Lakes basin.

C. Mount Daly (13,302 feet) (Class 3). On your way out, if the weather is still good, consider traversing across from the Capitol-Daly saddle at 12,500 feet to the summit of Mount Daly. Named for former National Geographic Society President Augustus Daly, this Class 3 ridge is super fun and gives you an amazing perspective of Capitol from afar.

CAPITOL LAKE—MOON LAKE
—CAPITOL PEAK—MOUNT DALY
—AVALANCHE LAKE

249

PIERRE LAKES BASIN LOOP TO MOON LAKE AND CAPITOL PEAK

49

Elevation Gain	4,000 feet for Pierre Lakes; 4,800 feet for Moon Lake; 5,800 feet for Capitol Peak
Round-Trip Distance	16 miles for Pierre Lakes; 24 miles for Moon Lake Loop; 26 miles for Capitol Peak Loop
Trailhead	Snowmass Creek (8,400 feet)
Difficulty Ratings	Class 1–3 hike with some on trails to the lakes but mostly rugged off-trail navigation, and some Class 2+ to Class 4 challenges on ridgelines for the traverses and peaks
Optimal Season	June 15 through October 1
Maps	Trails Illustrated #128; White River National Forest

COMMENT: This is a special place where there are no trails to access these amazing lakes, which occupy a massive glacial basin between Capitol Peak, Snowmass Mountain, and Clark Peak. When you are in the basin, you may feel more like you are in the Himalayas than in Colorado. All routes to get into this basin are rough, isolated, full of wildlife, and reserved for the experienced and strong alpinist. Don't take this place lightly and please leave no trace of your visit here.

The view of Snowmass and the waterfall leading into Pierre Lakes basin.

Sunset colors over Pierre Lakes basin are out of this world: Clark Peak (left) and Maroon Bells (center) with Snowmass (right).

GETTING THERE

Snowmass Creek (8,400 feet). For trailhead access see entry #48 for Capitol Lake from Moon Lake—Capitol Peak Traverse to Mount Daly—Avalanche Lake.

THE LAKES

1. Pierre Lakes (12,106 feet, 12,185 feet, 12,346 feet) (Class 3). *This hike isn't easy and includes some very challenging off-trail navigation.* Start from the gate at the Snowmass Creek Trailhead and hike through the aspens and pine on a partial ditch trail, the Maroon-Snowmass Trail #1975, for 1.4 miles to a viewpoint of a very large meadow across Snowmass Creek where you will arrive at a trail junction. Take a left turn (straight and south) and stay on Trail #1975. The trail passes through a wilderness gate at 1.75 miles and the wilderness boundary shortly after that. The hike for the next 2 miles is awesome through old-growth aspens primarily. Consider a visit here in September when the colors are popping.

Around mile 4 and 9,120 feet, you will arrive at the first significant switchback for the main Maroon Bells–Snowmass Trail. At this point, you are right near Snowmass Creek and can descend to the creek on a little switchback side trail by leaving the main trail to the right (straight) and not following the trail as it switches back to the left. You'll generally want to cross Snowmass Creek as close to Bear Creek as possible to avoid unnecessary bushwhacking on the far side, but it can be difficult to discern this drainage from Copper Creek, which is about 0.15 mile below Bear Creek. Crossing this creek in July is much more challenging and dangerous than in

September. In some years, fallen aspen trees in a few places can help get you across, but in most years you'll just have to ford the creek. Be sure to unbuckle your waist strap just in case!

After you cross Snowmass Creek, the terrain will naturally funnel you into the Bear Creek drainage and up the north side of the creek. A decent climbers' trail leads from Snowmass Creek into the drainage where navigation is fairly straight-forward up to Bear Creek Waterfall. The unmaintained route runs along Bear Creek through intervals of meadow, open rock, tall brush, and timber (at the 4.3-mile mark). Terrain is rough and grassy at times, but grades are generally moderate with easy navigation along the creek. Raspberries are found everywhere across open slopes. Be mindful of bears, especially where the vegetation gets thick. You'll find a big opening in the valley at the edge of a long rockslide from which you'll see Bear Creek Waterfall (5.1 miles, 9,650 feet). Cross this rocky section to a grove of willows between you and the base of the falls (5.3 miles, 9,850 feet). You can climb up and around this rugged portion, but it's best to stay low and punch through to the far side where you'll find cairns in some years leading up the right side of the waterfall (5.4 miles, 9,850 feet).

Reflection off Snowmass Massif in Pierre Lakes basin.

Left: It's always special to share the summit of Capitol with great friends. **Right:** Rugged columbines with Capitol and Pierre Lakes basin.

Cairns lead straight up with Class 3 scrambling in places. You can make out the easiest switchbacking climbing route by looking back and forth on the rocky cliffs as you ascend. You'll likely lose one route and pick up another by following natural lines. Dense brush can present a bigger challenge than rock or pitch on this scramble; the best way is often a hard-nosed punch right through it. The route climbs more than 750 feet across boulders, open ledges, and brush before tilting back down to glades above the waterfall (note the waterfall isn't even 300 feet tall, but the route leads you higher to avoid cliffs). Head toward the creek where a good path will soon emerge, leading you higher more easily (5.6 miles, 10,560 feet). Note your transition point from brush to open tree glades because it's difficult to find on the return. The waterfall descent is equally challenging and time-consuming. Routefinding is especially important on the return, as it's possible to get cliffed-out if you aren't careful.

Once above the waterfall, travel moderates to another long, open rockslide (6 miles, 10,570 feet). The valley is flat here, but the center is cluttered by willow, forcing you up the rock. Head straight across to find a grassy track that leads to a well-marked creek crossing (6.4 miles, 10,790 feet). This is where Bear Creek splits and the route crosses the north fork to a steep ridge between forks (the north fork leads to the lower lakes, and the south fork leads to the largest lake). The route follows some cairns and a faint use trail in some places up this steep ridge while favoring the south side and losing sight of the north side of the basin. Both route-finding and terrain become much easier as you pass tree line (7.3 miles, 11,525 feet) into alpine meadows along the south fork of Bear Creek. Follow the creek to a steep rocky ridge (7.8 miles), which you'll hike up to reach the Pierre Lakes basin with the lakes in close proximity (8 miles, 12,190 feet). Take your time to enjoy this place; there is a good chance this could be a once-in-a-lifetime destination. Each lake has some grassy banks and small but accommodating campsites so you can stay the night in a spectacular location.

THE LOOP

2. Wandering Dutchman Traverse to Moon Lake (Class 3). After a visit to the Pierre Lakes, mainly the largest lake at 12,185 feet, look south and travel up the basin toward the northern Pierre Lake for 0.5 mile on large boulders and relatively flat terrain. This area will really put your rock-hopping skills to the test. When you are on the east side of the upper lake, look north to view a significant notch between Capitol Peak to the west, Colorado's K2 closer to you to the northwest, and Clark Peak to your northeast. This notch is known as the Wandering Dutchman Couloir. This couloir is the key to exiting the Pierre Lakes basin. Ascend the gully to your north for 800 feet on some rocky slabs and minor climbing trail (Class 2–3). You will reach the notch and be able to look down a vast glacial valley to your north with Mount Daly in the distance. Most years, leftover snow and glacial firn will be present on the north side of the notch and can be very frozen and slick on your descent into the bouldered basin below, so use caution. Descend the basin for a good mile north and then head east to find Moon Lake at 11,745 feet. Your complete loop out of West Snowmass Creek basin back to the trailhead includes descending from Moon Lake to the east and finding the West Snowmass Creek Trail. (See the previous entry, #48, for more details.)

DR. JON'S EXTRA CREDIT

A. Capitol Peak (14,130 feet) (Class 4). From the notch at the top of the Wandering Dutchman couloir, turn left and ascend the upper basin to Colorado's K2 (13,664 feet). The climb of Capitol Peak is further described in the previous entry (#48). Have you ever heard of Satan's Ridge? It's the traverse from Capitol to Snowmass on one of the most dangerous ridges in the world. A few hearty souls have crossed this ridge. Have a look when you are on the top of Capitol; it's stunning.

B. Heckert Pass (12,525 feet) (Class 3). Do some map studying and exploring, and you can travel south from the southeastern corner of Pierre Lakes basin over Heckert Pass and find your way to Snowmass Lake for a great loop by connecting to the Maroon Bells–Snowmass Trail to return to the trailhead.

PIERRE LAKES BASIN LOOP TO MOON LAKE AND CAPITOL PEAK

SNOWMASS LAKE —SNOWMASS MOUNTAIN —FOUR PASS LOOP

50

Elevation Gain	2,600 feet for Snowmass Lake; 5,700 feet for Snowmass Mountain; 9,200 feet for Four Pass Loop
Round-Trip Distance	16 miles for Snowmass Lake; 21 miles for Snowmass Mountain; 40 miles for Four Pass Loop
Trailhead	Snowmass Creek (8,400 feet)
Difficulty Ratings	Class 1–2 hike, with some on trails to the lakes and Four Pass Loop and some Class 2+ to Class 3 challenges on ridgelines for the traverses and peaks
Optimal Season	June 15 through October 1
Maps	Trails Illustrated #128; White River National Forest

COMMENT: Snowmass Mountain is one of Colorado's best and isolated wild and scenic places. In recent years Snowmass Lake has become crowded in the summer as backpackers hike the Four Pass Loop. Starting in 2022, there will be a permit sys-

Idyllic Snowmass Lake.

Snowmass Lake from above.

tem implemented by the local Aspen Ranger District. More information on the new permit system can be found on recreation.gov by searching Snowmass Lake or Four Pass Loop in the Maroon Bells–Snowmass Wilderness. Practice leave no trace, carry a required bear canister, and consider a trip during the week or in late fall to avoid the crowds. Snowmass Mountain is a worthy fourteener objective but use caution on the namesake Snowmass snowfields when skiing or glissading in June or July.

GETTING THERE

Snowmass Creek (8,400 feet). For trailhead access, see entry #48 for Capitol Lake from Moon Lake—Capitol Peak Traverse to Mount Daly—Avalanche Lake.

Snowmass and Capitol from Buckskin Pass.

THE LAKES

1. Snowmass Lake (11,000 feet) (Class 1–2). From the trailhead, follow the Maroon-Snowmass Trail (#1975) for 8 miles to Snowmass Lake. At about 4 miles, catch a stellar view of Snowmass massif up the Bear Creek basin (Pierre Lakes basin) to the west. At 6 miles, you

Snowmass is rugged and steep near the summit.

will reach the second of two lakes and an interesting crossing on a logjam, which changes from year to year. Continue up the trail through some thicker pinewoods for the final 1.5 mile, reaching the lake at 11,000 feet.

THE HIGH RIDGE-TRAVERSE/CLIMB

2. Snowmass Mountain (14,092 feet) (Class 3). After a visit to Snowmass Lake, skirt around the south side of the lake on a well-worn climbers' trail through the willows to access the snowfield and the upper portion of the peak. In a strong snow year, you may reach the far side of the lake and then have to ascend snow for the first 500 feet above the lake to ascend a shallow gully. The gully in late summer holds a climbers' trail next to a splendid waterfall and affords access to the main snowfield and much gentler slopes on Snowmass higher up. Ascend slopes from 12,400 to 13,400 feet (usually moderate snow in early summer) before climbing to a notch at 13,700 feet on Snowmass's southeast ridge. Wrap around the west side of the ridge for 400 feet on Class 3 white granite to reach the top of Snowmass.

DR. JON'S EXTRA CREDIT: THE LOOP

A. Four Pass Loop (Class 2). Adventure awaits! After a night camping at Snowmass Lake, do your research to make the best decisions about days on the trail and destinations. By 2022, there will be a new permit system in place for the summer and fall seasons. Check recreation.gov for more information. If you have a high level of fitness, this loop can be done in an eight- to sixteen-hour day (24 miles around the loop) from Snowmass Lake. You could potentially just leave your camp at Snowmass Lake for two nights and do the loop in one big day or seek out other campsites. I recommend going clockwise on the loop for best views and grades.

SNOWMASS LAKE—SNOWMASS MOUNTAIN—FOUR PASS LOOP

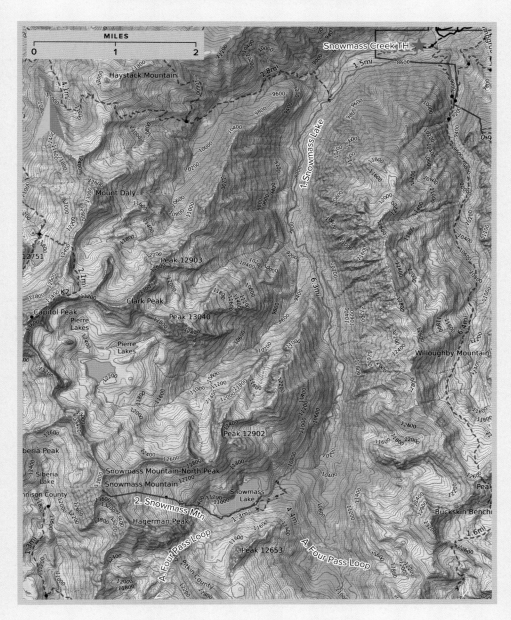

GENEVA LAKE —HAGERMAN PEAK —SNOWMASS MOUNTAIN

51

Elevation Gain	1,350 feet for Geneva Lake; 1,850 feet for Siberia Lake; 4,600 feet for Hagerman Peak; 4,800 feet for Snowmass Mountain; 5,285 feet for Snowmass to Hagerman High Traverse Loop
Round-Trip Distance	4.2 miles for Geneva Lake; 8.8 miles for Snowmass Mountain; 10.4 miles for Hagerman Peak Mountain; 10.2 miles for the Snowmass to Hagerman High Traverse Loop
Trailhead	Lead King Basin/Geneva Lake (9,700 feet)
Difficulty Ratings	Class 1–2 hike with some on trails to the lakes, and some Class 2+ to Class 3 challenges on ridgelines for the traverses and peaks
Optimal Season	June 15 through October 1
Maps	Trails Illustrated #128; White River National Forest

COMMENT: Snowmass Mountain is one of Colorado's best and isolated wild and scenic places. This alternative approach is the best way to enjoy the Maroon Bells–Snowmass Wilderness with far fewer people, and it gets you up high on a Centennial thirteener as well as a rugged fourteener. The wildflowers can be magical near Geneva Lake, so consider camping here to really make the most of it.

Reflection on Geneva Lake.

Looking west from near the summit of Snowmass while on the S ridge, you can spot Geneva Lake (left) and Little Gem Lake (right).

GETTING THERE

Lead King Basin/Geneva Lake Trailhead (9,700 feet). Travel Colorado Highway 133 south for 22 miles to a well-marked junction at the base of McClure Pass. Turn left (southeast) on County Road 3 and follow signs to Marble for 6 miles. Pass through Marble in a series of left and then right turns, three times to be exact. On the southeast part of town, the road turns to dirt, passes Beaver Lake on your right, and begins to ascend an ever increasingly rough dirt road. Following a significant creek crossing at mile 8.2 (2 miles past Marble) is a noticeable place to park a passenger car. The road requires a four-wheel-drive high-clearance vehicle from here. Stay left at any road junctions on FSR 315 and continue for 6.9 miles on this road as it passes a significant avalanche debris field from 2019, then switches back up Lost Trail Creek to 10,900 feet between Lost Trail Creek and Silver Creek, crosses Silver Creek, and then with spectacular meadow views and steep drop-offs, descends into Lead King Basin to a well-marked trailhead.

THE LAKES

1.   Geneva Lake (11,020 feet) and Siberia Lake (11,869 feet) (Class 1–2).
From the trailhead, follow the Geneva Lake Trail (#1973) for 2 miles to Geneva Lake. Make sure to stay left in the first 0.5 mile as the right fork is the Fravert Basin Trail to access the Four Pass Loop, while the left fork will allow you to ascend the basin steeply past some cliffs and an awesome waterfall on the north side of Lead King Basin, and you will arrive at the west side of Geneva Lake at mile 2.1 in the pine trees. You will have a nice view of Snowmass Mountain's "S" ridge, as well as Hagerman's

The traverse to Hagerman on the spine of the ridgeline is challenging.

south and west faces on your approach and when you get to the lake. Take advantage of several nice, designated camping sites near the trail above the lake's west and north sides. You can continue up the trail on the north side of Geneva Lake, pass a trail junction, and continue north on the valley's west side through some open meadows and reach Little Gem Lake (11,669 feet) about a mile north of Geneva Lake. The trail continues on a grassy shelf above the valley, steers north through some grassy openings between some rock features, parallels a creek, and arrives in a small tucked-in lake between some rock glacial features in another 0.6 miles. This is the gorgeous Siberia Lake.

THE HIGH-RIDGE TRAVERSE/CLIMB

2. Snowmass Mountain (14,092 feet) (Class 3). After a visit to Geneva Lake, follow the trail north toward Little Gem Lake and Siberia Lake as described above. After passing Little Gem Lake, continue through a grassy saddle and head east toward Snowmass Mountain to cross a creek that has seemingly emerged out of the rocks. Once across the creek, you will see the west face of Snowmass poised to stare you down. Do an ascending traverse from the creek crossing at 11,700 feet to the south to access the sharply defined S-ridge of Snowmass. Once you get to 12,200 feet, you can curve your way onto the ridge directly by climbing some small cliff bands (Class 3, minor Class 4). After the initial steepness on the ridge, the rock gets delightfully solid, and the best line is right on the crest for nearly 1,500 feet to the summit. You can look back down to Geneva Lake to check your progress as you ascend to the summit of Snowmass Mountain.

3. Hagerman Peak (13,841 feet) (Class 2+). From Geneva Lake, instead of taking the trail to Siberia Lake, take a right turn and head east along the lake's north-

Left: Siberia Lake and Siberia Peak looking northwest from near the top of Snowmass. **Right:** Near this river crossing, you can leave the trail to reach Hagerman's southwest slopes route.

ern shore, ford a creek, and then follow the trail south into the pine forest, leaving Geneva Lake. You'll pass signs that say, "Trail Rider Pass." Traverse into a separate valley around Hagerman's southwest ridge and enter a new basin, arriving at a creek at 11,480 feet. Before crossing the creek, leave the main trail, stay on a small climbers' trail for 200 yards, and ascend the basin past a nice campsite, continuing into a narrow drainage on grass. Continue north on the left side of the creek to 12,000 feet, turn left (west) on grass for 0.1 mile, and enter a small western valley drainage. Turn north again, climb some rocky benches for another 200 yards, and ascend a gully through rocky scree and rock to reach a final accommodating grassy bench at 12,500 feet. From here, the climb goes evenly and is consistently Class 2+ for 1,100 feet, reaching the ridge crest at 13,800 feet after a short, angled climb to the east. From the crest, scamper for another 200 yards over a false summit to then arrive on the true summit of Hagerman.

DR. JON'S EXTRA CREDIT: THE LOOP

A. Snowmass to Hagerman Traverse (Class 4). This connection, to create a loop between Snowmass and Hagerman, links both peaks that have been described in #2 and #3 above. From Geneva Lake, ascend the S-ridge on Snowmass. Then traverse the challenging southeast ridge of Snowmass for 0.6 mile to the summit of Hagerman Peak. Then, take care to descend the south face of Hagerman (Class 2) to return to Geneva Lake. You can do this loop in the opposite direction, but climbing up the S-ridge of Snowmass is preferred over descending it.

B. North Snowmass (Class 3). From the summit of Snowmass Mountain, traverse north to the 14,020-foot summit of North Snowmass. This scramble on solid rock gives you a super fun view down into Pierre Lakes basin and north to Capitol Peak.

GENEVA LAKE—HAGERMAN PEAK —SNOWMASS MOUNTAIN

CATHEDRAL LAKE —CATHEDRAL PEAK —"TRIPLE-C" TRAVERSE

52

Elevation Gain	2,000 feet for Cathedral Lake; 4,100 feet for Cathedral Peak; 5,200 feet for the high-ridge traverse loop and car-to-car to Conundrum and Castle Peak
Round-Trip Distance	6.5 miles for Cathedral Lake; 9.1 miles for Cathedral Peak; 11 miles for the Snowmass-to-Hagerman high-traverse loop
Trailhead	Cathedral Lake (9,900 feet)
Difficulty Ratings	Class 1–2 hike, with some on trails to the lakes, and some class 2+ to Class 3 challenging ridgelines for the traverses on the peaks
Optimal Season	June 15 through October 1
Maps	Trails Illustrated #127 and #148; White River National Forest

COMMENT: Cathedral Peak is truly one of the most stunning peaks in all of Colorado. The turquoise and green waters of Cathedral Lake make this journey well worthwhile. While Cathedral is not above 14,000 feet, you can combine a climb of Cathedral with a remote, challenging, and high traverse to the south to reach Castle Peak, the highest in the Elk Range. Choosing to traverse this spectacular high ridgeline will give you a new perspective of this corner of the Elk Range for sure, and you will be able to see many reasons why the Elk Range is so unique in its beauty and wildness.

Cathedral Lake.

Castle   Conundrum   Cathedral

Top: Castle (left) to Conundrum to Cathedral along the ridgeline heading north is one of Colorado's finest high-mountain traverses. **Bottom:** Cathedral and Castle's connecting ridgeline from Leahy Peak.

GETTING THERE

Cathedral Lake Trailhead (9,900 feet). From the town of Aspen, take Castle Creek Road from the roundabout on Colorado Highway 82 on the north side of town. This roundabout is shared with Maroon Creek Road. Follow paved Castle Creek Road for 11 miles to Ashcroft. Until late April or early May, the road will only be open as far as Ashcroft. After early May, continue past Ashcroft 1 mile to a marked road leading to Cathedral Trailhead. Turn right onto this dirt road and follow it as it switches back through aspen forests for 0.75 mile and reaches the Cathedral Trailhead and parking area.

Castle Creek Trailhead (9,900 feet). Use this trailhead for the car-to-car traverse of Cathedral to Castle and down. Continue past Ashcroft for 2 miles and an additional mile past the Cathedral Lake Trailhead dirt road turnoff described above to a marked road leading to Montezuma Basin. There is plenty of parking at this fork, and an information sign marks the trailhead/road toward Pearl Pass. If you like rougher roads, turn right onto a dirt road and follow it along the creek as it winds through a small aspen forest for 0.5 mile and reaches campsites and small places to park before the road gets steeper and much rougher. Depending on time of year, you can drive as far as you'd like as long as you don't value your vehicle! The first creek crossing at 10,200 feet on this rougher four-wheel-drive road is 4.5 miles from the summit of Castle Peak, and that distance is used for the car-to-car traverse description here.

Cathedral Lake.

THE LAKE

1. Cathedral Lake (11,866 feet) (Class 1–2). From the trailhead, follow the Cathedral Trail for 3.25 miles to Cathedral Lake. The trail corridor follows the right side (north side) of the basin and traverses some aspens and the creek all the way up the valley. There is a small flatter section of trail where the forest thins out and the trail traverses some scree before the terrain steepens right below the lake. Upon ascending the pine and steeper portion, you will reach a trail junction. Follow the left branch through the willows, and once again the trail flattens out, crosses a creek, and traverses willows to arrive at Cathedral Lake.

THE HIGH-RIDGE TRAVERSE/CLIMB

2. Cathedral Peak, south ridge (13,943 feet) (Class 3). After a visit to Cathedral Lake, head around the north side of the lake on some rocks and go to the lake's west end. From the west end of the lake, look to the west-northwest and spot the Cathedral massif. It is certainly stunning to admire from here. Hike west above some willows and grass and begin to ascend an old rock glacier to the west. In spring and early June, the rock glacier is buried under plenty of snow, and you can climb up into the broad and deep basin to the west and northwest of the lake. Stay west of the southeast ridge in the basin and aim for an obvious couloir that leads to the west and to Cathedral's south ridge at a 13,000-foot saddle. Ascend this couloir. You will need crampons in June or July, and the couloir is steep near the top. The top portion will melt out to dirt by late August or early September, so be ready for a tough scramble. From the saddle, follow Cathedral's south ridge on a loose climbers' trail ascending small ledges for 0.25 mile and 900 vertical feet to the summit.

DR. JON'S EXTRA CREDIT: THE HIGH-RIDGE TRAVERSE/LOOPS

A. Cathedral Peak, Pearl Couloir, to South Ridge Traverse Loop (Class 3). This Tour de Cathedral is awesome, especially when done in late May or early June

Cathedral

Left: Use caution along the ridges once a little snow dusts the high peaks. **Right:** Near the top of Castle with Cathedral and the long Triple-C Traverse to the right ridgeline.

to take advantage of nice snow conditions in the Pearl Couloir. From Cathedral Lake, look at Cathedral Peak and find the sharp southeast ridge coming directly toward you. Find the Pearl Couloir by leaving the lake on its north side and hiking north into the basin on piles of glacial talus to the right (east side) of Cathedral's prominent southeast ridge. After about a half mile, you will be to the east of the southeast ridge; look to your left and spot the Pearl Couloir tucked into the ridgeline among the stunning "cathedral towers." It's a gorgeous line that you can climb in a westerly direction to near the summit ridge for about 1,600 feet. Ascend the couloir. Halfway up, there is a choke point where the couloir cuts between the ridgeline and east face; climb to a prominent notch within 150 feet of the top. From the notch, turn left and head a bit farther west for one-eighth mile toward the summit. Descend Cathedral's south-ridge route back to Cathedral Lake as described above.

B. Cathedral to Conundrum to Castle Traverse ("Triple-C" Traverse) (Class 3–4). After ascending either the south ridge or the Pearl Couloir on Cathedral, this car-to-car connection to create a loop between Cathedral and Castle is super fun! Most of the ridgeline for 2 miles between Conundrum and Cathedral is easy Class 2–2+ with a few Class 3 moves on solid rock. You only need to take it to Class 4 if you get off route too much. The views on this tour won't quit! You will traverse over Conundrum Peak on the way to Castle and hike Castle's northwest ridge to the summit. From the top of Castle Peak, it is not too difficult to descend the well-worn climbers' trail down Castle's northeast ridge and into Montezuma basin for 4.5 miles and a car shuttle somewhere near Castle Creek Trailhead and the prominent creek crossing of avalanche debris at 10,200 feet.

CATHEDRAL LAKE—CATHEDRAL PEAK —"TRIPLE-C" TRAVERSE

AMERICAN LAKE —HAYDEN PEAK —ELECTRIC PASS PEAK

53

Elevation Gain	2,000 feet for American Lake; 4,200 feet for Hayden Peak; 4,600 feet for Electric Pass Peak Ridge Traverse Loop
Round-Trip Distance	6.4 miles for American Lake; 10 miles for Hayden Peak (after visiting American Lake); 11 miles for the Hayden Peak to South Hayden to Electric Pass Peak High-Traverse Loop
Trailhead	American Lake (9,400 feet)
Difficulty Ratings	Class 1–2 hike with some on trails to the lakes, and some Class 2+ easy ridgelines for the traverses on the peaks
Optimal Season	June 15 through October 1
Maps	Trails Illustrated #127 and #148; White River National Forest

COMMENT: Hayden Peak, named for Ferdinand V. Hayden from the original US Geological Surveys of the 1870s, is one of the easiest but scenic peaks in the Elk Range. Unlike the higher thirteeners and fourteeners of the very rugged and loose rock nature, Hayden is somewhat gentle, grassy with only some steep loose rock sections, and not nearly as steep or dangerous as its higher neighbors. If you combine

American Lake on a crisp bluebird morning.

Hayden with a loop of neighboring Electric Pass Peak, you will get high enough to breathe in the thin cool mountain air and view the fourteeners of the Elk Range in very scenic style without having to labor for their summits. Take plenty of water, and enjoy your excursion of solitude, which will be normal once you leave the American Lake Trail.

GETTING THERE

American Lake Trailhead (9,400 feet). From the town of Aspen, take Castle Creek Road from the roundabout on Colorado Highway 82 on the north side of town. This roundabout is shared with Maroon Creek Road. Follow paved Castle Creek Road for 10 miles to just short of Ashcroft. The marked trailhead will be on your right just across the paved road from the Elk Mountain Lodge.

American Lake is a stunning fall hike, especially in aspens near the trailhead.

THE LAKE

1. American Lake (11,365 feet) (Class 1–2). From the trailhead, follow the American Lake Trail (#1985) for 3.2 miles to American Lake. The trail rises steeply, switchbacking through the aspen for the first mile before reaching a spruce and pine forest. From this point to the lake, the trail levels off with periodic ascents of easy and moderate grades. On a rainy day, the forest aroma is bucolic. The trail continues its ascent, passing through several sets of forest and meadows that are alive with wildflowers from mid-July to August. About 0.5 mile before the lake, the trail emerges into a fantastic wildflower oasis surrounded by scree. From here, you can also see to the west into a valley that leads to Hayden Peak. Next, the trail briefly reenters the forest before it crosses yet another large scree field with soothing sounds of a waterfall just ahead and to the left. If you are climbing Hayden and decide to visit the lake first, this is where you need to return to on the trail for 0.25 mile in order to travel northwest for your climb of the peak (see next description for climb). Cross through some final trees to find American Lake tucked into a small idyllic basin right before your eyes.

THE LOOP AND HIGH-RIDGE TRAVERSE

2. Hayden Peak, east ridge (13,561 feet)(Class 2). After a visit to American Lake, head back down the American Lake Trail for 0.25 mile to reach the prominent small meadow with waterfall sounds as previously described. The trail heads east through this meadow, then turns north and then west to return to the trailhead. At 11,250 feet, look for the prominent ridgeline in the pine forest on a hill crest and follow it around to the north and then west to enter into Hayden Peak's eastern glacial cirque valley. Continue into the basin in a northwest direction, find an old miner's use trail, and ascend slopes along a rock glacier for 1 mile in the valley to gain the slopes to Hayden's east ridge. Once on the ridge above timberline, travel west for several hundred yards to reach the summit. The views of the Elk Range from this broad summit and ridgeline are excellent. You can return to the trailhead by descending the valley into the cirque basin and finding the American Lake Trail.

3. Hayden Peak ridge traverse to South Hayden (13,540 feet) and Electric Pass Peak (13,620 feet) Loop (Class 2-3). This is a spectacular ridge traverse that is great to hike and climb and delivers the best views all the way. Leave Hayden's summit and travel the 1.25-mile ridge over South Hayden and ascend to the top of Electric Pass Peak. Along the journey from Hayden to South Hayden Peak, you will encounter two separate ridge sections that require some Class 3 moves and can be quite treacherous on loose rock. The best advice is to stay on the ridge crest for safest

Hayden's ridgeline gives you awesome views clear to the Maroon Bells, Capitol, and Snowmass.

Left: Hayden's ridgeline has a couple of short Class 3 scrambling sections, so be ready for some loose rock too. **Right:** Electric Pass Peak, with Cathedral and Castle in the distance down to Cathedral Lake. *Photo by Dreama Walton*

passage. From the top of Electric Pass Peak, you can actually follow some well-worn climbers' trails in a counterclockwise fashion from the north to the west, then to the south, and east around Electric Pass Peak to then drop back down to the east into American Lake basin on grassy terrain. From the top of Hayden to Electric Pass Peak and back to American Lake is 2.75 miles. You can even extend your ridge traverse if you'd like and tag 13,318-foot Leahy Peak in the process.

DR. JON'S EXTRA CREDIT

A. Hayden Peak, Electric Pass Peak to Cathedral Lake Traverse Loop (Class 3). This longer extended tour is brilliant. Leave a vehicle at the Cathedral Lake Trailhead (see the Cathedral Lake entry, #52), which is only a ten-minute drive and 3 miles from the American Lake Trailhead. Hike to American Lake, climb Hayden Peak, traverse to Electric Pass Peak, and then descend the very nicely defined Electric Pass Peak Trail to Cathedral Lake and down for 3 miles to the Cathedral Lake Trailhead. This awesome tour is about 12 miles total for a lot of extra scenery. The car-to-car loop works equally well in the opposite direction.

B. Leahy Peak (13,318 feet) (Class 2). After ascending Electric Pass Peak on your loop journey, follow the east ridge of Electric Pass Peak to 13,318-foot Leahy Peak, yet another easy thirteener on these massive ridgeline systems.

American Lake—Hayden Peak—Electric Pass Peak

AMERICAN LAKE—HAYDEN PEAK —ELECTRIC PASS PEAK

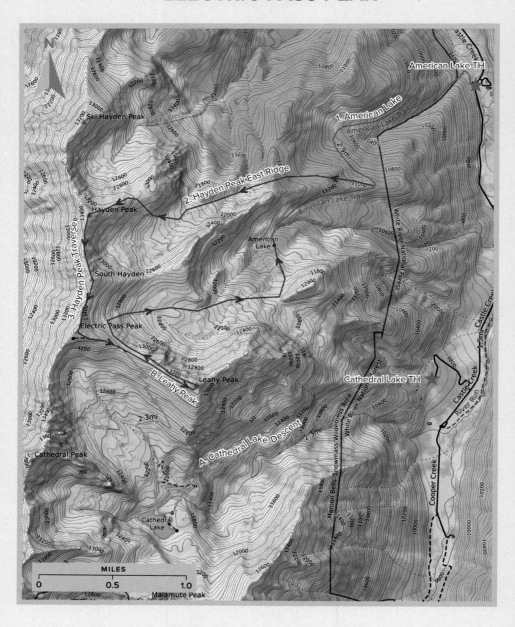

TWIN LAKES —CONUNDRUM HOT SPRINGS—CASTLEBRA VIA COFFEEPOT PASS

54

Elevation Gain	1,600 feet for Upper Twin Lake; 2,300 feet for Conundrum Hot Springs; 5,000 feet for Castlebra; 5,500 feet for Castlebra Loop over Peak 13,550' back to Coffeepot Pass (add 1,200 feet for the lower, passenger car parking option for all of these options)
Round-Trip Distance	6 miles for Twin Lakes; 11.6 miles for Conundrum Hot Springs; 12.5 miles for Castlebra to Peak 13,550' to Coffeepot Pass Loop (add 10 miles round-trip to each of these if parking at the lower, passenger car option)
Trailheads	Twin Lakes (10,400 feet) or Conundrum Creek (8,600 feet)
Difficulty Ratings	Class 1–2 hike with some on trails to the lakes, and some Class 2+ to 3 ridgelines for the traverses on the peaks
Optimal Season	June 15 through October 1
Maps	Trails Illustrated #127 and #148; White River National Forest

COMMENT: The Conundrum Hot Springs are certainly a draw for many but have become quite crowded over the years. The peaks surrounding the hot springs, by contrast, see very few visitors. In order to take advantage of solitude and an alternative approach to Upper Conundrum Basin, consider an adventure to Twin Lakes,

Copper Lake near Triangle Peak, Triangle Pass, and East Maroon Pass.

Coffeepot Pass, and several thirteeners in the upper basin, such as Castlebra, Hillard, Keefe, and Peak 13,550'. You can also take a day excursion from Twin Lakes or the hot springs to hike over Triangle Pass to explore Copper Lake. So many places to see, so little time.

GETTING THERE

Twin Lakes Trailhead (10,400 feet). From the town of Gunnison, follow Colorado Highway 135 north toward Crested Butte. Pass through Almont, and 2 miles before reaching Crested Butte, turn right (northeast) on CR 738/FSR 738, also known as Pearl Pass Road. The road is paved initially, passing through a subdivision, and then becomes gravel after several miles. Passenger cars can make it to the 5-mile mark on the road reasonably well until a junction with the East River Valley. It's best to park passenger cars at some primitive campsites near the East River and the Main Brush Creek before crossing the West Brush Creek. For the remaining 5 miles of four-wheel-drive road, you will need a high-clearance vehicle. Continue past a road intersection at mile 6 as FSR 738 gains elevation following Middle Brush Creek. At 10,400 feet, Twin Lakes Trailhead is on your left (mile 9.5).

Conundrum Creek Trailhead (8,600 feet). Take Castle Creek Road from the roundabout on Colorado Highway 82 on the north side of Aspen. This roundabout is shared with Maroon Creek Road. Follow paved Castle Creek Road for 4 miles to a road junction for Conundrum Creek Road. Take a right and head up the paved road passing some large houses for 0.25 mile to a marked trailhead located within a newly devastated (as of 2019) avalanche run-out zone. (Note: not shown on map.)

Left: The scree gully of Castlebra from Conundrum Hot Springs. **Right:** Castlebra summit with the west ridge of Castle visible.

THE LAKES

1. Twin Lakes (11,800 feet) (Class 1–2). From the trailhead, carefully cross Middle Brush Creek on foot and follow the Twin Lakes Trail (#402) northwesterly for 3 miles to Upper Twin Lake. The trail stays on the east side of the creek up until a crossing 0.5 mile below Lower Twin Lake. Willows might be thick near the lakes, and you can avoid them by staying farther west of the creek as you ascend the upper valley. While the trail stays west of the lakes, there are several small use trails leading down into the glacial cirque, allowing you to arrive at the banks of upper Twin Lake.

THE LOOP AND HIGH-RIDGE TRAVERSE

2. Conundrum Hot Springs (11,200 feet) with climb of Castlebra (13,812 feet) (Class 2–3). From Twin Lakes, ascend a dying-out climbers' trail to the northwest from Upper Twin Lake, following a creek on some grassy, then rocky slopes for 0.75 mile to the 12,750-foot summit of a col known as Twin Peaks. The final 200 feet to the Twin Peaks col is super steep, so instead of climbing to the col, 0.25 mile below in the basin, aim to the northwest on a use trail and access a 12,500-foot open saddle that separates Upper Twin Lakes basin with West Brush Creek basin. You will still be on the south side of the massive divide ridgeline to your north and Triangle Peak to your west. Continue northwest for 1 mile to the upper northerly portion of West Brush Creek to the 12,750-foot saddle of Coffeepot Pass. From this saddle, you can look down into Conundrum Basin toward timberline to the north and see the vicinity of Conundrum Hot Springs. Reservations are required to camp at the hot springs; visit recreation.gov in advance to book your campsites. An alternative to the crowded campsites is a set of perfectly legal campsites on the grassy benches at 12,500 feet on the north side or even the south side of Coffeepot Pass. There are a few springs and small tarns nearby to gather water. From here, you get excellent views and solitude and can descend 1,300 feet in 1.66 miles into the valley by catching the trail to your northwest just below Triangle Pass to access the hot springs. Using the

Looking down the north gully of Castlebra; Hilliard and Keefe Peaks are on the opposite side of the basin.

Left: Soaking up the Conundrum Hot Springs. **Right:** Triangle Pass is close to Coffeepot Pass (right).

campsites in this loop will save you the effort of hauling your gear back out of the Conundrum Basin after a long day climbing peaks.

After a nice soak in the hot springs, leave the springs and climb up a direct scree gully to the southeast, ascending steeply in a U-shaped glacial trough for 2,600 feet to the summit of Castlebra. The view from Castlebra is exceptional, with Castle Peak and other Elk Range classics as your panorama. From the top of Castlebra, traverse south for 1 mile to the top of Peak 13,550', and then back west for 0.75 mile to reach the Twin Peaks col and eventually Coffeepot Pass and the nearby grassy benches campsites over one more minor 13,000-foot summit (Peak 13,162').

DR. JON'S EXTRA CREDIT

A. Triangle Pass (12,900 feet) to Copper Creek Loop (Class 2). This is a fun day tour that leaves the high campsites near Coffeepot Pass, jumps onto the Upper Conundrum Basin Trail, crosses over 12,900-foot Triangle Pass, and heads west down Trail #1981 to Copper Creek. You will catch the East Maroon Trail to head north from Copper Lake for two miles and then find another spur trail clockwise to return to Triangle Pass and Coffeepot Pass. This little excursion is fun and remote and a nice break from peakbagging coming from your high camp.

B. Hillard Peak (13,383 feet) and Keefe Peak (13,468 feet) (Class 2+). Both of these peaks are prominently displayed from Coffeepot Pass and are west of Conundrum Hot Springs, waiting to be climbed.

C. Conundrum Hot Springs (11,200 feet) via Conundrum Creek Trailhead (Class 1). You can do the standard 18-mile round-trip hike from Conundrum Creek Trailhead coming from Aspen, but you will be lumped in with the masses if you do. Visit recreation.gov for permit system guidelines.

TWIN LAKES—CONUNDRUM HOT SPRINGS —CASTLEBRA VIA COFFEEPOT PASS

MAROON LAKE—CRATER LAKE—WILLOW LAKE —MAROON BELLS TRAVERSE

55

Elevation Gain	500 feet for Crater Lake; 3,800 feet for Willow Lake; 4,900 feet for South Maroon to North Maroon Traverse Loop
Round-Trip Distance	3.0 miles for Crater Lake; 12 miles for Willow Lake; 10 miles for Maroon Bells Traverse Loop
Trailhead	Maroon Lake (9,600 feet)
Difficulty Ratings	Class 1–2 hike on trails to lakes, and then tundra and Class 3–4 climbing on solid rocks and scree off trails
Optimal Season	June through October, but July through September is ideal
Maps	Trails Illustrated #128; White River National Forest

COMMENT: A stunning place that is one of the most photographed on earth, the Maroon Bells are a Colorado icon. If you choose to hike here, take only pictures and please come early to avoid the crowds. While this guidebook isn't necessarily intended to push people to the busy places, this entry is classic Colorado in every way, so please tread lightly and enjoy. The Maroon Bells parking and Maroon Lake access is heavily regulated now by the Aspen Ranger District. Please visit aspenchamber.org for more information on obtaining a permit to visit this pristine area.

Friendly mountain goats will always greet you on North Maroon.

Descending from Buckskin Pass on the Four Pass Loop, Pyramid Peak (left) and the Maroon Bells (right) are magnificent.

GETTING THERE

Maroon Lake Trailhead (9,600 feet). From the town of Aspen, take Maroon Creek Road from the roundabout on Colorado Highway 82 on the northwest side of town. This roundabout is shared with Castle Creek Road. Follow paved Maroon Creek Road for 9.5 miles to Maroon Lake and a paved parking area. Until early May, the road is only open for 3 miles, from Colorado Highway 82 to just past the T-Lazy-7 Ranch.

From Memorial Day weekend through Labor Day weekend (and sometimes through early October) the road is closed from 8:00 a.m. until 5:00 p.m., but a shuttle bus travels from the Aspen Highland ski resort to Maroon Lake. You can also get special parking permits for Maroon Lake; visit aspenchamber.org well in advance of when you would like to visit. For more information, call the White River National Forest Ranger Station in Aspen at 970-925-3445.

THE LAKES

1. Crater Lake (10,080 feet) (Class 1). This is a great hike to take the family on. Walk along the banks of Maroon Lake initially, and then when you reach the far western end of Maroon Lake, follow a well-worn trail through the gorgeous aspen forest. You will ascend for about a mile into a rolling boulder-field meadow after a set of trail switchbacks. Finally, descend and pass through a final aspen grove before taking the trail left and emerging at Crater Lake below the Maroon Bells.

2. Willow Lake (11,800 feet) (Class 2). This hike requires a bit more effort but is worth it to separate yourself from the crowds and gain some solitude. Hike 1.4 miles from Maroon Lake toward Crater Lake as described above. You can visit Crater Lake if you desire or simply turn right 0.1 mile before Crater Lake and continue on the Maroon Snowmass Trail for 2.5 miles as it climbs toward Buckskin Pass. Crater Lake will be visible below you to your left as will the Maroon Bells. Ascend several switchbacks in the pine forest, pass some stellar waterfalls and creeks, and make your way into the krumholtz of Buckskin basin. At 11,800 feet, you will reach a signed trail junction right above tree line. The left branch climbs to Buckskin Pass; the right heads into Willow basin. Continue to the right (northeast) as the trail climbs higher into the alpine. At 12,000 feet, you will pass a gorgeous green spring pool in a small bowl to your left. Keep going. The trail heads east into the upper basin and then takes a steep climb on three switchbacks to gain Willow Pass at 13,000 feet (mile 4.6 from the trailhead). From the pass to your southeast down in the basin, Willow Lake will appear, tucked into a broad cirque in the basin at tree line. There is also a three-pass loop that circumnavigates Willoughby Mountain and includes Willow Pass, Buckskin Pass, and East Snowmass Pass. You could make night one at Willow Lake, spend a second day hiking over East Snowmass Pass to East Snowmass Trailhead, and then follow the Snowmass Creek Trail up and over Buckskin Pass and back to Maroon Lake. This 23-mile loop is a nice alternative excursion to the much more crowded Four Pass Loop in the area.

THE HIGH-RIDGE TRAVERSE (LOOP)

3. Maroon Bells Traverse, south (14,156 feet) to north (14,014 feet) (Class 4). Leave Crater Lake and head southwest passing several campsites along the river for 1.5 miles en route to the East Maroon Creek crossing and the South Maroon Peak Trail junction. Look for the well-marked South Maroon Peak Trail along the northern banks of the creek. This is also a great place to fill water bottles before climbing higher. The excellent South Maroon Trail climbs from the valley floor for a strong 0.75 mile before getting very steep and somewhat disappearing in the grassy ledges at 12,500 feet. The best way to routefind can be to wrap around west and look for use trails. Your goal should be to find a prominent rib/minor ridgeline between 12,500 and 12,700 feet. It is possible to wrap far west and then climb up this ridge on a use trail to gain the main South Maroon Peak ridgeline at 13,100 feet. From here, you will be heading to the northeast toward South Maroon. Stay on the ridge's west side

Left: Traversing to North Maroon from South Maroon. *Photo by Chris Tomer* **Right:** Ice skating on Maroon Lake in November or December in a dry fall can be amazing.

as you traverse a relatively easy set of ledges (Class 2+ and Class 3). Careful route-finding for the last 800 feet of this route is key to keeping it all Class 3. Above 13,600 feet, you can climb directly on the ridge on two separate occasions to then reach the final summit ridge and the summit of South Maroon.

From South Maroon's summit, the challenge to traverse to North Maroon is obvious. Start by staying directly on the ridge crest. Downclimb a Class 4 cliff onto a small slabby ridge crest. Then drop into a shallow gully again on the left (north-west) side of the ridge to then make your way into the 13,922-foot connecting saddle between South Maroon and North Maroon. You can also peer down the Bell Cord couloir toward Pyramid Peak from here. While the dangerous downclimbing on the traverse to North Maroon is over, you have to make a tough choice. It's possible to stay on the ridge crest and climb exposed dangerous mudstone (Class 5), or you can slip along ledges on the west (left) side of the ridge, following a series of ledges and small chimneys on several occasions to the final headwall pitch to the summit. The routefinding is delicate and tedious if you have never done this traverse, so I recommend going with someone you trust who has been on this route before. Do not leave your routefinding up to staring at someone else's secondhand photos of where they may have climbed or attempting to follow wrongly placed wayward cairns, neither of which will help you here.

Once you reach the top of North Maroon, carefully descend the northeast ridge route of North Maroon through a series of ledges and gullies (Class 4 downclimbing) to then cross a large rock glacier and connect with the North Maroon Trail and finally the Maroon-Snowmass Trail, returning to the trailhead at Maroon Lake.

Top: Maroon Lake. **Bottom:** Willow Lake from Willow Pass on the Three Pass Loop.

DR. JON'S EXTRA CREDIT (THE LOOPS)

A. Four Pass Loop backpacking (Class 2). This 27-mile backpacking loop is simply sensational. Do your research to make the best decisions about days on the trail and destinations. By 2022, there will be a new permit system in place for the summer and fall seasons. Parking at Maroon Lake already requires a reservation as well. If you have a high level of fitness, this four-pass loop from Maroon Lake can be done in an eight- to sixteen-hour day. I recommend going clockwise on the loop for the best views and grades.

B. Maroon Lake ice skating (Class 1). In the fall between November 1 and December 15, especially in a really dry spell of cold evenings and shortening days, the ice skating on the lake is one of a kind. Most years the road is open until almost Thanksgiving, so take advantage of this rare opportunity to drive to Maroon Lake and skate!

C. Triple feat (Class 4). On a perfect summer or early fall day, a lack of afternoon thunderstorms and a strong desire to climb can lead you to do the Maroon Bells Traverse but then for extra fun, climb Pyramid on your way back down from Crater Lake. Allow eight to sixteen hours for this challenge, gaining 9,000 feet in over 18 miles.

MAROON LAKE—CRATER LAKE —WILLOW LAKE—MAROON BELLS TRAVERSE

CHAPTER 8

SANGRE DE CRISTO RANGE

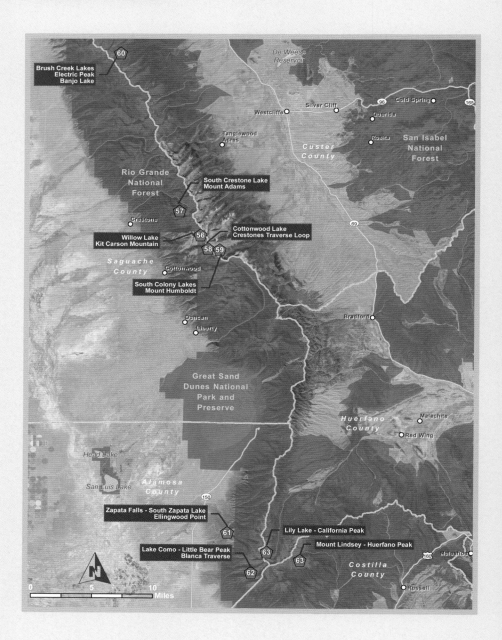

Brush Creek Lakes
Electric Peak
Banjo Lake

South Crestone Lake
Mount Adams

Willow Lake
Kit Carson Mountain

Cottonwood Lake
Crestones Traverse Loop

South Colony Lakes
Mount Humboldt

Zapata Falls - South Zapata Lake
Ellingwood Point

Lily Lake - California Peak

Lake Como - Little Bear Peak
Blanca Traverse

Mount Lindsey - Huerfano Peak

De Weese
Reservoir

Westcliffe
Silver Cliff
Cold Spring
Querida
Rosita
San Isabel
National
Forest

Custer
County

Rio Grande
National
Forest

Crestone

Saguache
County

Cottonwood

Duncan
Liberty

Bradford

Great Sand
Dunes National
Park and
Preserve

Huerfano
County

Malachite

Red Wing

Head Lake

San Luis Lake

Alamosa
County

Costilla
County

Russell

Muleshoe

0   5   10
Miles

WILLOW LAKE
—KIT CARSON MOUNTAIN

56

Elevation Gain	2,675 feet for Willow Lake; 5,265 feet for Kit Carson Mountain; 5,500 feet for the return loop over Challenger Point
Round-Trip Distance	7 miles for Willow Lake; 10.5 miles for Kit Carson Mountain north-ridge traverse of Kit Carson Avenue, return via Challenger Point
Trailhead	Willow Creek/South Crestone (8,900 feet)
Difficulty Ratings	Class 1–2 hike on trails to the lakes, and some Class 2, 3, and 4 exposed climbing on ridgelines for the traverses on the peaks
Optimal Season	June 15 through October 1
Maps	Trails Illustrated #138; San Isabel and Rio Grande National Forests

COMMENT: Kit Carson Peak in the Sangre de Cristo Range is a fourteener that is steep on all sides. The famous Prow is a well-known and sharp rock buttress that gives the Kit Carson massif a distinct shape when viewed from the San Luis Valley. Kit Carson Peak includes Challenger Point to the west (14,081 feet) and Kat Carson to the east, which is only a shade below 14,000 feet. The Sangre de Cristos can be very

Willow Lake with Kit Carson.

windy and dry and are known particularly for their affinity to harbor some incred-ible thunderstorms. I've heard many stories over the years of people who got caught out on the high ridgelines when a storm brewed up quickly, and it made hair stand up and zippers buzz. Get an early alpine start for this one so you don't get zapped out of the sky.

GETTING THERE
Willow Creek Trailhead (8,900 feet). From the north (Salida), drive over Pon-cha Pass by traveling south on US Highway 285. From the US Highway 285/Colo-rado Highway 17 junction, take Colorado Highway 17 south for 13.8 miles, passing through the small town of Moffat. When you are 0.4 mile south of Moffat, turn left (east) on a paved road, and head toward the town of Crestone. From the south (Ala-mosa), travel north on Colorado Highway 17 through the town of Hooper. From the Colorado Highway 112/Colorado Highway 17 junction in Hooper, drive 16.8 miles and turn right (east) on the paved road from Moffat. Travel 12.4 miles east to get to Crestone. From the center of the town of Crestone, take Galena Street east, following a dirt road for 2.3 miles to the well-marked trailhead (also called South Crestone Trailhead) and pit toilet.

THE LAKE
1. Willow Lake (11,575 feet) (Class 1–2). From the trailhead, you will follow the Willow Lake Trail (#865) for 3.5 miles to Willow Lake. To start, hike east for 100 yards, turn right (south), cross the creek in the woods, emerge in a meadow, and turn

Left: Kit Carson near the trail junction to Challenger Point. **Right:** Looking down the valley from the cliffs above Willow Lake.

14,165'

North Ridge

Kit Carson Mountain boasts Kat Carson/Columbia Point (left), and Challenger Point (right).

left. Follow the sandy trail through an initial meadow and the start of the Willow Creek Trail. The trail makes a couple of super long switchbacks in the north-facing pine forests before it crests a ridgeline and reaches Willow Lake basin and some great views after the first 1.5 miles. Once in the upper basin, you will continue up the very well-defined Willow Lake Trail for another 2 miles. The trail climbs a gorgeous basin and ascends across some cliffs, and you will enter a hanging valley above the gorge and flatter terrain in the woods before reaching Willow Lake. Pass several campsites just before arriving at the picturesque lake, which has a signature waterfall flowing into the upper end from the cliffs at 11,700 feet.

THE LOOP AND HIGH-RIDGE TRAVERSE

2. Kit Carson Mountain, north ridge (14,165 feet) (Class 4). After a visit to Willow Lake, continue on the Willow Lake Basin Trail as it circles around the north end of the lake for 0.25 mile to gain the cliffs above the lake. From here, you will get a nice view of Kit Carson, stark in its appearance to the east-southeast. Follow the trail along the creek for a strong mile toward Kit Carson. In the first 0.25 mile, you will cross the creek to its south side and pass a trail junction that takes hikers right (south) and steeply up the standard route on Challenger Point and over to Kit Carson. Make note of this trail split, look toward Challenger Point and the route,

Left: Challenger Point ridgeline prior to an oncoming storm; the Great Sand Dunes and Blanca Massif are visible in the distance. **Right:** A plaque commemorates the Space Shuttle Challenger disaster.

and study it a bit, as you will be descending this north face to complete the loop. Continue west by taking the left fork of the trail up the flatter valley. In summer, wildflowers and lots of green grass will dominate this place. The trail will begin to fade out, but simply stay on the right side of the basin and follow the creek as you ascend the basin. Farther up the basin along Willow Creek at 12,000 feet, the trail fades out completely. Before you reach a smaller upper tarn, turn right (south) and ascend grassy benches to the base of Kit Carson's prominent north ridge. Stay to the left (east) of the steep ridge, ascending toward the mouth of the Outward Bound couloir. At 12,500 feet, you can head west on some grassy ledges to get onto the ridge. The ridge begins on grassy benches at 12,600 feet and 0.9 mile above Willow Lake and gradually gets more difficult as you ascend. In the first 400 feet, the grass will give way to pleasant and solid conglomerate. Use the knobs to your advantage and climb the north ridge. Most of the route is Class 3 initially, and then if you stay right on the crest of the spine, the difficulty doesn't exceed Class 4, but there will be moments of exposure and airyness the higher you climb. Climb and enjoy some fine conglomerate for nearly 1,200 feet as you ascend! At 13,950 feet, you'll reach a crest with the summit ridge and join the standard route that comes from the south side. Follow the crest of the ridge to the west, staying on the safer, southern side for 150 yards and 100 vertical feet to the small and accommodating summit.

The safest way down is not by descending the north ridge; instead, descend back only to the ridge crest you climbed up to the east for 150 yards, then follow a series of small gully and ledge systems down the south face of Kit Carson to its

The waterfall at Willow Lake is paradise.

famous catwalk at 13,500 feet (easy Class 3). Finding the catwalk known as "Kit Carson Avenue" (Class 2) is key to your exit to the west and traversing around to the connecting saddle between Kit Carson and Challenger Point. Once off the Avenue ledge, you will have to travel farther west on use trails (Class 2+), do a short 150-foot ascent for 0.25 mile to the top of 14,081-foot Challenger Point, and then continue down to the west ridge and then the north-face route on Challenger to make your way safely back to Willow Lake in the basin to complete the loop.

DR. JON'S EXTRA CREDIT

A. Kat Carson/Columbia Point (13,981 feet) (Class 3–4). This eastern satellite summit of Kit Carson Mountain (also known as "Kitty Kat Carson") was also recently named "Columbia Point" in honor of the 2003 Space Shuttle Columbia that exploded. Instead of dropping down from the summit ridge crest to reach Kit Carson Avenue, you can just traverse high on the ridge for 0.25 mile to the 13,640-foot connecting saddle between Kit Carson Mountain's summit and Kat Carson in the distance to the east. This saddle is very prominent as it separates the Outward Bound couloir to the north and the narrow south couloir. From the saddle, ascend some challenging but fun conglomerate for 0.25 mile in a couple of sections to the summit of Kat Carson. Everything on the north side of the ridge drops off dramatically, so stay away from that edge! Return to this saddle and back over Challenger Point as previously described.

WILLOW LAKE
—KIT CARSON MOUNTAIN

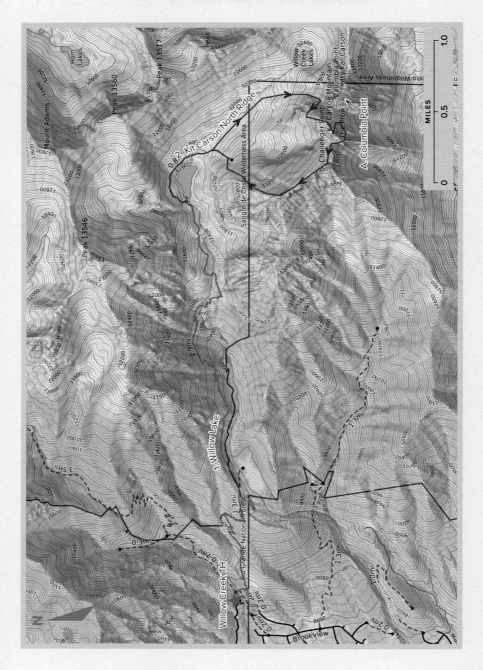

SOUTH CRESTONE LAKE
—MOUNT ADAMS

Elevation Gain	2,900 feet for South Crestone Lake; 5,031 feet for Mount Adams
Round-Trip Distance	7.6 miles for South Crestone Lake; 11 miles for Mount Adams Loop
Trailhead	Willow Creek/South Crestone (8,900 feet)
Difficulty Ratings	Class 1–2 hike on trails to the lakes; Class 2+ on Mount Adams; some Class 2, 3, and 4 exposed climbing on ridgelines for the extra-credit traverses on the peaks
Optimal Season	June 15 through October 1
Maps	Trails Illustrated #138; San Isabel and Rio Grande National Forests

COMMENT: Mount Adams, the Sangre de Cristo's northernmost Centennial thir-teener, is a relatively obscure and unknown peak for most mountaineers. It's tucked away only about 2 miles north of Kit Carson but visited by few. Mount Adams has several ridgelines extending from its summit, and they all can be climbed in a mod-erately technical fun style with loop linkups. Be safe and enjoy being all alone on this peak, as I've rarely seen another person on these isolated, high, and scenic ridgelines.

Ascending grassy slopes on the northwest ridgeline variation to Mount Adams.

Adams's northwest ridge with North Crestone Lake below.

GETTING THERE

Willow Creek Trailhead (8,900 feet). To get to Crestone, see entry #56 for detailed trailhead directions. From the center of the town of Crestone, take Galena Street east, following a dirt road for 2.3 miles to the well-marked trailhead (also called South Crestone Trailhead) and pit toilet.

THE LAKE

1. South Crestone Lake (11,780 feet) (Class 1–2). From the trailhead, continue straight (east) and follow the Crestone Lake Trail (#860). The trail passes through a gorgeous high-desert juniper forest before reaching spruce and pine higher up. Cross to the south side of Crestone Creek and then back to the north side of the creek after 3 miles. You will reach South Crestone Lake at 11,780 feet after 3.8 miles. From the lake, the west-northwest face of Mount Adams is still tucked away out of view up the valley to the east.

THE LOOP AND HIGH-RIDGE TRAVERSE

2. Mount Adams, Northwest Ridge to West Ridge Loop (13,931 feet) (Class 2+). After a visit to the banks of the South Crestone Lake and a brief study of Mount Adams to your east, follow the valley southeast for 0.7 mile to the base of the face at 12,400 feet. Finally, after several hours of approach, look to your left (north), and ascend to a 12,780-foot saddle below Adams's northwest ridge. The climbing is mostly solid grassy benches and rocky bands that are pretty enjoyable. From the saddle, navigate the ridgeline toward the summit to gain the upper northern part of the ridge at 13,750 feet. Follow the north ridge south to the summit; you must gain the summit block by traversing to the southeast on an interesting grassy ledge to keep the final pitch a Class 2+ and gain the true summit. Enjoy the view, and then look to descend the west ridge of Adams on some solid rocky bands. You'll descend to a 12,900-foot saddle before dropping north on talus and rubble to return to the head of the valley at 12,400 feet to complete the loop and back to South Crestone Lake. An alternate, more scenic route to climbing Adams is to leave South Crestone Lake to the north, ascending grassy slopes to gain the ridgeline to the north of the lake. This is known as the northwest ridgeline variation. Cross a 13,153' subsummit and drop to a saddle before gaining the northwest ridge proper.

Left: Traversing to the southeast along the knife-edge ridgelines. **Right:** Final summit ridge on Adams.

DR. JON'S EXTRA CREDIT

A. Bear's Playground Traverse to Kat Carson Peak (13,981 feet)—Kit Carson Mountain (14,165 feet) and Challenger Point (14,081 feet) (Class 3–4).
From Mount Adams, you will get to see several spectacular ridgelines extending to the east and south. Closest to you is a narrow ridgeline that leads to the southeast for 2.4 miles over four thirteener summits on the ridge to a very broad and flat plateau feature known as Bear's Playground. Upon reaching Bear's Playground from Mount Adams's extended southeast ridge, you will be able to do a horseshoe-shaped traverse back to the west over a flat peak called Obstruction Peak (13,799 feet) to then ascend a long and ever increasing in difficulty line toward the west to the summit of 13,981-foot Kat Carson. This eastern satellite summit of Kit Carson Mountain was also recently named "Columbia Point" in honor of the 2003 Space Shuttle Columbia that exploded. Reach this summit and further extend the loop as described in entry #56 for Kit Carson. Descend on the ridge toward Kit Carson for 0.25 mile to the 13,640-foot connecting saddle between Kit Carson Mountain's summit and Kat Carson where you came from. This saddle is very prominent as it separates the Outward Bound couloir to the north and the narrow south couloir. From the saddle, descend to Kit Carson Avenue and back over Challenger Point as previously described. You can then descend for 3.5 miles from Willow Lake back to the same trailhead, as the trails only split a mere 100 yards from the parking lot.

B. North Crestone Lake (11,780 feet) (Class 2–3). North of the basin you hiked up from South Crestone Lake to 12,400 feet, you can explore another col to the other side on rugged terrain to locate the scenic North Crestone Lake.

SOUTH CRESTONE LAKE—MOUNT ADAMS

COTTONWOOD LAKE —CRESTONES TRAVERSE LOOP

58

Elevation Gain	3,900 feet for Cottonwood Lake; 5,900 feet for Crestone Peak; 6,250 feet for Crestone Peak to Crestone Needle Traverse Loop
Round-Trip Distance	10 miles for Cottonwood Lake; 11.5 miles for Crestone Peak; 12.5 miles for Crestone Peak to Crestone Needle Traverse Loop
Trailhead	Cottonwood Creek (8,440 feet)
Difficulty Ratings	Class 1–2 hike on trails to Cottonwood Lake; some Class 2, 3, and 4 exposed climbing on ridgelines for the traverses on the peaks
Optimal Season	June 15 through October 1
Maps	Trails Illustrated #138; San Isabel National Forest

COMMENT: Crestone Peak and Crestone Needle in the Sangre de Cristo Range are known for their conglomerate rock and challenging climbing in the summer and fall. The climbing is on some of the best stable rock in all of Colorado. The steep couloirs that fill with snow in good winter years melt out, and the ledge systems and gullies that are left behind become ultra-classic climbs and viewpoints with stunning views. Consider a backpack into the wilderness with a climb of either peak described here to really enjoy the scenery and wildlife. Bighorn sheep are often spotted around Cot-

Sunset at Cottonwood Lake.

Crestone Needle and Cottonwood Lake far below near Broken Hand saddle.

tonwood Lake, and mountain goats tend to greet climbers regularly on the upper steep and imposing ledges.

GETTING THERE

Cottonwood Creek Trailhead (8,440 feet). Several miles south of Crestone, this trailhead is on private property, but with proper leave-no-trace ethics, permission to use the trailhead from the parking area is permitted. From the north (Salida), drive over Poncha Pass by traveling south on US Highway 285. From the US Highway 285/Colorado Highway 17 junction, take Colorado Highway 17 south for 13.8 miles, passing through the small town of Moffat. When you are 0.4 mile south of Moffat, turn left (east) on a paved road, and head toward the town of Crestone. From the south (Alamosa), travel north on Colorado Highway 17 through the town of Hooper. From the Colorado Highway 112/Colorado Highway 17 junction in Hooper, drive 16.8 miles and turn right (east) on the paved road from Moffat. Travel 12 miles east to the entrance of the Baca Grande Chalets Grants.

Turn right (south) into the Baca Grande Chalets Grants following the paved Camino Baca Grande. If you somehow end up in the town of Crestone, you missed this turn. Proceed south, crossing Crestone Creek at 0.8 mile and cross Willow Creek at 2.2 miles. The road will turn to dirt after 3.5 miles at Spanish Creek, and then before crossing Cottonwood Creek at mile 5, park at the signed trailhead near a water tower and shed just before the trailhead. There is parking on the north side of the creek. Stay away from the creek and the Tashi Gomang Stupa as they are located on private property. The Cottonwood Trail begins on the north side of the creek heading east.

Left: Crestone Needle and the spectacular waterfall greets you on the way up the valley.
Right: Descending the Red Gully on Crestone Peak.

THE LAKE

1. Cottonwood Lake (12,315 feet) (Class 1–3). From the trailhead, continue straight (east) and follow the Cottonwood Creek Trail (#861/FSR 743). This trail stays on an old mining road corridor for the first mile, then switches back, and ascends through thick pine forest and aspen for 3.6 miles before reaching a trail junction near Cottonwood Creek and South Cottonwood Creek. In the final mile to the junction, split-up rocky slabs and some tricky conglomerate terrain are tough, but well worth the effort. When it's time to go higher into Cottonwood basin and beyond, turn left (northwest), then north, and follow the trail up some rocky outcroppings with the creek still cut deeply in rocks to your right. Next, you will climb steeply to eventually get to tree line and then emerge from the trees into more willows and rocks in the flatter basin. Next you will see that a wide switchback wraps an easy contour to the base of a prominent waterfall and a narrow Class 3 move that goes up the terrain left of the creek.

Above the waterfall and beyond the boulders, a meadow brings you to the base of another large rock wall. Following cairns to the top (nothing exceeds Class 2), the forest quickly gives way to the willows. The trail through the willows has been getting better over the years, so hopefully you can find it and ascend through the willows much easier than you thought. As you slowly work your way through the elevation, the Crestones come into view at the head of the basin above the waterfall. When you see Crestone Peak's Red Gully, you will emerge into a flat area at 12,260 feet between rocky outcroppings and willows with a wall of rock above you and meet an easy trail that leads to Cottonwood Lake. Turn right (east) and walk 0.25 mile to the shores of the lake.

Left: The crux knife-edge pitch on the traverse from Crestone Peak to Crestone Needle.
Right: Getting near the summit on the final pitch; Kit Carson Mountain is in the distance.

THE LOOP AND HIGH-RIDGE TRAVERSE

2. Crestone Peak (14,294 feet) to Crestone Needle (14,197 feet) Traverse (Class 4). After a visit to Cottonwood Lake, travel west for 0.4 mile and let the trail take you to a beautiful basin under Crestone Peak's Red Gully. Head north to access the face and Red Gully couloir of Crestone Peak. From here the climbers' trail that was built in the late 1990s will take you up to the base of the couloir. From the base of the couloir, climb nearly 2,000 feet to the 14,180-foot saddle between Crestone Peak (left) and Northeast Crestone (right). The safest route for the lower two-thirds of the climb in the Red Gully is to actually traverse and climb up on the right side of the couloir to mitigate any rockfall. At 13,600 feet, reenter the Red Gully by veering into the right side of the gully by traversing small ledges to the left. Climb loose rock and stable red conglomerate straight up to the 14,180-foot saddle/notch, then from the notch, traverse the steep face along ledges, and travel west-northwest to reach the summit.

While the summit is exhilarating, there is more work to be done. If the weather and time allow, you can go for the "Crestones Traverse" to Crestone Needle. Descend the Red Gully on Crestone Peak and then veer to the left as you descend to the 13,600-foot ledge between the peaks. This ledge is often well marked by cairns from previous fourteener climbers. You may have come up this same ledge on your ascent when avoiding the middle section of the gully. Do a descending traverse to the east across a ledge system to get to just below the 13,400-foot connecting saddle between Crestone Peak and Crestone Needle. You will have to overcome several rock bulges and minor chimney gullies (Class 2+ to 3) along the way. From this saddle, look northeast to locate the prominent Black Gendarme and climb to the right of the Black Gendarme up to a small chimney (Class 4–5), overcome a tough low Class 5 move (the route's crux), and then ascend a deep couloir to a narrow, rocky, razor's-edge traverse. This move can feel a bit exposed. The north side of this large razor rock drops off into nothing on the north face, so a fall here would be fatal. The stone rock wall feature blocks the col. A Class 4 move to gain easier terrain is necessary to the right, and downclimbing once you've committed to the razor's edge is not an option. Once you clear this crux, traverse back and forth twice on reasonable conglomerate inset ledges from 13,700 feet for 250 feet to reach the final Class 4 ridgeline pitch. Some parties choose to use a rope on the pitch. A 30-meter rope will suffice and can be anchored to a large rock, and sometimes old slings are left behind, but trusting your own sling is the best choice. This airy summit pitch is simply amazing. You feel super exposed, but the conglomerate knobs for the final 100 feet are such a nice gift. Once clearing the final summit pitch, the ridge gets easier for the final 80 vertical feet on solid rock, which is quite fun. The summit of the Needle is yours.

To get down and make this a loop, descend the south face of Crestone Needle. To access the south face, leave the summit on the sharp southeast ridgeline for 100 yards and then angle down into the south face in a prominent gully. You should select the right of two couloirs when descending, but then traverse to the east to the eastern couloir on the way and always keep an eye out for rockfall depending on climbing situations with others around you. Once down to 13,200 feet, the gully ends, and you can angle southeast to pick up the Broken Hand/Crestone Peak climbers' trail to get back down to Cottonwood Lake.

DR. JON'S EXTRA CREDIT

A. East Crestone Peak (14,241 feet) (Class 3–4). After reaching the top of Crestone Peak, descend to the 14,180-foot saddle at the top of the Red Gully. From here, traverse and scramble (Class 3) west for 150 yards to the summit of East Crestone.

B. Broken Hand Peak (13,573) (Class 3–4). After returning to the saddle between Crestone Peak and Broken Hand Peak, climb the ridge southeast for two-thirds mile to 13,573-foot Broken Hand Peak. It's a short and sweet but challenging summit. This summit will give you a true perspective of the Crestones and the entire area.

C. Upper Sand Creek Lake (11,745 feet) (Class 3). Travel southeast along high ridgelines for several miles once you've climbed Broken Hand Peak, and if you can locate the majestic Upper Sand Creek Lake, you will be rewarded.

COTTONWOOD LAKE—CRESTONES
TRAVERSE LOOP

SOUTH COLONY LAKES —MOUNT HUMBOLDT —ELLINGWOOD ARETE

Elevation Gain	2,900 feet for South Colony Lake; 3,225 feet for Upper South Colony Lake; 5,280 feet for Humboldt Peak; 5,400 feet for Ellingwood Arete to Crestone Needle summit
Round-Trip Distance	8 miles for South Colony Lake; 9 miles for Upper South Colony Lake; 13 miles for Humboldt Peak; 11 miles for Ellingwood Arete to Crestone Needle Traverse Loop; add 5.4 miles round trip total to all distances for two-wheel-drive trailhead at 8,780 feet, which is 2.7 miles below the South Colony Trailhead at 9,900 feet
Trailhead	South Colony (8,780 feet)
Difficulty Ratings	Class 1–2 hike on trails to South Colony Lake; Class 2 hike to Humboldt Peak; exposed technical climbing Class 5–5.9 for Ellingwood Arete on Crestone Needle
Optimal Season	June 15 through October 1
Maps	Trails Illustrated #138; San Isabel National Forest

COMMENT: Humboldt Peak is a worthy and rewarding hiking objective that stands in the shadow of Crestone Peak and Crestone Needle to the east. Humboldt's summit serves as a vantage point for viewing the stellar Crestones from a safe distance. The

From the top of Ellingwood Arete on Crestone Needle, Humboldt (left) and Upper Colony Lake are visible.

Above: The trail in the basin near South Colony Lake gives you a nice view of the Ellingwood Arete, the prominent ridgeline on Crestone Needle. *Photo by Dreama Walton* **Left:** Peering down Ellingwood Arete to South Colony Lake; Humboldt is across the valley.

only super technical route in this book, Ellingwood Arete is featured here for the technical climber simply because it is what high-mountain traditional climbing is all about in Colorado: ultra-sensational.

GETTING THERE

South Colony Trailhead (8,780 feet). From the Shell gas station on the south end of Westcliffe, travel south on Colorado Highway 69 for 4.5 miles. Turn right (south) on Colfax Lane and follow the road as it turns to dirt for 5.5 miles to a T junction. Turn right (west) and follow the road as it ascends the valley. There is a parking area 1.5 miles from the T junction. Passenger cars have to park here because the road becomes extremely rough 1 mile beyond this parking area. In four-wheel-drive high-clearance vehicles, you can drive another 2.7 miles up the road and into the national forest (1.4 miles) and to the South Colony Trailhead beyond. Do not park along the road on private property below the national forest boundary.

THE LAKES

1. South Colony Lake (11,650 feet) and Upper South Colony Lake (12,040 feet) (Class 1–2). From the passenger-car South Colony Trailhead in the valley, hike up the road for 2.7 miles to the summer South Colony Trailhead at 9,900 feet, which is well marked. Cross the South Colony Creek to the southwest side on a footbridge and continue 2.5 miles up to the end of the old four-wheel-drive road. In the middle of a small meadow at 11,000 feet near historical kiosk signs, find a small sign that splits the trails to the south and southwest sides of the basin. Stay right (west-northwest) at this trail junction and find your way up toward South Colony Lake through the trees (1.3 miles). At 11,400 feet, you will emerge below the lake with the iconic Crestone Needle above you to the west and Humboldt's relatively steep south couloir gully above you to the north. Proceed to the west up to 11,600 feet and South Colony Lake. Follow the excellent trail toward Upper South Colony Lake for 0.5 mile to your northwest. This lake, at just over 12,000 feet, is impressive.

THE LOOP AND HIGH-RIDGE TRAVERSE

2. Humboldt Peak (Class 2). Leave Upper South Colony Lake zigzagging an excellent trail up grassy slopes to reach a 12,800-foot connecting saddle on Humboldt's west ridge. It will take some effort on the steep trail as it ascends past many boulders to the east and slabby rocks to a ridge crest at 13,950 feet. The trail gets rocky and less like a trail right near the ridge crest, so use caution but just stay high on the crest, and you will be in the right place. Follow the easy final flat portions of the west ridge east to reach the rocky summit. If you so choose, there is a way to descend the southeast slopes of Humboldt into a broad couloir and down the southeast slopes for 2,000 feet to link back up with the South Colony Trail. If you'd rather not test your off-trail routefinding, returning back the way you came on the trail is often the best plan. Plus, you can revisit the lakes again on the way.

DR. JON'S EXTRA CREDIT

A. Ellingwood Arete, Crestone Needle (14,197 feet) (Class 5.6–5.9). This technical route is committing but a Colorado trad-climbing classic. The six- to eight-pitch (Class 5.6–5.9), 1,700-foot vertical route is an excellent conglomerate rock route, one of the best in all of Colorado. From both South Colony Lake and Upper South Colony Lake, the prominent ridgeline of the north face of Crestone Needle stares you in the face. Bring your technical climbing gear and have a blast! Descend the south face and gullies route on Crestone Needle back to South Colony Lakes to make this a tantalizing and "adrenal flushing" Tour de Crestone Needle.

SOUTH COLONY LAKES—MOUNT HUMBOLDT—ELLINGWOOD ARETE

BRUSH CREEK LAKES —ELECTRIC PEAK —BANJO LAKE

60

Elevation Gain	3,000 feet for Lower Brush Creek Lake; 3,150 feet for Upper Brush Creek Lake; 5,200 feet for Electric Peak; 6,400 feet for Banjo Lake
Round-Trip Distance	11 miles for Lower Brush Creek Lake; 11.5 miles for Upper Brush Creek Lake; 19 miles for Electric Peak Loop; 19–20 miles for Banjo Lake
Trailhead	North Brush/Rainbow (8,425 feet)
Difficulty Ratings	Class 1–2 on trails to Brush Creek Lakes; Class 2 minor trail and off trail above timberline and on the high ridges and peaks
Optimal Season	June through October
Maps	Trails Illustrated #138; San Isabel National Forest

COMMENT: Brush Creek Lakes are the gateway to some stunning solitude in the Sangre de Cristo Wilderness. Electric Peak and Banjo Lake are certainly rewarding destinations for those who want to make the extra effort to see the views and the terrain in this northern part of the Sangre de Cristo Range.

GETTING THERE
North Brush Creek Trailhead/Rainbow Trailhead (8,425 feet). From Westcliffe, take Colorado Highway 69 north for 10 miles, passing through the small extinct

Banjo Lake from the summit of Electric Peak. To the south, along the spine of the Sangre de Cristos, you can see thirteeners DeAnza, Gibbs, and Marcy.

town of Hillside. Just north of Hillside after a significant curve on the highway, turn left (west) on Lake Creek Road (FSR 198) and travel west for 2 miles. Next turn left (southwest) on a marked trail for Brush Creek Lakes. Follow this dirt road for 0.8 mile to a fork. The south fork (left) leads to the South Brush Creek Trail, while the right fork continues west (on a very rough four-wheel-drive road) to higher parking areas at 1.2 miles and 2.0 miles. If you value your vehicle, park at this very first trail split at 8,425 feet; if not, you can head up the rough road for an extra 1.2–2 miles to 8,900 feet and beyond to shorten your journey.

THE LAKES
1. Brush Creek Lakes (11,410 feet and 11,555 feet) (Class 1–2). From the low parking area, follow the four-wheel-drive road west for 1.2 miles to where the road eventually turns south crossing the north fork of Spruce Creek. At mile 2, this rough road (FSR 331) reaches a marked trailhead for Brush Creek Lakes right near an old silver mining building at 9,400 feet. Turn left on this trail as it climbs steeply through aspens and works its way south in 1 mile to cross a ridge and drop into North Brush Creek. Once into the basin, the trail descends and then travels southwest for 2.5 more miles through beetle-kill pine forest to Lower Brush Creek Lake at 11,410 feet. Upper Brush Creek Lake is an additional 0.25 mile past the lower lake, and both lakes have excellent camping near their shorelines.

THE LOOPS AND HIGH-RIDGE TRAVERSE
2. Electric Peak (13,598 feet) Traverse Loop. From a camp at either Brush Creek Lake, it's 8 miles round-trip to do this loop, so start early. Leave the area of Upper Brush Creek Lake on a faint climbers' trail that traverses some rocky outcroppings to the southwest of the lake and also passes a smaller unnamed lake as it gains elevation to a broad 12,300-foot grassy saddle to the east of Lakes Peak. From

Far left: Sunrise on Brush Creek Lake. **Middle:** Brush Creek Lakes from the top of Lakes Peak. **Right:** Looking north to Lakes Peak and Thirsty Peak across the northern Sangre de Cristos.

this saddle, you can look to your south and spot Electric Peak. It is possible to do an ascending traverse of this basin to the south for 0.75 mile to reach a 12,400-foot saddle between Electric Peak to the south and Lakes Peak to the north. From this saddle, follow rocky and gently grassy ridgelines for another 0.5 mile to reach the top of Electric Peak. If you aren't up for the entire loop described here, you can descend back the way you came and save your legs; if you want to take the scenic tour, descend the northeast ridge of Electric Peak. You can descend the rocky terrain of Electric Peak's northeast ridge for 1,500 feet, keeping the steep portions of the ridge away from you to the south. You will get dramatic views of Banjo Lake too. Once down to 12,000 feet on a broad eastern shoulder of Electric Peak, look for a faint climbers' trail that will traverse you back to the northwest into the sweeping basin north of Electric Peak. Finding this old climbers' trail is key to this loop because you want to be able to make your way back to Brush Creek Lakes by way of the broad grassy saddle you crossed earlier.

DR. JON'S EXTRA CREDIT

A. Banjo Lake (12,385 feet) (Class 2+). Tucked into a large east-facing cirque at the head of South Brush Creek is the scenic Banjo Lake. You can attempt to descend by way of Electric Peak's steep south ridgeline to get to the banks of the lake, or there are a few ways off of Electric Peak's northeast ridge to get into the basin.

B. DeAnza, Gibbs, Marcy, and Silver thirteeners (Class 2). The southern extension of the ridge from Electric features four more 13,000-foot peaks. In 2008, I did a very large loop of these peaks from the Gibson Trailhead that included Lakes of the Clouds, Silver, Marcy, Gibbs, DeAnza, and Electric as well as Lakes Peak, then down North Brush Creek to the Rainbow Trail and back to Gibson Trailhead. What a fun 27-mile marathon day that was! Anything is possible; do some research and go for it!

BRUSH CREEK LAKES
—ELECTRIC PEAK—BANJO LAKE

ZAPATA FALLS
—SOUTH ZAPATA LAKE
—ELLINGWOOD POINT
—TWIN PEAKS

61

Elevation Gain	2,900 feet for South Zapata Lake; 5,042 feet for Ellingwood Point; 5,950 feet for Ellingwood Point to Twin Peaks Traverse Loop
Round-Trip Distance	10 miles for South Zapata Lake; 14 miles for Ellingwood Point; 15.5 miles for Ellingwood to Twin Peaks Loop
Trailhead	Zapata Falls (9,000 feet)
Difficulty Ratings	Class 1–2 hike on trails to South Zapata Lake, and some Class 2–3 climbing on ridgelines for the traverses on the peaks
Optimal Season	June 15 through October 1
Maps	Trails Illustrated #138; San Isabel and Rio Grande National Forests

COMMENT: Everyone climbs Ellingwood Point from the standard Lake Como approach. This alternative to that route is only slightly more difficult with a visit to South Zapata Lake, and you'll likely have it all to yourself. The only places you will see people will be near the trailhead due to Zapata Falls and possibly on the summit of Ellingwood. The north ridge on Ellingwood is a super-underrated route, a Class 3 rock scramble with minimal exposure and excellent vistas.

South Zapata Lake with Ellingwood beyond.

Accessing the scree gully to gain the ridge.

GETTING THERE

Zapata Falls Trailhead (9,000 feet). From east of Alamosa on US Highway 160, go north on Colorado Highway 150 toward Great Sand Dunes National Park for 11 miles to a marked dirt road for Zapata Falls (BLM Road 5415) leading to the east. Follow the rough road for 3.5 miles as it passes through sandy soils and rougher cobblestones and gets gradually rougher, dead-ending at the developed trailhead. The trailhead is quite popular for people who visit the Zapata Falls, which are only 0.25 mile from the trailhead. Park at the developed restrooms, and if you have your National Parks pass, display it on your dashboard to avoid having to pay the parking fees.

THE LAKE

1. South Zapata Lake (11,900 feet) (Class 1–2). From the Zapata Falls Trailhead, hike through juniper and semiarid desert vegetation for 0.25 mile to Zapata Falls. From the falls, the South Zapata Trail (#852) switches back to the southeast (right) and begins to gain elevation. You'll leave the crowds behind and parallel

Near Ellingwood's summit with Lily Lake below.

Descending Ellingwood's north ridge; California Peak is on the horizon. *Photo by Carrie Besnette Hauser*

the South Zapata Creek for several miles as you climb into the basin above. After 1.5 miles, pass an old cabin frame in a grassy meadow and continue to climb more steeply. Eventually you will enter pine forest and make your way into a beautiful high-mountain basin with Ellingwood Point off into the distance. You will pass through an excellent stand of pine trees at mile 4 that provides the last best coverage from storms, as well as great campsites. If the weather is really good, leave the trees behind and cross a large meadow in the glacially cut basin, arriving at the shores of Zapata Lake at 11,900 feet. There is a nice rocky shelf among boulders and grass that can sustain some camping if you want to be near the lake; just be sure to stay 100 feet or more away from the water when camping here.

THE LOOP AND HIGH-RIDGE TRAVERSE
2. Ellingwood Point (14,042 feet) to Twin Peaks (13,534 feet and 13,580 feet) Traverse Loop (Class 3). From the southeast side of Zapata Lake, follow a use trail for 0.25 mile to the southeast into the upper basin. Locate a shallow scree gully that ascends to a prominent col above the basin to the south in the direction of Ellingwood Point. Climb the gully for 1,100 feet, which is Class 2 but will challenge your footing with lots of loose rock. Once you reach the col at 12,900 feet, you will turn left (east) and hike up rock slabs and a partial use trail on a high broad ridge-

Looking down the gully to South Zapata Lake; this gully provides access to the north ridge of Ellingwood.

line for 0.25 mile to gain the north ridge of Ellingwood. Once reaching the ridge at 13,600 feet, follow some boulders for 150 feet or so to your south, and then the north ridgeline and ridge crest of Ellingwood beckon you to climb. The ridge is steep on both sides, but keep in mind the east side is most dangerous, so climb ledges and rock features on the western (right) aspect. Follow the ridge for several hundred feet on a series of ramps and rock steps to gain the summit ridge at 14,000 feet. From here, turn east (left) again, scramble up a short gully, and walk across solid granite rocks to the summit.

On your return from the summit, you can descend the same way to the 12,900-foot col and (1) return down the gully that empties back into the basin to South Zapata Lake, or (2) follow the ridgeline west and then north for 0.5 mile to the summit of 13,534-foot South Twin Peak. This remote thirteener sees very few people. From this thirteener summit, head north again for three football-field lengths and a 150-foot saddle that separates the two peaks to its higher twin: the 13,560-foot North Twin. Backtrack to a minor saddle/cirque of the southern peak and then descend directly north on easy rock slabs back to South Zapata Lake. This loop not only allows you to climb a fun thirteener as a bonus, but it's much easier descending to South Zapata Lake than taking the scree col you came up earlier in the day for Ellingwood Point.

DR. JON'S EXTRA CREDIT

A. Blanca Peak (14,345 feet) (Class 2+). After reaching the top of Ellingwood Point, consider the weather and your strength. Blanca Peak is a nice climb and not too far away to your south. Just remember that you will have to climb back up to Ellingwood Point to make it back into Zapata Basin—a pretty big day!

ZAPATA FALLS—SOUTH ZAPATA LAKE
—ELLINGWOOD POINT—TWIN PEAKS

LAKE COMO
—LITTLE BEAR PEAK
—BLANCA TRAVERSE
—UPPER COMO LAKES

62

Elevation Gain	3,740 feet for Lake Como; 6,037 feet for Little Bear; 6,669 feet for Little Bear to Blanca Traverse Loop
Round-Trip Distance	12 miles for Lake Como; 15 miles for Little Bear; 17.5 miles for Little Bear to Blanca Traverse Loop
Trailhead	Lake Como (8,000 feet)
Difficulty Ratings	Class 1–2 hike on trails to Lake Como, and some class 2, 3, 4, and 5 exposed climbing on ridgelines for the traverses on the peaks
Optimal Season	July 1 through October 1
Maps	Trails Illustrated #138; San Isabel and Rio Grande National Forests

COMMENT: Blanca Peak is the sentinel of the Sangre de Cristo Range. The mountain towers over the San Luis Valley and in the right weather delivers a super-long and rewarding climb and traverse when combined with Little Bear Peak. Little Bear by itself is one of Colorado's most challenging peaks. Start early and don't take any of these peaks lightly. The Little Bear to Blanca traverse is one of Colorado's finest high-ridge traverses. It's challenging, airy, and steep and will test you to the max.

Lake Como with Little Bear waiting in the wings.

Left: The infamous Hourglass. **Right:** The Hourglass makes for some challenging climbing.

GETTING THERE

Lake Como Trailhead (8,000 feet). From east of Alamosa on US Highway 160, go north on Colorado Highway 150 for 3.2 miles to an unmarked road leading to the northeast. Follow the road for 2 miles as it passes through sandy soils. At 8,000 feet, the road starts to get rough with large round cobblestones. Most of the time, you can drive up a fence line as the road climbs for several hundred feet more. The road turns left while curving through juniper trees and becomes very rough. Consider parking lower if you value your vehicle, but definitely park in the juniper forest before you reach significant switchbacks. Any elevation you gain before you start your hike will help, but not at the expense of your automobile.

THE LAKE

1. Lake Como (11,740 feet) (Class 1–2). From 8,000 feet in the San Luis Valley, follow Lake Como Road for 5 miles to Lake Como. The south-facing aspects of the road's switchbacks are generally hot and relentless, but once you enter Holbrook basin and travel northeast, the trees will give shade, and a refreshing creek crossing/road washout will create some drama if you let it at 10,900 feet. Continue up four more switchbacks on the road to Lake Como at 11,740 feet. At one point on a straightaway at 11,400 feet, Little Bear Peak will appear like a siren song in the basin in front of you, begging you to come climb. Arrive at Lake Como and follow the road around the lake's north side. There is good camping on the southeast end of the lake near a creek that flows into the lake.

The traverse to Blanca is along the spine on the ridge, clearly seen here.

THE LOOP AND HIGH-RIDGE TRAVERSE

2. Little Bear (14,037 feet) to Blanca (14,345 feet) Traverse (Class 4–5).

From the east side of Lake Como, follow the four-wheel-drive corridor up through evergreen trees for 0.25 mile to a small meadow along a creek at 11,950 feet. Do not keep going on the road toward Blue Lakes (Upper Como Lakes) at 12,200 feet. Instead, leave the road near a prominent rock glacier that is across the creek. Cross the creek and climb directly up the rock glacier on a small climbers' trail. After 100 feet, you will be on some boulders, and the rock glacier flattens out. Above you to the south, there is a steep rocky scree gully of both dirt and talus. A climbers' trail will ascend this steep gully, and the climb is very loose in most places. Climb this gully for 800 feet, aiming for a prominent notch on the west ridge of Little Bear. Once on the ridgeline in the notch at 12,900 feet, turn left (east) and follow yet another minor use trail on ledges staying on the right side (south side) of the crest. At times, there is a minor trail; at other times you are just contouring and heading east, slightly ascending toward Little Bear Peak. Keep in mind that this west ridgeline of Little Bear drops off on the north side, so you will want to stay on the south side of the ridge. After 0.75 mile of traversing, the climbers' trail will ascend onto a western face of Little Bear just below a feature known as the Hourglass. Traverse into the bowl toward the Hourglass couloir on a small use trail for an additional 0.25 mile. The difficulty of this traverse is no more than Class 2+ if you take care to follow the correct ascending traverse line. Once reaching the base of the Hourglass, the trail ends, and it's time to climb solid rock. Assess the terrain closely. You can climb directly up the bottom of the Hourglass mainly on the north (left) side. If it has rained the night before, there may be water running down the main part of the gully where it is the narrowest. Take care on this crux move and only go up if you feel comfortable coming down. Once past the Hourglass, you have a solid 500 vertical feet left to finish. Turn left, climb the upper gully on some small cliffs, and then traverse back right on a prominent ledge into a deep inset couloir. From here it's fun Class 3 for 150 yards to make it to the top of Little Bear. You've done it!

But wait, there's more. You can either descend Little Bear back to Lake Como the way you came or go for the Little Bear to Blanca Traverse, a tough and exposed Class 5 journey. The 2-mile ridgeline between the two peaks is a classic. Some people choose to use a rope in this traverse, but a rope is very hard to anchor, making protection marginal. It's best to dial in your scrambling and climbing skills, take some time to get it done, and be safe.

If you choose to commit to the traverse, give yourself at least two to four hours. After the initial drop-offs from the summit of Little Bear, most of the traverse is ascending because Blanca is over 300 feet higher than Little Bear. Some sections of the ridgeline are as narrow as a foot wide, and the exposure is incredible. You'll pass a feature known as Captain Bivwacko Tower partway across. Keep it together; when in doubt, stay on the crest of the ridge, and enjoy the just over 1-mile journey to the top of Blanca Peak. Descend Blanca Peak's northwest face route back to Lake Como for 3 miles.

The view from Blanca's summit southeast to some isolated lakes and the Spanish Peaks on the horizon.

DR. JON'S EXTRA CREDIT
A. Ellingwood Point (14,042 feet) (Class 2+). After reaching the top of Blanca Peak following your traverse from Little Bear, you must descend the northwest face of Blanca. This descent takes you down to the connecting saddle between Ellingwood and Blanca. If you have the energy and the weather is good, go for your third fourteener of the day. You've got this! For the insatiable high-ridge traverser, you can ascend the south face or southeast ridge of Ellingwood and descend the southwest ridge for a full Tour de Ellingwood on the highest ridge crests possible (Class 3).
B. Take a dip in Upper Como Lakes or Lake Como. If it's a hot summer day, nothing makes your accomplishment feel even better than taking a dip in one of the many lakes you pass on your way back down the valley. Soak it up; you've earned it!

LAKE COMO—LITTLE BEAR PEAK
—BLANCA TRAVERSE—UPPER COMO LAKES

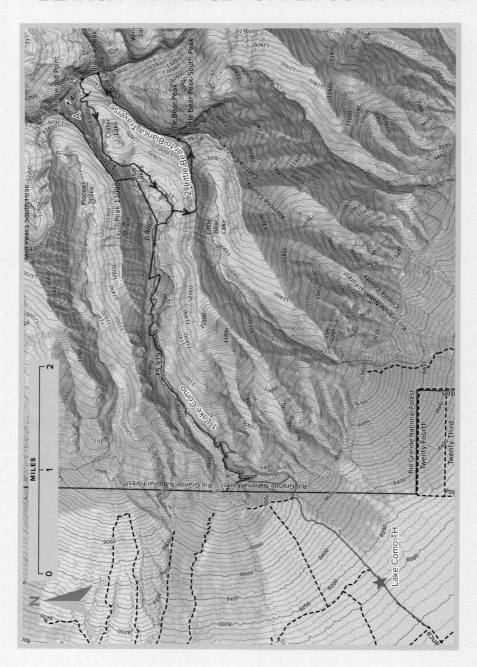

LILY LAKE—CALIFORNIA PEAK—MOUNT LINDSEY —HUERFANO PEAK

63

Elevation Gain	2,000 feet for Lily Lake; 4,300 feet for California Peak Loop; 3,800 feet for either Mount Lindsey Peak or Huerfano Peak
Round-Trip Distance	10 miles for Lily Lake; 12 miles for California Peak Loop; 8–9 miles for Mount Lindsey and/or Huerfano Peak
Trailhead	Upper Huerfano River (10,680 feet)
Difficulty Ratings	Class 1–2 on trails to Lily Lake; Class 2–3 off-trail scrambling on the high ridges and peaks
Optimal Season	June through October
Maps	Trails Illustrated #138; San Isabel and Rio Grande National Forests

COMMENT: Lily Lake is tucked into a far corner of the Sangre de Cristo Range that few will ever see. Unless you hike to the lake and put in the effort, the only other places that the lake is visible from is near Blanca Peak's summit on the north ridge. If you look down into the Huerfano basin, you will see the lake perched up in the corner of a gorgeous glacial tarn. "Huerfano" means "orphan boy" in Spanish, and you'll understand this on your visit. The climbing in this area around Lily Lake is

Lily Lake deep in the heart of the Sangre de Cristo Range.

fun too: this loop to explore the high ridges includes a summit of Colorado's eighty-fourth highest peak: California, a very remote-access peak, and so solitude will be your reward.

GETTING THERE

Upper Huerfano River Trailhead (10,680 feet). This trailhead is south of Gardner off of Colorado Highway 69. Take Exit 52 from Interstate 25 north of Walsenburg and travel 0.3 mile south toward the town of Walsenburg. Turn west onto Colorado Highway 69 north, driving 25 miles north to the town of Gardner. Pass through Gardner for 0.8 mile more and take a right turn (southwest) on the Redwing Spur of Colorado 69 (paved). You can also reach this spur turn by traveling south from the town of Westcliffe. Measure your distance once you have started on the Redwing Spur. There will be signs telling you how far you are from the Huerfano River Trailhead (approximately 22 miles). The road is paved for the first 7 miles and then turns to dirt. You will pass the Singing River Ranch at mile 12 where the road gets rougher although stays passable for most passenger cars. You will pass Aspen River Ranch at mile 17, cross a meadow with an awesome view of aspens and Blanca Peak at mile 19.5, and reach the boundary of the San Isabel National Forest at mile 20.5. A high-clearance vehicle is needed from the national forest boundary. At mile 21.2, you will reach the Lower Huerfano Trailhead junction for the Zapata Trail (useful for this loop description). Continue south for an additional 1.1 miles to mile 22.3 to the

Left: The route to Lily Lake is spectacular as you cross under the massive northeast faces of Blanca and Ellingwood. **Right:** The author on the ridgeline with Peak 13,640' emerging from the clouds. *Photo by Dreama Walton*

The Huerfano River valley from above with Huerfano and Lindsey Peaks.

Upper Huerfano Trailhead, located above a steep section of road above the Huerfano River and a deep gully/meadow. There is some car camping near the trailhead, but please be respectful of others while using this fragile area.

THE LAKES
1. Lily Lake (12,340 feet) (Class 1–2). Descend into the Huerfano River valley for the first 0.5 mile of this trail. You'll cross a beautiful meadow with nice views of Blanca and Ellingwood and their steep eastern faces. Follow a gorgeous trail back into the pine forest with a moderate grade. After 1 mile, there is a Lily Lake sign on the trail; turn right (northwest), and follow the trail for several miles as it heads for the upper basin toward Blanca and Ellingwood. The trail traverses several small meadows and then switches back up some steep rocky terrain on the northwestern corner of the Huerfano River basin for the last mile to the lake. You won't see the lake until you clear some rocky outcroppings right before the lake, and suddenly Lily Lake appears tucked into a large glacial cirque with dramatic cliff backdrops on nearly all sides.

THE LOOP AND HIGH-RIDGE TRAVERSE
2. California Peak (13,849 feet) Traverse, south-to-north ridge loop (Class 2). From Lily Lake, leave the basin and head north-northwest on some boulders,

Left: A gorgeous meadow in the lower Huerfano River basin, with Iron Nipple in the distance. **Right:** The author with his sister, Krista, on the summit of Lindsey in 1999.

talus, and scree for 0.25 mile to 12,600 feet in the basin. Climb an additional 0.25 mile north to the east ridge of Peak 13,577' at 13,450 feet. You will see an unnamed upper basin lake to your left en route. From the ridgeline, continue north for 100 yards to the top of Peak 13,577'. From here, it's all academic on easy Class 2 boulders; hike the gentle ridge north for 1.2 miles to the top of California Peak. One-third of the way across the ridge, you will climb over another unnamed summit at 13,420 feet, and you'll be able to spot Lost Lake in a glacial cirque down below the ridge to your east. After spending a little time on the summit of California, to continue on this loop, follow the ridgeline north for 2.5 miles, pass over Peak 13,476', and then reach an 11,860-foot saddle near some fallen bristlecone pine trees where you will meet up with the Zapata Trail. Head east and descend to tree line on the Zapata Trail through some gorgeous aspen and meadows for 1.7 miles to the Lower Huerfano Trailhead (10,200 feet). At one point you'll see a large rock glacier to your right (south) as you descend into the basin. From the Lower Huerfano Trailhead, hike up the four-wheel-drive road for 1.1 miles to reach your car parked at the Upper Huerfano Trailhead to complete the loop.

DR. JON'S EXTRA CREDIT
A. Mount Lindsey (14,042 feet) or Huerfano Peak (13,828 feet) (Class 2+).
Many people come here to climb the big peaks. Mount Lindsey is one of those peaks, along with Huerfano, and both are worth the side trip as it's always tempting to climb high on peaks you see from a distance, even when you are visiting a lake like Lily.

LILY LAKE—CALIFORNIA PEAK
—MOUNT LINDSEY—HUERFANO PEAK

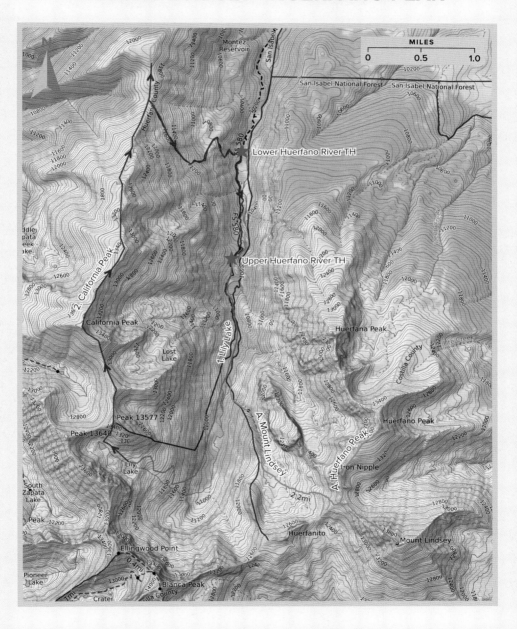

MILES

0   0.5   1.0

Montez
Reservoir

San-Isabel National Forest   San-Isabel National Forest

Lower Huerfano River TH

Upper Huerfano River TH

Huerfano County

FS 580

2. California Peak

California Peak

Lost
Lake

Huerfana Peak

Middle
Zapata
Creek
Lake

1. Lily Lake

A. Mount Lindsey

Costilla County

Huerfano Peak

Peak 13577

Peak 13640

Lily
Lake

South
Zapata
Lake

Peak

Ellingwood Point

Pioneer
Lake

Crater

Blanca Peak

Huerfanito

Mount Lindsey

Iron Nipple

2.2mi

0.4mi

A. Huerfano Peak

Deer Creek

CHAPTER 9

SAN JUAN RANGE

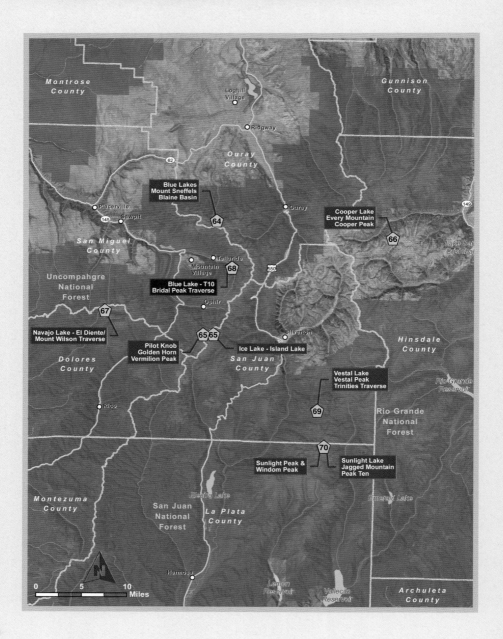

BLUE LAKES —MOUNT SNEFFELS —BLAINE BASIN —TEAKETTLE MOUNTAIN

64

Elevation Gain	1,650 feet for Lower Blue Lake; 2,160 feet for Middle Blue Lake; 2,400 feet for Upper Blue Lake; 4,810 feet for Mount Sneffels; 5,500–7,500 feet for adding Teakettle Mountain depending on routes for extra credit
Round-Trip Distance	7 miles for Lower Blue Lake; 8 miles for Middle Blue Lake; 8.75 miles for Upper Blue Lake; 11 miles for Mount Sneffels; 15 miles for Teakettle Mountain for extra credit
Trailhead	East Dallas Creek—Blaine Basin/Blue Lakes (9,340 feet)
Difficulty Ratings	Class 1–2 on trails to Upper Blue Lake; Class 2–3 off-trail scrambling on the high ridges and peaks (Teakettle extra credit has a Class 5 summit tower)
Optimal Season	June through October
Maps	Trails Illustrated #141 and #146; Uncompahgre National Forest

COMMENT: A climb of Mount Sneffels, a true monarch of this corner of the San Juan Mountains in the 15,566-acre Mount Sneffels Wilderness, is always a treat. Now, combine the approach of Mount Sneffels with two of the most gorgeous lakes in all of

Upper Blue Lake reflection, Mount Sneffels Wilderness.
Photo by John Fielder

Upper Blue Lake. *Photo by Chris Tomer*

Colorado: sold. Not only will you see the stunning blue and turquoise glacial waters with your own eyes, but you can also attempt Sneffels by its classy and fun southwest ridge, which is not its standard route. Then, if you love loops, take advantage of dropping into Blaine Basin and basically circumnavigating the mountain as a whole. Yes! This Tour de Sneffels is one of the best adventures in this entire guidebook; just don't tell anyone else about it. At 14,150 feet, Sneffels is the third highest in the San Juan Mountains. It was named by Frederic Edlich during the 1874 Hayden Surveys because he thought it resembled Mount Snaefell in Jules Verne's *Journey to the Center of the Earth.*

GETTING THERE

East Dallas Creek Trailhead (9,340 feet). This trailhead is sometimes referred to as the Blaine Basin/Blue Lakes Trailhead because two trails start from here. From the town of Ridgway, travel west on Colorado Highway 62 for 5 miles from the Colorado Highway 62/US Highway 550 junction in Ridgway. Turn left (south) on Ouray County 7 (East Dallas Creek Road) and follow the dirt road for 9 miles to the trailhead; stay left at 0.3 mile, stay right at 2 miles, and enter the Uncompahgre National Forest at 7 miles. Upon entering the national forest, the views of Sneffels beckon.

THE LAKES

1.   Blue Lake (10,980 feet), Middle Blue Lake (11,500 feet), and Upper Blue Lake (11,720 feet) (Class 1–2). This hike is gorgeous! Just beyond the trailhead gate, you will pass the Blaine Basin Trail junction, which branches off toward the east. Note this is where you will return if you complete the entire loop for climbing Sneffels, returning via Blaine Basin. Follow the Blue Lakes Basin Trail (#201), which ascends southwesterly while traversing along the east fork of Dallas Creek. The trail climbs steadily up the valley between Mount Sneffels and 13,041-foot Wolcott Mountain. The early portions of the route cross Engelmann spruce forests, while showing expansive views of the Sneffels Range in the open areas. At 1.6 miles from the trailhead, the trail crosses a small stream, and then begins heading toward the southeast to make the final climb up to Blue Lakes.

The trail switches back a couple of times on the western aspect of the basin, then traverses up to the Lower Blue Lake at mile 3.5 and 10,980 feet. There is good camping here in the trees near the lake. This first lake is the largest of the three. And morning reflections can be stunning. From the western shoreline, you may be able to frame Mount Sneffels in the lake.

Next depart the lower lake and ascend 500 feet, leaving the timberline behind to arrive in 0.5 mile farther southeast at Middle Blue Lake. You can continue higher for another one-third mile to reach Upper Blue Lake at 11,720 feet. The elevation gain opens up views of Mount Sneffels as well as Dallas Peak (13,809 feet) and Gilpin Peak (13,694 feet).

From the summit of Dallas Peak, below Mount Sneffels, you can see all three Blue Lakes in the basin.

THE LOOPS AND HIGH-RIDGE TRAVERSE

2. Mount Sneffels (14,150 feet), southwest ridge traverse (Class 3). From the south shores of Upper Blue lake, ascend a series of switchbacks on the relatively good Blue Lakes Trail for 0.5 mile to 13,000-foot Blue Lakes pass. Once on the pass, turn left (north), and you will see the southwest ridge. From the pass, view Sneffels and get ready to have some fun! Follow the use trail up to the left side of the pinnacles at the base of the ridge at 13,150 feet. From here, you have 1,000 feet of climbing on loose Class 2–3 terrain to the top. Beyond the first pinnacles, look for a gully along the ridge crest, which is what you'll climb for the next section of the route. Continue to the gully and climb for an additional 100 feet on loose rock. Gain access to another small gully, turn left, and climb the gully again for another 100 feet. You will reach the ridge crest again near 13,500 feet. Climb and then bypass a sharp pinnacle to its right (east) side. Pass a formation near 13,700 feet known as "Kissing Camels" and then scramble to the ridge crest for the last 450 feet on the crest to reach the top on better and better solid rock the closer you get to the summit. From the top of Sneffels, you command a view of the San Juans and so many other peaks in all directions. Enjoy!

A signature look at Teakettle near the summit.

Blue Lake. The colors of the water are from glacial rock flour.
Photo by Chris Tomer

To descend for the circumnavigation loop of Sneffels, drop the initial steep 150 feet by angling southeast toward the scree col and exit crack that take you into Lavender Col. Once to the entrance of Lavender Col, depending on snow depth or time of year, you can descend the gully for 500 feet on loose rock (Class 2+) into the top of a scree col at 13,500 feet. This is where the south face and the east slopes of Sneffels split in a reasonably broad saddle. You will see a climbers' trail (standard route) off Sneffels head south into Yankee Boy Basin, but for your loop, you can turn left and descend on another climbers' trail to the southeast, then east for 1,000 feet of the broad but relatively steep east slopes of Sneffels. When you reach the basin below at 12,500 feet, take another left turn and descend into Blaine Basin on a broken climbers' trail and rock glacier and back toward a meadow at 10,800 feet to find the Blaine Basin Trail #203 and eventually the trailhead at East Dallas Creek.

DR. JON'S EXTRA CREDIT
A. Teakettle Mountain (14,042 feet) (Class 3–5). Teakettle is a thirteener across the ridgeline to the east from Sneffels. It is an iconic San Juan gem that is often admired from a distance but rarely climbed. But the peak is quite easy to access. From the four-wheel-drive parking area at 11,300 feet in Yankee Boy Basin, the peak is straight up and relatively direct to reach through a series of gullies. You can also take a side detour to climb this peak by descending to the south and east from Sneffels into Yankee Boy Basin while on the climb described here. Some hearty mountaineers have also traversed the challenging ridgeline from Sneffels to Kismet to Teakettle. Potosi, Teakettle's neighbor to the southeast, can also provide some awesome high-ridge traversing. Do a little research and see what is possible on both peaks.

BLUE LAKES—MOUNT SNEFFELS
—BLAINE BASIN—TEAKETTLE MOUNTAIN

ICE LAKE—ISLAND LAKE —PILOT KNOB —GOLDEN HORN —VERMILION PEAK

65

Elevation Gain	2,430 feet for Ice Lake; 2,600 feet for Island Lake; 3,918 feet for Pilot Knob; 4,000+ feet to add Golden Horn or Vermilion
Round-Trip Distance	7.4 miles for Ice Lake; 8.5 miles for Island Lake; 11 miles for Pilot Knob; 13 miles for Pilot Knob to Golden Horn to Vermilion loop back to Ice Lake
Trailhead	South Mineral (9,820 feet)
Difficulty Ratings	Class 1–2 hike on trails to lakes and then tundra; Class 3–4 climbing on solid rocks and scree off trails
Optimal Season	June through October, but July through September is ideal
Maps	Trails Illustrated #141; San Juan and Uncompahgre National Forests

COMMENT: A stunning but often-crowded hike, the Ice Lake Basin is a place you have to visit. The colorful blue lake water combined with the dramatic backdrop of golden, orange, and vermilion rocks and aesthetics of wildflowers in full bloom in July make this place an instant Colorado classic. Wildfire activity in 2020 as well as

Ice Lake, one of Colorado's great wonders, with Pilot Knob (center) and Vermilion Peak (left).

Top: Are these blue waters Caribbean or Colorado? **Bottom:** Fields of columbines in the basin.

overcrowding in recent years are prompting officials to create a permit system. Please visit recreation.gov or the Uncompahgre National Forest website for more information on obtaining a permit to visit this pristine area.

GETTING THERE

South Mineral Trailhead (9,820 feet). This is the popular access from Silverton to Ice Lake, Island Lake, and Vermilion's east side. From Ouray, follow US Highway 550 south to Red Mountain Pass. Go 7.8 miles south on US Highway 550 from the top of Red Mountain Pass or 2 miles northwest on US Highway 550 from Silverton. Turn south on San Juan County Road 7, which is marked for South Mineral Basin. Follow Road 7 (South Mineral Creek Road) for 4.4 miles. You can park along the road anywhere on the straight (left) fork after 3.7 miles, up until the road ends at mile 4.4. The right fork at mile 3.7 gets steep; later in the spring, four-wheel-drive vehicles can drive 1 mile from here to get up to the 10,360-foot parking on Clear Creek Road. The road beyond the parking at 9,820 feet becomes much rougher.

THE LAKES

1. Ice Lake and Island Lake (Class 2). Follow the Ice Lake Trail from the meadow and parking lot as it switches back through some pine trees initially. The historic snow in the winter of 2018–19 created some catastrophic avalanches and leveled the forest through part of the first mile of the trail. Follow trail switchbacks and enjoy some views of the destruction as well as the waterfalls in the creeks as you ascend higher. After the first 1.5 miles and more switchbacks, the trail reaches a middle flat basin with campsites and meadows. Enjoy the flatter terrain, cross a

Island Lake; the route to U. S. Grant Peak (left) is very clear.

creek, and then the trail steepens once again. Once you pass the 12,000-foot level, you will rise above krummholz and smaller trees, travel north, and then west into the tundra and wildflower zone and reach Ice Lake after 3.7 miles. Island Lake is an additional mile or so farther northwest up the trail and around the corner through even more spectacular wildflowers.

THE HIGH-RIDGE TRAVERSE
2. Pilot Knob (13,738 feet) (Class 4). Leave Island Lake and head west and southwest, passing two small ponds en route to the northeast-facing scree gully of Pilot Knob. Ascend the minor gully through the path of least resistance. The yellow-orange rock slope will direct you. From this small saddle, follow the ridge south for 250 feet to the summit. At one point, you can find a narrow couloir that gains access to the final summit tower. A Class 3 climb with an occasional Class 4 move are required on solid rock once the use trail ends.

DR. JON'S EXTRA CREDIT (THE LOOP)
A. Peak-to-Peak Pilot Knob to Golden Horn to Vermilion (Class 3+). There are so many options in this basin. From the top of Pilot Knob, you can travel along the ridgeline south and connect both Golden Horn (13,870 feet) and Vermilion (13,894 feet). The Vermilion Dollar Couloir is a fun couloir to climb in early summer if you brought your ice ax and crampons. On the way back to Ice Lake, stop by Fuller Lake and enjoy the relative solitude. Another fun and interesting option separately would be to climb Ulysses S. Grant Peak from the banks of Island Lake.

ICE LAKE—ISLAND LAKE—PILOT KNOB —GOLDEN HORN—VERMILION PEAK

COOPER LAKE —EVERY MOUNTAIN —COOPER CREEK PEAK

66

Elevation Gain	2,100 feet for Cooper Lake; 3,041 feet for Every Mountain; 3,650 feet for Every Mountain Traverse Loop with Cooper Creek Peak
Round-Trip Distance	8.0 miles for Cooper Lake; 11.0 miles for Every Mountain Traverse
Trailhead	Cooper Creek/Cooper Gulch (10,650 feet)
Difficulty Rating	Class 1–2 hike on four-wheel-drive road, trails, and tundra and rocks/scree off trails
Optimal Season	June through October, but July through September is ideal
Maps	Trails Illustrated #140 and #141; Uncompahgre National Forest

COMMENT: A beautiful and secluded hike, the Cooper Lake basin is a place you can explore and not see another soul, even in the middle of the summer. The popular fourteeners nearby and the popularity of the Alpine Loop Road can make the drive to the trailhead busy, but once you start your hike, get ready for some rocky mountain solitude. Adding the high-ridge traverse of some Bicentennial thirteeners that are rarely climbed not only gives you great views, but also adds to the feeling that you are truly exploring a wild and isolated place.

Cooper Lake with Gudy Peak above.

GETTING THERE

Cooper Creek (10,650 feet). Travel 2.5 miles south from the center of Lake City on CO Highway 149. Turn right on County Road 30 (Lake San Cristobal) and begin measuring distance on the Alpine Loop Road. Pass Lake San Cristobal after the first couple of miles and follow CR 30 for 12.1 miles to a Y intersection. Continue right on CR 30 as it climbs out of the valley and becomes rougher and narrower, following some dramatic road cuts and steep drop-offs. Pass the Silver Creek/Grizzly Gulch Trailhead (access to Sunshine, Redcloud, and Handies fourteeners) at 16.2 miles. The unmarked trailhead for Cooper Lake is located right after crossing Cooper Creek at a historical marker at 17.0 miles. There are three or four parking spaces on the left (south) side of the road. You can also travel an additional 0.25 mile west to a second unmarked parking area that intersects the faint four-wheel-drive hiking trail for Cooper Lake.

THE LAKE

1. Cooper Lake (Class 2). Start from the Cooper Lake Trailhead (second parking area) and follow the faint old four-wheel-drive road for 0.4 mile to the north-northeast across a meadow and into the woods. From the first parking area, it's possible to walk 0.25 mile north through the open bushes and meadow to locate the trail

Left: The trailhead is small but right along the road; Redcloud and Sunshine Peaks are in the distance. **Right:** Travelling along Cooper Creek in a stunning isolated valley.

Looking toward Every Mountain (left) and Cooper Creek Peak (right).

before it gains elevation into the woods to the trail register. After the register, continue northeast for a mile as the trail rises through the pine forest and opens up into some meadows before crossing Cooper Creek at mile 1.4. The Cooper Creek valley is gorgeous, and you will travel through several meadows and then trees, passing old cabin ruins and finally getting far above the timber. The wildflowers in July are excellent. C.T. Peak (13,312 feet) and Gudy Peak (13,566 feet) rise to the west and Peak 13,484' is prominent to the northeast at the head of the valley alongside Cooper Creek Peak (13,689 feet). In a broad meadow past timberline, the faint trail crosses back to the west of Cooper Creek at mile 2.5 and begins to climb up the western flank of the valley. At mile 3.3, the path curves to the north and then northwest, and the valley drops away from you as you travel northwest into a small but deep basin. At 3.6 miles, the valley levels out, and you might think that there will be a lake tucked into this area. Unfortunately, the lake is still higher, requiring a steeper hike on a small use trail to bypass a headwall. Stay to the left (south) on this use trail, and carefully make your way up through a small access point near the small creek outlet. The trail eases up a bit once you climb off of the talus-sloped trail. Continue on the use trail into a tucked-away basin and over a couple of glacial moraine hills to arrive at Cooper Lake at mile 4 at 12,750 feet.

Top: Elephant heads are abundant here.
Bottom: Looking up valley to Cooper Creek Peak.

THE LOOP AND HIGH-RIDGE TRAVERSE

2. Every Mountain Traverse (13,691 feet) (Class 2+). Leave the comfortable northeast edge of Cooper Lake and ascend scree and talus slopes to the north to reach the top of Every Mountain. It's possible to stay on this high ridge and travel east toward Cooper Creek Peak. In 0.7 mile, there is a way to get onto old mining trails and drop back south to the Cooper Creek Trail in the lower basin, allowing you to head back to the trailhead. If you are ambitious and the weather is good, traverse the ridge for another 0 .75 mile to the summit of Cooper Creek Peak.

DR. JON'S EXTRA CREDIT (THE LOOP)

A. Cooper Creek Peak (13,689 feet) (Class 2+). Instead of heading all the way to Cooper Lake initially, from mile 2.5 on the Cooper Lake Trail, follow Cooper Creek for an additional mile to the northeast and then east into the eastern basin of Cooper Creek Creek. From there, it's possible to climb some grassy slopes and talus to the top of Cooper Peak. Study the map and choose your route wisely, but a counterclockwise traverse loop from east to west from Cooper Creek Peak to Every Mountain and down to Cooper Lake, returning to the basin following the trail, is certainly a fun adventure waiting for you! If you are early and ambitious, the rugged trio of Cooper Creek Peak to Every Mountain to Gudy Peak and then a return to the western shores of Cooper Lake is certain to make your day full.

COOPER LAKE—EVERY MOUNTAIN
—COOPER CREEK PEAK

NAVAJO LAKE —EL DIENTE/MOUNT WILSON TRAVERSE

67

Elevation Gain	1,300 feet for Navajo Lake; 4,300 feet for El Diente; 4,800 feet for Mount Wilson Traverse from El Diente; 6,617 feet for adding Wilson Peak
Round-Trip Distance	11.5 miles for Navajo Lake only; 11.6 miles for El Diente only; 15 miles for Mount Wilson Traverse from El Diente; 18.4 Miles to add Wilson Peak to the loop
Trailheads	Kilpacker (10,100 feet); Navajo Lake (9,350 feet)
Difficulty Ratings	Class 1–2 hike both on trails and across tundra/scattered alpine forest ecozone with no trails; Class 3 and 4 scrambling is required on El Diente and on the traverse as well as to Mount Wilson and Wilson Peak
Optimal Season	June through October
Maps	Trails Illustrated #141; San Juan and Uncompahgre National Forests

COMMENT: The three fourteeners above Telluride are scenic, iconic, and dangerous. El Diente, Mount Wilson, and Wilson Peak are beautiful but require serious care when climbing and traversing their slopes. The peaks aren't super technical, but the loose rocks are notorious for causing problems for the average person who thinks these peaks are just a hike. CARRY A HELMET AND USE IT! If you get even

Summit of Mount Wilson; El Diente (left) and Wilson Peak (right) on a spectacular skyline.

Navajo Lake.

slightly off route, you can get into trouble in a hurry. On the positive side, if you plan on visiting or camping at Navajo Lake or any of the basins, you will be treated to stunning scenery and amazing wildlife encounters. Be safe and enjoy the journey!

GETTING THERE

Kilpacker Trailhead (10,100 feet). This trailhead is open by about May 1 most seasons. Take CO Highway 145 south from the roundabout on the west side of Telluride to Lizard Head Pass. Continue on Highway 145 for 5 miles to Forest Road 535. Turn right and follow dirt Forest Road 535 for 5 miles to the signed Kilpacker Trailhead located at the end of a grove of pine trees in a vast meadow.

Navajo Lake Trailhead (9,350 feet). Follow the directions for Kilpacker Trailhead above but instead of turning into the Kilpacker Trailhead, continue west on Forest Road 535 for 1.5 miles as it descends to a switchback and turn right into Navajo Lake Trailhead.

THE LAKE

1. Navajo Lake (11,160 feet) (Class 1–2). Follow the Kilpacker Trail (straight ahead from the fourteener signage) west in a large open meadow for 0.5 mile until you reach the forest and a junction with a spur trail that leads down to the Navajo Lake Trailhead. From the junction, stay right and follow the trail another 1.8 miles through a mix of open meadows and timber to the junction of the El Diente trail at 10,280 feet. Stay left at the junction and follow the Kilpacker Trail #207 and signs

Top: The final summit pitch on El Diente.
Bottom: Traversing to Mount Wilson from El Diente.

to Navajo Lake Trail. The trail will drop almost 250 feet over 1 mile to a creek and intersect with the Navajo Lake Trail (#635). Turn right (north) and continue up the stunning valley for 2.5 miles to Navajo Lake. Along the way, there are some stellar meadow viewpoints, and the final mile to the lake features a series of switchbacks that climb above a large cliff band (with waterfalls off to the right) to gain access to the lake. You will intersect the Woods Lake Trail junction a half mile before you reach Navajo Lake. Follow the signs to Navajo Lake. There is excellent camping along the southern and northern banks, and the Colorado Fourteeners Initiative has recently rerouted the trail (as of 2021) with some excellent rock work around and above the lake and into the upper basin.

THE LOOPS AND HIGH-RIDGE TRAVERSE

2. El Diente (14,159 feet) to Mount Wilson (14,246 feet) Traverse (Class 3–4). Start from Kilpacker Trailhead and follow the Kilpacker Trail (#207) for 2.3 miles as described above for heading to Navajo Lake. At mile 2.3, you will intersect with the signed "El Diente Route" trail. Turn right and ascend through stunning meadows into Kilpacker Basin. This trail takes you on a journey for almost 3 miles, as you will see a stunning waterfall and leave the timber and meadows behind. At 12,600 feet, you will emerge into a narrow flat and rocky basin after climbing on a well-worn rocky trail along a scree field. This is a good place to fill up water near a creek before you turn north to head up the broken ledges of El Diente. You may want to put your helmet on here. The climb of El Diente begins with loose rock and scree for 800 feet as you follow a faint climbers' trail to a small buttress outcropping at 13,400 feet. From here ascend a narrow inset gully (Class 3). At 13,750 feet, reach the base of the ridgeline and turn west toward El Diente. It's important you do not get to the crest of the ridge just yet. Instead, stay on the southern side of the ridge, following a ledge system known as the "Organ Pipes" for 200 yards or so and then climb up 100 feet into a narrow gully to the ridge crest. At 13,900 feet, pass to the north side of the ridge following a narrow, exposed ledge for 150 feet to a notch. Once in this notch, ascend another small gully to the westernmost high summit block (Class 3.) Enjoy this small perch summit also known as "The Tooth."

Next up is the traverse to Mount Wilson. The ridgeline is 1 mile across, and with careful routefinding, does not exceed Class 4. Return to the location on the ridge where you traversed below the Organ Pipes. You will intersect where you climbed up from El Diente's south-face route. As you continue across the traverse, stay to the south side of the ridgeline for one-third mile and bypass some tricky towers by making some traversing Class 3 and 4 moves on small ledges of solid rock. Next it is okay to traverse to the ridge crest where the terrain becomes easier, and you can boulder hop along the spine of the ridge with amazing vistas before descending (Class 4) to a prominent saddle. From this saddle, you are three-fourths of the way finished and have two choices: (1) climb 150 feet of Class 4 or even 5 rock and stay on the ridgeline, traversing to the last saddle/notch, which is just north of the summit; or (2) descend around the towers to the north into the highest reaches of Kilpacker Basin, turning west, and climbing one of two gullies to either reach the notch to the north of the summit, or take the southern westerly facing gully to the notch to the south of the summit (which is also the entrance to the Boxcar gully/couloir).

Whichever route you choose, have fun exploring! There are at least three ways to climb to the summit for the last 150 feet from either notch on the north side of the peak or the south, and you can choose your own adventure (Class 4–5). Once on the summit, you command a view of the entire San Juan Range, from Grand Junction to Durango, out to the La Sal Mountains and Moab and even northeast to the Elk Range near Aspen on a clear day.

To descend off Mount Wilson's summit block, you have two choices: (1) the northeast-facing block has a prominent step crack that takes you down to the east for 50 feet then back north to the mini saddle 150 feet below, or (2) stay on the northern ridge crest and descend some large boulders right on the crest with a

Traversing along the ridgecrest from El Diente.

couple of Class 5 downclimb moves. Either way you choose, some parties use a rope to protect.

Once below the summit block, you can descend Mount Wilson's rocky north face, heading to the northeast initially then down a climbers' trail into the basin and to an idyllic spring near the Navajo Lake Trail at 12,200 feet before turning west on the Navajo Lake Trail and back down to the lake and trails to get back to civilization.

DR. JON'S EXTRA CREDIT

A. Navajo Lake from Navajo Lake Trailhead (Class 1–2). If you are looking for a shorter hike to Navajo Lake and a bit more fall aspen leaf peeping, start from the Navajo Lake Trailhead and hike to Navajo Lake for 4.5 miles (9 miles round-trip).

B. El Diente Mount Wilson Traverse from Kilpacker and returning via Kilpacker Basin (Class 3–4). While the traverse is still challenging, returning into Kilpacker Basin by way of the southern couloirs and valley and trail you hiked in on will get you 13 miles round-trip instead of the longer loop with the visit to Navajo Lake.

C. Wilson Trifecta: Tap the Rockies (Class 3–4). After traversing Mount Wilson from El Diente and descending to 12,200 feet in upper Navajo Basin, if it's early enough in the day and the weather is good, fill your water up in a natural spring and go for your third peak of the day by climbing Mount Wilson. This is the iconic peak of the Coors beer can and will add an additional 3.4 miles and 1,800 feet, for a total of over 18 miles and 6,600 feet for your entire day.

NAVAJO LAKE—EL DIENTE/MOUNT WILSON TRAVERSE

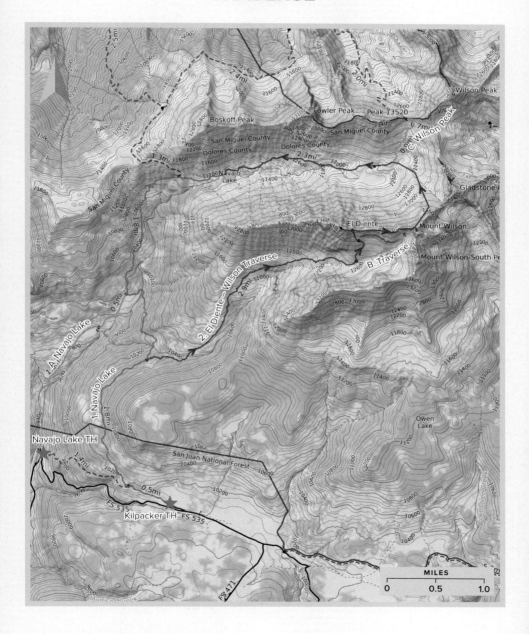

BLUE LAKE—T10 —T11 (BRIDAL PEAK) TO LEWIS LAKE TRAVERSE

68

Elevation Gain	3,160 feet for Blue Lake; 4,491 feet for Bridal Peak and Traverse Loop with Lewis Lake
Round-Trip Distance	9.6 miles for Blue Lake from lower parking (parking at the falls cuts off 3.6 miles round-trip); 13.8 miles for Bridal Peak Traverse Loop with Lewis Lake
Trailheads	Bridal Veil (9,020 feet) or Bridal Veil Falls (10,660 feet)
Difficulty Ratings	Class 1–2 hike on four-wheel-drive road, trails, and tundra; Class 2–3 on ridgelines above the lake
Optimal Season	June through October, but July through September is ideal
Maps	Trails Illustrated #141; San Juan National Forest

COMMENT: This is the signature hike for visiting Telluride. Bridal Veil Falls is a 356-foot waterfall with a historic power plant building. Continue farther in the basin to reach Blue Lake and the peaks beyond. The views from the ridgelines and summit of Bridal Peak (T11) are unmatched, and all the lakes you will see are gorgeous hues of teal and blue.

Blue Lake and old mining relics with Bridal Peak (T11) visible above the lake to the right.

Left: Hiking up to the historic house above Bridal Veil Falls. **Right:** More mining history in the valley toward Lewis Lake.

GETTING THERE

Bridal Veil Trailhead (10,650 feet). Travel 1.5 miles east from the center of Telluride on Main Street (Colorado Avenue). The road passes the Pandora Mill on the left, and where the road turns to dirt and gets dramatically rougher, it begins to switchback. There is ample parking to begin the hike. You may drive to the bottom of the falls but a high clearance, four-wheel-drive vehicle is necessary. The road can get very busy with hikers, bikers, and OHV traffic, so driving should only be considered if you are unable to bike or hike. No vehicles are permitted beyond the top of the falls. The gate just before the power plant is the trailhead heading into the Bridal Veil Basin.

THE LAKE

1. Blue Lake (12,180 feet) (Class 2). Start from Bridal Veil Trailhead, and there are two options here. You can hike up the rough road for 2 miles to Bridal Veil Falls and continue past a closed gate to access Bridal Veil basin. There is also a new Bridal Veil Trail that shortens your hike by 0.5 mile to reach the falls from the trailhead, but it's steep and rough. Once you pass the falls and power plant, continue up the road on the Bridal Veil Trail (#636) in a narrow basin for an additional mile to reach timberline. Once in the upper basin, the road switches back a few more times, then flattens out near some old mining buildings and reaches the lake after 5 miles. Stay left at any road forks. Blue Lake is best to visit early in the morning for the reflection in calm conditions.

THE LOOP AND HIGH-RIDGE TRAVERSE

2. Bridal Peak (T11) Traverse to Lewis Lake (13,511 feet) (Class 2+–3). This loop adds an additional 1,331 feet of elevation gain and 4 more miles in a loop, for

Left: Blue Lake; Three Needles are visible upper left. **Right:** Ingram Lake near Black Bear Pass.

a total of nearly 14 miles. Leave the comfortable southern edge of Blue Lake and ascend scree and talus slopes to the south to nearly reach a saddle between Three Needles to the north and Bridal Peak to the southwest. You can avoid the crest of the jagged ridge by simply bypassing it on Class 2 small talus and slabby rock on the north side of the ridge on your way to Bridal Peak. From here at 13,250 feet, there is a large break in the ridgeline a few hundred feet from the summit of Bridal Peak, and you can scramble up easy Class 2 to gain the ridge. The last bit to the summit is Class 2+ via Bridal Peak's east ridge. The views from Bridal Peak are some of the best in Colorado: Columbine Lake to the south, Blue Lake to the north, and the colorful San Juan peaks in all directions, including La Junta and Wasatch Peaks to the west.

Descend Bridal Peak by following a social trail down the west ridge of Bridal Peak and continue southwest on grass and wildflower tundra to a minor saddle, where you will cross a minor game trail. The trail leads to the northwest to Lewis Lake but can be difficult to follow. Reach Lewis Lake and locate a small dam of a concrete strip and pick up the Lewis Lake Trail (another road converted into a trail), pass the Lewis Mine, and continue through some awesome meadows down to the Bridal Veil Trail. Total distance from Lewis Lake to Bridal Veil Trail: 2.5 miles.

DR. JON'S EXTRA CREDIT (CHALLENGING TRAVERSE)
A. Blue Lake to Three Needles (13,481 feet) to T10 (13,477 feet) Traverse and Muddy Lake Basin (Class 4). This very challenging traverse collects the summits of Three Needles and both T10 summits heading north along the ridge from Blue Lake. It's possible to continue to Black Bear Pass or descend into Muddy Lake before returning to the trailhead. Study the route and the weather carefully before launching and go early!

BLUE LAKE—T10—T11 (BRIDAL PEAK)
TO LEWIS LAKE TRAVERSE

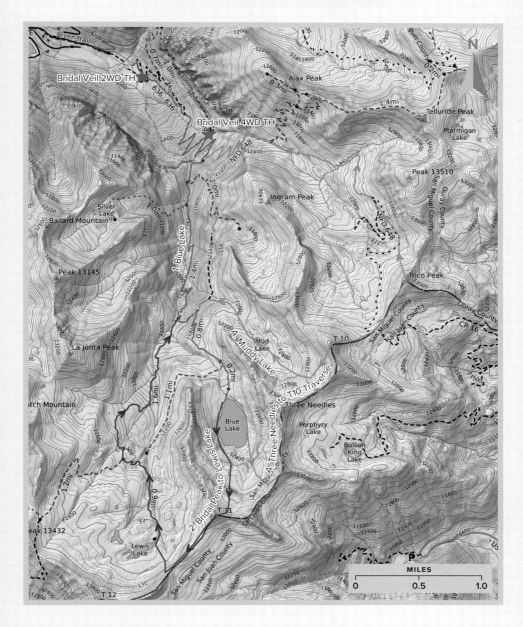

VESTAL LAKE —VESTAL PEAK —TRINITIES TRAVERSE —FIVE PEAK TRAVERSE

69

Elevation Gain	**FROM ELK PARK TRAILHEAD:** 3,375 feet for Vestal Lake; 5,280 feet for Vestal Peak; 6,200 feet for Trinities Traverse; 8,750 feet for adding Vestal and Arrow Peak to Trinitas Loop
	FROM MOLAS TRAILHEAD: 5,055 feet for Vestal Lake; 7,000 feet for Vestal Peak; 7,775 feet for Trinities Traverse; 10,450 feet for adding Vestal and Arrow Peak to Trinitas Loop
Round-Trip Distance	**FROM ELK PARK TRAILHEAD:** 11 miles for Vestal Lake only; 12.2 miles for Vestal Peak only; 15 miles for Trinities Traverse through Vestal Lake; 17 miles to add Vestal and Arrow Peak to the Trinitas Loop
	FROM MOLAS TRAILHEAD: 17.5 miles for Vestal Lake only; 18.7 miles for Vestal Peak only; 21.5 miles for Trinities Traverse through Vestal Lake; 23.5 miles to add Vestal and Arrow Peak to the Trinitas Loop
Trailheads	Elk Park (8,860 feet); Molas (10,620 feet)
Difficulty Ratings	Class 1–2 hike both on trails and across tundra/scattered alpine forest ecozone with no trails; Class 3, 4, and 5 scrambling required on the traverses; Wham Ridge is Class 5.4
Optimal Season	June through October
Maps	Trails Illustrated #140; San Juan National Forest

COMMENT: One of the most amazing and isolated places in all of Colorado, Vestal Lake, Vestal Peak, the Trinities, and Arrow Peak are the epitome of wild, rugged, and remote. Vestal Lake is tucked into an awesome nook just below Vestal Peak, and the scenery looks fake. Hardened peakbaggers and skilled ridge-traversing alpinists can test themselves on these peaks and go for the famous Five Peaks Traverse from Arrow to Vestal and the Trinities. This loop is difficult, dangerous, hard-earned, and fun, all packed into one long day if you have the strength to get them done.

GETTING THERE
Elk Park Trailhead (8,860 feet). You can access this trailhead and the Elk Park Trail best by riding the Durango and Silverton Narrow Gauge Railroad. Elk Park is located in the Animas River canyon 6 miles south of Silverton. You can only reach

Elk Park by foot or railroad but not by road. Access the trailhead by taking a morning train from Durango or an afternoon train from Silverton. Visit durangotrain.com for information on train departures, schedule, and fares. The train only runs from May through October generally.

Molas Trailhead (10,620 feet). Access this trailhead if you prefer to avoid the expensive train fees and the tourist crowds. If coming from the north, from the gas station at the junction of US Highway 550 and Colorado Highway 110 just south of town, travel US Highway 550 5.5 miles toward Molas Pass. At mile 5.5, there is a turnoff to a marked dirt road and trailhead on your left, on the north side of Molas Pass. A sign for Molas Lake and Molas Trail marks the turn for the trailhead parking off of US Highway 550. If coming from Durango to the south, drive 40 miles to Molas Pass, and the trailhead is 1.1 miles on the north side of the pass on the right side. The trail and dirt parking lot are about 100 yards off of US Highway 550. The Molas Trail is part of the Colorado Trail here, and this trail is accessible in winter.

THE LAKE

1. **Vestal Lake (12,235 feet) (Class 1–2).** Follow the Colorado Trail from Elk Park. From the train tracks, you will cross a field and ascend a spur trail into the forest to the northeast for 0.25 mile before meeting up with the actual Colorado Trail. Pass into the Weminuche Wilderness and a trail register. From here, hike 2.75 miles, staying on the north side of Elk Creek to a beaver pond at 10,000 feet. Look south, up a remote basin, and you'll spot Arrow Peak drawing you in. At the east end of the beaver pond, leave the Colorado Trail on an unmarked trail and traverse some boulders for 100 yards to get back into the woods south of the pond. You'll pass some flat campsites in the woods, and in 0.15 mile, you'll have to cross the mini gorge of Elk

Sunset at Vestal Lake; Trinities (left), Vestal (center), and Arrow (right) at one of Colorado's best lake vistas.

Left: Wham Ridge of Vestal. **Right:** Getting steeper above Vestal Lake on Wham Ridge.

Creek. In late summer, the crossing is easy on some logs; in early summer, this may be a challenge. Once across the creek, rejoin the Vestal Creek Trail 150 feet above the creek on some benches as it traverses west and then southwest through the deep pine forest. The trail has been becoming much easier to follow in recent years. After the first 0.25 mile south of Elk Creek crossing, you will ascend steeply into Vestal basin. Follow the trail for a steep mile, stay well above Vestal Creek (to your west), and cross some open meadows and then some more forest. There are two or three borderline Class 3 moves on the actual trail as it gets steep in the woods and on the valley side hills. At 11,100 feet, emerge into a meadow near the creek, and then turn southeast and then east for the next 0.5 mile as the trail just keeps going. At 11,400 feet, the trail will flatten out into a meadow that is known as Lower Vestal Meadow. There are some good campsites on rocky outcroppings and in pine trees north of the creek near this meadow. You will see Arrow and Vestal to your south about 0.75 mile away and nice and high above you. From here, turn south, find a use trail through some willows, and climb steeply for 500 feet to get past the tree line. Above timberline, follow a set of rocky slabs and grassy benches through a shallow small shelf valley for 0.25 mile to reach the banks of the stunning Vestal Lake. Note when coming from Molas Trailhead, you will first have to descend into the Animas River basin via the Colorado Trail for 3.25 miles and down 1,680 feet to reach the Elk Park Trailhead. This drop will give you some hard work to ascend back to your car at the trailhead at the end of the trip.

THE LOOPS AND HIGH-RIDGE TRAVERSES

2. Vestal Peak (13,864 feet), Wham Ridge Loop, and Trinities Traverse Loop (13,805 feet) (Class 3–5.4). Wham Ridge is one of the best pure rock climbing mountaineering routes in all of the United States. Start from Vestal Lake and aim for the west end of the stark north face of Vestal, known as the Wham Face. Your goal is to climb as far as you can on grassy benches from 12,300 to 12,600 feet, traversing higher and across the north face to get to Wham Ridge proper (Class 2+). The grassy ledges are delightful; in July, they will be loaded with columbines, sunflowers, and other gorgeous plants. You may even encounter a mountain goat or two in this area, so be on the lookout. Once you have made the crest of the ridge at 12,650 feet, you will start up the beautiful and ever-steepening ridge. The difficulty up the rock slabs goes from Class 2+ to Class 4 in a hurry, and once you get above 13,000 feet, several Class 5 moves will be needed. One in particular, the route's crux, is a crack that forces you to step east out onto the face and climb a super fun and solid slab at 13,200 feet

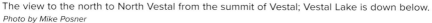

The view to the north to North Vestal from the summit of Vestal; Vestal Lake is down below. *Photo by Mike Posner*

for 50 feet with several high-intensity crack moves (Class 5.4). Some parties will protect this section with a 30-meter rope, several small cams, and a sling, but once you are past the crux, the difficulty goes back to Class 4 for the last 500 feet of ledge systems to the top. You will make the top of a subsummit on Vestal first and then have to traverse some ledges and climb to the true summit. From the top, views of the entire San Juan Range surround you.

To descend, take the south face as it splits the face with a small rib ridgeline. Take the southeastern gullies (left) down to a ledge that provides you with the ability to traverse to the east toward the Trinities. Once on the flat connecting saddle between the Trinities and Vestal at 13,100 feet, you can choose to continue east or circle down on a rock glacier to the north on a use trail to some rock benches back for a swim in Vestal Lake.

3. Trinities Traverse Loop (13,805 feet) (Class 4). From the 13,100-foot ridgeline between Vestal and West Trinity, continue east up the relatively easy Class 2+ southwest ridge of West Trinity (13,765 feet). Follow rocky ledges along the ridgeline for 0.3 mile to the summit. The downclimbing between peaks when going west to east

A view of Middle Trinity from West Trinity along the Trinities Traverse; the Kodiak High Route is visible in the mountains to the right.

Near the summit of Vestal with Arrow behind.

is no harder than Class 2+. Next be ready for Class 4 climbs of two separate chimneys to reach the top of Trinity. East Trinity (13,745 feet) is no more difficult than Class 3. When descending the east ridge of East Trinity and looping back around to Vestal Lake, you will visit a beautiful unnamed lake below the north face of the Trinities. This whole traverse is so fun on a clear fall bluebird day, so settle in and enjoy.

DR. JON'S EXTRA CREDIT

A. Trinitas, the Five Peaks Traverse (Class 3–5.4). If you are really feeling invincible, leave Vestal Lake, climb Arrow Peak first (Class 3), traverse to Vestal's Wham Ridge, and continue across to the Trinities. I spent a really fun and long day on this Five Peaks "Trinitas" Traverse in 2016, and it's one of the all-time classic ridge traverses in Colorado. From the Molas Trailhead, it's more than 10,000 feet of vertical gain in more than 23 miles.

B. Consider doing the Kodiak High Route (Class 2–3). This spectacular high route from the south side of Vestal and the Trinities saddle extends for nearly 10 miles to Jagged pass and connects to Sunlight basin. (See entry #70 for more options.) Consider a backpacking adventure to these scenic wild and high places, and there are so many lakes up in this high alpine to see along the way!

VESTAL LAKE—VESTAL PEAK—TRINITIES TRAVERSE—FIVE PEAK TRAVERSE

SUNLIGHT LAKE—JAGGED MOUNTAIN—SUNLIGHT AND WINDOM PEAKS

70

Elevation Gain	4,200 feet for Sunlight Lake; 6,000 feet for Jagged Mountain; 6,200+ feet for Sunlight and Windom Peaks
Round-Trip Distance	29 miles for Sunlight Lake; 31 miles for Jagged Mountain; 30+ miles for Sunlight and Windom Peaks
Trailhead	Vallecito (7,900 feet)
Difficulty Ratings	Class 1–2 on trails to Sunlight Lake or Jagged Lake; Class 2–4 off-trail scrambling on the high ridges and peaks; Class 5.0–5.2 climbing on the upper 1,500 feet on Jagged
Optimal Season	June through October
Maps	Trails Illustrated #140; San Juan National Forest

COMMENT: Last and certainly not least; last and certainly best. Jagged is the "Jagged King" of all Colorado mountains. Located far away from roads, towns, or any civilization, every time you set eyes on Jagged, it makes you feel like you can just forget what is going in in the real world. Some people take two days to approach Jagged and won't summit until day three. Jagged was first climbed in 1933 by Dwight

Hidden Surprise Lake to the south of Jagged Mountain. *Photo by Mike Posner*

The spires of Jagged are all nearly the same height.

Lavender, and he noted just how hard it was to even identify which pinnacle was the true summit. Even to this day in the summer, Jagged can go weeks without anyone climbing to its summit. If you choose to venture into this area, you will also have options to visit several of the lakes in the area, all of which make this part of the wilderness even more special.

GETTING THERE
Vallecito Trailhead (7,900 feet). Approach this trailhead from either Bayfield or Durango. From the south or east from US Highway 160 in Bayfield, turn north onto La Plata County Road 501 for 13 miles to Vallecito Reservoir's west side. Continue straight (left) at mile 18.5 on La Plata County 500. The road dead-ends at Vallecito Campground and Trailhead along the river at mile 21.5. From the north or west from Durango, travel northeast on Florida Avenue (La Plata County 240) from downtown Durango off of US 550. Travel 16 miles out of town, follow the signs to Vallecito Reservoir. Turn left on La Plata County 501 at mile 26 to reach the reservoir then follow County Road 500 to reach the Vallecito Campground and trailhead at mile 29.

THE LAKES
1. Sunlight Lake (12,033 feet), Upper Sunlight Lake (12,340 feet), and Jagged Lake (12,700 feet) (Class 1–2). After circling around the Vallecito Campground to start, travel through a beautiful gorge and series of valley meadows along the Vallecito River for 11.3 miles to 9,600 feet in a scenic valley. You will cross to Vallecito River's south side at mile 7 on the way. From mile 11, look to your west to locate the Sunlight Creek valley. Leave the main trail at a marked junction and ford the Vallecito River once again, crossing to the west side. From the river crossing, pick up the Sunlight Basin Trail and follow it for 2.5 miles as it climbs steeply through pine and aspen forests. Higher up in the basin, you will navigate through some cliff bands to ascend into an upper basin at 11,000 feet, following a beautiful creek with

brook trout visible as you hike. Here you will notice the forest is all beetle kill, and the trail has been getting easier to follow in recent years. In a small meadow, the trail stays left of a rock wall at 11,200 feet and climbs again to reach timberline. Follow the trail and emerge from the thicker forest in a scoured basin next to the creek to 11,500 feet. From here, continue west and then southwest for 0.5 mile up to Sunlight Lake at just over 12,000 feet. Sunlight Lake is located in the flattest part of the basin near some krummholz trees to the east of Sunlight Peak. If you aren't looking to visit Sunlight Lake but instead just climb Jagged, you can find a use trail from the steep meadow at 11,500 feet to then ascend north through rocky outcroppings and above tree line through a shallow set of rock gullies and high alpine for 1 mile north to Jagged Lake at 12,700 feet. Jagged Lake is about 1 mile northeast of Jagged, and you will get a nice view of the north face of Jagged from the lake.

THE HIGH-RIDGE TRAVERSE

2. **Jagged Mountain, north face (13,824 feet) (Class 5–5.2).** Jagged is arguably the most rewarding, isolated, fun, and awesome peak to climb in all of Colorado. The north-face route is the best, most practical way to climb Jagged. After inspecting the route from a distance and observing how complex the line is, launch from the shores of Jagged Lake. Study the face carefully as it will be sure to test your routefinding skills. There is a deep snow couloir in the center of the north face. Jagged's main 13,824-foot summit is the first summit west of the deep notch (to the right) at the top of this couloir. The route on the north face also goes west (to the right) of the snow

The north face of Jagged; the route is center then center-right.

couloir and reaches the deep notch west of the main summit. You will not be able to see the upper route as you will be traversing high on the face to a notch west (farther right) of the main summit and then traversing the final finishing portions high and on the back side of the notch on the southwest face for the final 150 feet.

When leaving the banks of Jagged Lake, ascend to the south on boulder fields and scree that give way to solid rock slabs and grassy benches for 500 feet to get above 13,000 feet. Your goal is the bottom of the prominent inset snow couloir (which may be devoid of snow by late August), and you will reach this by performing an ascending traverse to the southeast (Class 2+). The introduction is over, and now you have to climb.

Next ascend a steep granite slab for 10 to 15 feet that runs parallel to the couloir and climb a crack (Class 4). Climb 20 more feet of Class 3 rock and sneak around a corner (to the east, left) and up an exposed northeast-facing ramp for 50 feet (Class 4). From the top of the ramp, zigzag above on some grass ramps and climber-created steps for 100 feet and do not go into the notch couloir; instead, when the climb gets harder than Class 3 in this section, turn west (right) and zigzag some more to a shallow gully. Climb the gully but then do a down-and-up traverse west on some ledges for 40 to 50 feet to pass a gendarme, climb another 75 feet or so, and look for a chimney and a rounded rock climb, which is a second crux of this route. Ascend the chimney-like gully for 100 feet and then south over the Class 4 rounded rock (25 feet up) and continue to zigzag up the ledges again. For the last 100 feet until the western notch, you will have to navigate a cruxy 5.0–5.2 chimney system, There are

Ascending Peak Ten with Sunlight Lakes and the Sunlight-Windom Massif in view.

Camp in Sunlight Basin for Jagged and other peaks in the area.

two chimneys in fact, one to the east and one farther west. I prefer the west because it's harder but easier to protect and quite fun to climb. From the top of the route's third crux, scramble to the western notch of Jagged and take a turn around to the southwest side of the peak. You can look down Jagged's southwest face and get a nice view too. The summit is calling. Traverse 30 feet southwest, climb 40 feet east on ledges, and then problem-solve the final 150 traversing feet on several exposed ledges and one more fun but easy chimney for 40 feet to get to the summit crest. Carefully walk across the summit block, which is the size of an après-ski sun deck at your favorite ski resort. Nice work!

Descend the same way you came up using some slings for two or three rappels of the chimneys and cruxes with a 30-meter rope, add some nifty downclimbing, or if you brought a 60-meter rope, you can rappel off the north side, passing the upper of the route's major cruxes to easier ground and then downclimb the rest. You'll certainly remember the views and the experience of this summit forever.

DR. JON'S EXTRA CREDIT
A. Sunlight and Windom (14,042 feet) (Class 3–5). From Upper Sunlight Lake at 12,340 feet, you can traverse into a basin to the southwest and then climb west to a 13,000-foot col in between Sunlight and Windom at the head of Chicago Basin. It's rugged but a fun alternative way to climb both of these popular fourteeners.
B. Peak Ten, south face ledge (13,500 feet) (Class 4–5). Peak Ten is to the north of Sunlight Lake and to the southwest of Jagged. Reaching the summit of this thirteener is a true problem-solving task.
C. Upper Hidden Surprise Lake (Class 2–3). Explore this lake to the northwest of Sunlight Lake, and you can combine it with a climb of Knife Point, which is just shy of 12,900 feet.

SUNLIGHT LAKE—JAGGED MOUNTAIN
—SUNLIGHT AND WINDOM PEAKS

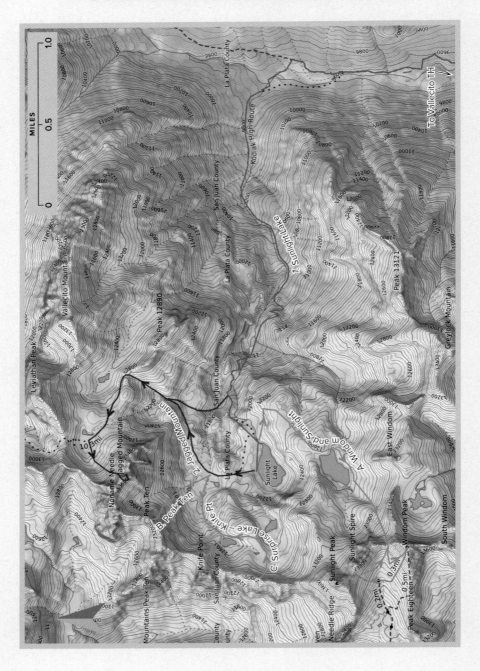

APPENDIX

AVALANCHE, SNOWPACK, LODGING, AND WEATHER RESOURCES

10th Mountain Division Hut Association: huts.org

American Alpine Club: americanalpineclub.org

Colorado Avalanche Information Center: avalanche.state.co.us

Colorado Mountain Club: cmc.org

Crested Butte Avalanche Center: cbavalanchecenter.org

Great Sand Dunes National Park: nps.gov/grsa

National Avalanche Center: avalanche.org

National Oceanic and Atmospheric Administration: noaa.gov

Red Mountain Pass Cabins: skihuts.com

Rocky Mountain National Park: nps.gov/romo

San Juan Huts: sanjuanhuts.com

For all backcountry permits in areas that require wilderness permitting, visit recreation.gov.

Sun setting on Capitol Peak. Grateful for all of my climbing and photography partners over the years that have made this book possible. Thank you!

ACKNOWLEDGMENTS

I have nothing but gratitude to be able to share some of my favorite summer and fall adventures in the backcountry of Colorado while exploring the mountains by hiking, climbing, swimming, and even ice skating. This book is for everyone who loves getting lost in the remote corners of Colorado. Without the love of my best friends, family, and business partners, this book would never have been possible.

I want to thank my many wilderness partners over the years who have helped motivate me to explore and to capture content and photos: John Fielder, Torrey Udall, Mike Posner, Aaron Jenniges, Erin Snow, Colin O'Brady, Amy Charity, Jen Martin, Tim Loes, Jenny Fox, Carrie Besnette Hauser, Jenna Besaw, Brad Burgtorf, Connor Drumm, Chris Tomer, Mike Lewis, David Duncan, Kevin Duncan, Andrew Hamilton, Andrea Sansone, Jennifer Broome, Jose Oberholzer, Celine Oberholzer, Deandre Lansdowne, Chris John, Bob and Lauren Pietrack, Adam Murray, Naomi Jane Atherton, Stacia Glenn, Jesse Willms, Ingrid Arneburg, Zack Wilson, and Dreama Walton.

Major thanks to my dear friends and longtime mentors John Fielder and Carrie Besnette Hauser for adding some of their best photos to this book to help accent some of these special places.

My publisher/editor at the Colorado Mountain Club Press was the amazing Sarah Gorecki. Without you, there is no way I could ever bring these places to life like I do. Our masterful copyeditor Gretel Hakanson and layout designer Takeshi Takahashi have been amazing to work with as well. Also, Sarah Jenniges, your special work on the overview maps and other advice on map editing is always appreciated. To the Colorado Mountain Club Press and Executive Director Keegan Young: thanks so much for giving all my fun books a chance. To some of my sponsors over the years: Zeal Optics, Sierra Designs, Silver Oak, Honey Stinger, Fisher Space Pen, Mountain Hardwear, Lifeproof, Four Points, Garmin, the Ingrid Arneburg Foundation, and the Steadman Clinic, thanks so much for supporting all my adventure days out there to gather the information I needed to produce this book. Andrew Hamilton, you are the ultimate Colorado mountain man and high-ridge traversing machine. I am super grateful for your insightful contribution to this book.

Thanks to my family: my parents, Bob and Barb; my brother Jared and his family (Michelle, Kash, and Kaden); my sister, Krista, and her husband, Zack; and my brother Robbe and his family. Now everyone knows what the heck I was always doing when I would just disappear for a week in our mountains with my camera and notepad in hand.

If there is anyone else I might have forgotten along the way, thank you and come explore with me!

ABOUT THE AUTHOR

Photo by Naomi Jane Atherton

Dr. Jon Kedrowski, author of *Sleeping on the Summits: Colorado Fourteener High Bivys* (2012) and *Skiing and Sleeping on the Summits: Cascade Volcanoes of the Pacific Northwest* (2016), as well as *Classic Colorado Ski Descents* (2017), grew up in Vail, Colorado. Jon first climbed each of Colorado's fourteeners in the late 1990s before he turned 18. Over the years, he has skied from every fourteener, and in 2016, he skied each Colorado fourteener during the same winter season. Jon has explored every lake and location in this guidebook, as his climbing résumé in Colorado includes multiple ascents of the 58 official Colorado fourteeners and three hundred of Colorado's 584 thirteeners.

Jon has advised or led climbing expeditions to each of the Seven Summits except for Vinson Massif in Antarctica, which is high on his bucket list. In 2012, Jon summited Mount Everest and has since led five different expeditions to Mount Everest (2012, 2015, 2018, 2019, 2021, guiding clients to the top in 2019 and 2021). He has been featured on several documentaries about his climbing and skiing adventures on the Discovery Channel, Smithsonian, NBC, DatelineNBC, CBS, ABC, FOX, and CNN. In 2019, Jon made the summit of Manaslu at 8,163 meters / 26,781 feet without the use of supplemental oxygen and was part of the first expedition to K2 (8,611 meters / 28,250 feet) in 2021 that put ten Nepali climbers on the summit for the first time ever in winter. He is also a regular contributor to KDVR Fox 31 Denver and KWGN CW2 in Denver for stories about the great outdoors in Colorado. He is the owner of a company called Dr Jon's Adventures that leads expeditions all over the world.

Jon's favorite hobbies include skiing, mountaineering, and photography. He loves to travel, mountain bike, trail run, river raft, play basketball, and play golf while enjoying the gorgeous summer and fall seasons in Colorado. For more about Dr. Kedrowski, visit jonkedrowski.com and drjonsadventures.com or @drjonkedski on Instagram and Twitter.

Recreate with
RIMS

Give back to the land you love with the CMC RIMS (Recreation Impact Monitoring System) mobile app: If you spot a downed tree, trail erosion, trash, or poor signage while you're exploring the places in this book, open the app and submit a quick report so that land managers can address the issue. Learn more and get started at cmc.org/RIMS.

cmc.org/RIMS

Illustration by Jesse Crock

Join Today.
Adventure Tomorrow.

The Colorado Mountain Club is the Rocky Mountain community for mountain education, adventure, and conservation. We bring people together to share our love of the mountains. We value our community and go out of our way to welcome and include all Coloradoans—from the uninitiated to the expert, there is a place for everyone here.